René Griffiths

Ramblings
— of a —
Patagonian

Artisan Media Publishing (uk)

ARTISAN MEDIA PUBLISHING (UK)

First published in Great Britain in 2014 by
Artisan Media Publishing (UK)
22 Palace Avenue, Llandaff, Cardiff CF5 2DW
artisanmediapublishing@outlook.com

A CIP catalogue record for this book is available from the British Library.

ISBN 978-0-9929833-0-7

Cover design by Mathew Bevan
www.mathewbevandesign.co.uk
Print design by *anɢove* graphic communication
www.neilangove.ltd.uk

Typeset in 11 pt Minion Pro on 80 gsm Munken Cream Wove

Printed and bound by
CPI Group (UK) Ltd, Croydon, CR0 4YY
www.cpibooks.com/uk

CONTENTS

DEDICATION

Dedicated to my family, and all the friends and colleagues
who have contributed to the experiences, adventures
and stories included in this book.

ACKNOWLEDGEMENTS

My thanks go to Shirley Cheal and Paul McNichol for their observations, ideas and assistance with the early drafts of this book. Also, my thanks to Terry Breverton of Glyndŵr Publishing for his contribution of the appendix on Michael D. Jones, and to those friends and photographers who agreed to their images being included in the book as it neared completion.

At this stage I thought the book was finished but then I happened upon John Humphrys' *Lost for Words: The Mangling and Manipulating of the English Language*. Reading this caused me to completely re-write my manuscript and to throw the first and many subsequent drafts into the fire (thanks, John!) but I must acknowledge the sobering effect his words had when I realized the extent of my particular mangling of the English language. Priscilla Harriman's meticulous editing and insightful comments on the resulting final draft are very much appreciated, and any errors, omissions or manglings now are my own. And my special thanks to Yvonne Cheal whose assistance throughout has been invaluable, and without whom the book may well have been started, but it would definitely not have been finished.

Finally, thanks to David Higham Associates for permission to use a quotation from Dylan Thomas' 1948 screenplay *The Three Weird Sisters*.

Illustration Credits

I would like to thank the following companies and individuals for permission to reproduce their images in the photographs section: The Trustees of the British Museum; Yvonne Cheal; Haydn Denman; Gaucho Cyf.; Dilwyn Goch; Fredy Griffiths; Paul McNichol; Keith Morris; Media Wales Limited; Jasper Winn.

PREFACE

THE author, Eugenio René Griffiths, was born in 1950 on a farm in Bryn Crwn, Gaiman, Patagonia, Argentina. As part of a revolutionary idealism to create a new Wales in South America, his ancestors emigrated from Wales to Patagonia in 1882, following the first exodus from Wales in 1865. As a result, René was brought up with Welsh as his first language and Spanish his second.

René is an insatiable traveller and *troubadour*. As a Welsh-speaking 'gaucho', he came to Wales for the first time in 1972. After spending a year at Coleg Harlech, improving his Welsh and studying Welsh literature, René added English and French to his linguistic repertoire. He bought a ranch in Cholila, in the Andean region of Patagonia – land once owned by Butch Cassidy and the Sundance Kid – to return to farming in 1989.

This book is a collection of stories and an array of anecdotes. They range from his childhood journeys to school on horseback, to appearing at London's Royal Albert Hall as a singer and guitarist, to becoming the lead actor in the Welsh film Gaucho and undertaking many more film roles, television parts, and appearances on music and light entertainment shows. From becoming a well-known singer in Wales and Europe, to wine making in France, and becoming the first guanaco breeder in the world back in Patagonia.

His writing reflects the influence of both the Latin American and Welsh cultures in a witty and humorous way. This is a travelogue that rambles through many countries, stories and experiences. Ramblings of a Patagonian is a unique voyage from Patagonia to Wales, and from Wales back to Patagonia, traversing many other countries in between. And why written in English? As René says, 'Because the English language is an exuberant jungle of exotic words that fuses with the way I think.'

— 1 —

SCHOOL

THE president of the Argentine Republic, Juan Domingo Perón, was busy up and down the country repairing and building beautiful schools with red roofs, but for some reason he missed mine. The people in the area said that he had run out of materials, and consequently it eventually closed down. But not completely. Some goats and horses made good use of it when it rained. My horse visited the school whenever he could. He waited for a while at the same old post and then came back home, carrying just the image of René Griffiths on his back.

That was in the 1950s in Bryn Crwn, near Gaiman in Patagonia, where Diana, the Princess of Wales, went to have a Welsh cup of tea in English in the 1990s. The name 'Patagonia' confuses many people because it is not a country – it's just a vast area of land covering the southern part of Argentina and Chile, similar to 'The Lake District' in England, or 'The Camargue' in France.

The Fifties were very confusing years for me and my school friends. The word 'modern' entered our vocabulary in two languages, Welsh and Spanish, and took a seat alongside us. It was easy to remember because both languages used exactly the same word at that time. Our old (to me) teacher was a Welsh Patagonian lady and her Spanish was well mixed up with the Welsh language, so we understood her. Then they sent us a new teacher from Buenos Aires – well, that was a mess! We couldn't understand her and she couldn't understand us. Sometimes she would break down in tears with frustration and, although we were too young to be frustrated, we cried with her a lot, to see what happened.

She stopped us playing with the *boleadora*[1] because it belonged to the Indians and was a hunting tool and an instrument of war. To us it was just a toy that you could hurt your nasty little enemy with and it never broke. But that wasn't good enough for her. She gave us a ball to kick and we kicked it all day long until it broke. Then she brought 'modernism' to our little school. She ceremoniously presented us with a plastic ball. That was an intelligent ball – to begin with it was 'modern' because it was made of plastic, but it was the worst instrument of torture we had yet come across. When it was hot it became a lazy ball. It didn't want to play with us, making our play time very hard. When it was cold, at about ten below zero, it became an iron ball and it really hurt our toes. Then, if you hit the ball with your head it would knock you out for the rest of the day. You had only two choices if you wanted to play with it – have a terrible headache afterwards or limp all the way back to the classroom.

We had to do something about that, so we came up with an idea. If we could keep a fire going all day in the field, we could warm up the modern ball from time to time and then keep playing all day without headaches or bad toes. We collected the wood, we made the fire and we threw the ball in. Then we pulled it out, then it went in again, and so on. It really worked – no headaches, no bad toes, until one day

1   *boleadora* – a weapon made of three leather thongs approximately one metre long, with a stone ball at the end of each thong. Used for hunting wild animals by entangling the thongs in the animal's neck or legs

the ball got tired of us and caught fire. It began to change in shape and in a few seconds it had gone forever.

I always looked forward to going to school, but one Monday morning it took a long time to catch my horse, and my mother had forgotten to iron our white overalls, so we were very late when we set off. The weather was getting worse by the second, with wind and rain. Hundreds of leaves from the top of the poplars were slapping my face. They were blinding both me and my horse and it was quite difficult to saddle up. I really wanted to go to school that day, more than any other day, because I had a very special present to give to my teacher. It was a huge toad that I had found by the irrigation canal, and I was going to hide it in her handbag. When I finally set off at full gallop with one of my sisters on the back of the horse, we went through a couple of cross-country tracks. The ground by now was very wet and sticky for the poor horse, and somehow he managed to perform an unwelcome somersault. He then promptly bolted home with his tail in the air, leaving my sister and me half-conscious in a pool of water and mud. I desperately searched for my precious toad but he was gone, too. I was in a terrible temper and blamed my sister for what had happened, while trying to find my pencils and books in that nightmare of sticky, dark clay.

When we arrived at the school after walking the last mile on foot, no one could recognize us, and after trying to explain a bit, even the teacher laughed at us. Oh yes, that laughter hurt me a lot and she would pay for it! I knew where the bats were hanging upside down in one of the ceilings of the school and it was easy to grab them by the backs of their necks, so they couldn't twist their heads to bite you with their sharp teeth. I caught a couple of the bats and threw those inside my beloved teacher's handbag instead of the toad. After that I decided there was a pain in my stomach somewhere, so she sent me home. I never found out exactly what happened to those ugly, shining bats, but I later heard she found them in her handbag and wet herself, but was too embarrassed to tell anybody.

She was a good teacher but a bit stupid. She gave us a lot of time to scratch our heads and to look out of the window like little monkeys behind bars, nostalgic about their jungle – or in this case about the desert. But no, she was wrong. We were not nostalgic at all. The reason we were looking out of the window was that a little Shetland pony was trying to mount a big mare that was tied to the fence and we couldn't help the situation. I mean, we couldn't help the little pony do the job correctly. That way of mating was a total mess and the little pony was getting very tired. We were sure that if our fathers were there they would help. They would bring a bigger stallion, or perhaps they could put the mare on her knees. Well, we thought of everything possible to help the little pony, until the teacher came to look through the window too, and she went red. After that, we couldn't look through the window any more because soon afterwards some beautiful long curtains with lots of flowers were nailed over the windows – but it was not the same.

School became a bit boring as the years rolled slowly through the salty scrubland of the valley of Chubut. So to relieve the boredom from time to time, two plus two made five in order to see the teacher coming towards me at full trot, waving a ruler, her hands spread out, displaying the full expanse of two big breasts charging aggressively down the room and stopping just in front of my nose. When I thought she had stopped totally the ruler would crash on top of my head but it didn't hurt as much as the *boleadora*.

My teacher told me that Señor Juan Domingo Perón was the President of the country and that he was going to help us create a new Argentine Republic. She said he was a very nice man with a lot of money. But in order for him to help us there were certain rules to obey and she wrote them down: 1) Do not speak Welsh or any Indian language in the school; 2) Do not play with *boleadoras*; 3) Do not race horses in the play ground; 4) Do not chase hares with the dogs at play time.

We tried our best to speak Spanish because Señor Perón had a lot of money – that was why he was building so many schools around the place – and probably he would build a little shed for me and my friends to play in when it rained. Or perhaps he would build a better corral for the pigs and the milking cows – but, although we tried very hard to speak properly, we couldn't find the word for 'pillow' and 'pantry' in Spanish, or the word 'nain' (grandmother in Welsh) or 'choique' (ostrich in Tehuelche Indian). The teacher couldn't either. My father didn't want to talk about 'that rubbish' and my mother said that pillow always has been pillow and pantry has always been pantry, and why should they change our grandmother's name now that she was so old? But we were learning fast now.

We learnt that in Paris there was a tower, made out of iron, which they called 'Eiffel', and somewhere in London was a river and everybody called it 'Thames'. Of Africa, we learned that the river Nile was the longest in the world. The teacher left us with the feeling of wanting to be there, on that river Nile, but we didn't know where Africa was. No other countries, continents or rivers existed in our classroom; either they were too complicated to teach or my teacher didn't know them. So on the subject of Europe we got ten out of ten, especially about the Eiffel Tower.

One very dry afternoon, on my way back from school, the wind from the west brought tons of dust from the desert and covered the whole sleepy valley with an unpleasant blanket of microscopic powdery grey stuff. The birds couldn't fly and my horse couldn't see. All the way home, alongside the road, there were sparrows, pigeons, parrots and falcons and other birds that I couldn't recognize. All of them were balancing on their fragile legs with their eyes closed, like drunken people waiting for a bus. I dismounted from my dusty horse and caught some peregrine falcons, put them into a bag and brought them home with me to wash. As they couldn't see anything, they didn't try to escape.

— 2 —

THE PICTURE

ARRIVING home from school was always a satisfying time. After taking the sheepskin and the cinch that I used as a saddle without stirrups off the back of my horse, I would brush the sweat from him a bit and let him loose in the field until the next morning. Then, feeling extremely hungry, I would run with my stomach empty straight to the pantry of the house, and scoop spoonfuls of honey from the barrel.

Then I would prepare a mug of cocoa to drink with bread, salted butter and more honey.

My family house was big, cool and lovely in the summer and freezing cold in winter. My father, when he was in the house, would spend his entire time in the kitchen, eating, drinking wine or smoking at the table. To my mother the kitchen was the most important place in the house as well, and cooking, washing dishes and arguing with my father were her favourite distractions. The rest of the house consisted of a very big living room where nobody lived, three bedrooms and a large pantry. That living room was kept clean and tidy for everyone to practise music for the Eisteddfod and chapel events. Leading from the living room was a passageway to the bedrooms and pantry. On the wall above the entrance to this long passage was a frightening religious picture, hanging on a strong nail. Once inside the passage, there were two bedrooms to the right, and then opposite were two more bedrooms – but my mother used one of them as a home dairy to make sausages, cream and butter, and to kill chickens. Many sacks of wheat were put on top of salty legs and other parts of pigs, so they could dry and cure into ham and bacon ready for the winter. The jams, honey, biscuits, bread, cakes and sweets were kept in another much smaller pantry close to the kitchen.

In order to get to any of those bedrooms or the large pantry I couldn't avoid seeing 'the Picture'. It didn't matter what was I doing in the house, 'the Picture' was always looking at me, and consequently my entire life, I am sure, has been disturbed and 'traumatised' by those early days. After swallowing that big cocoa and milk drink, I cleaned the eyes of the falcons well, and passed underneath 'the Picture' once more to put them in my room to rest for the night. My mother wasn't happy with this, and my father told me to kill them, as peregrines killed the chickens and baby turkeys. But I couldn't do that. I loved birds as a child, and especially the peregrine falcon. I still think it is a magnificent bird today. In the morning the two birds were fit and flying around my room. I couldn't catch them but I opened all the windows and doors of the house and they flew out like bullets.

Just to open the windows and doors of the house was a challenge, as there were so many of them, and each time I passed from one part of the house to another I had to pass under 'the Picture'. Although we were not a fanatically religious family, the gates of hell were very important at home because my mother, with all the best intentions in the world, had obtained this religious picture somewhere and she hung it on the wall, above the entrance to the passage leading from the living room, where everybody could see it and where nobody could miss it.

I would have been too young to register all the details in that picture, but the main image clearly showed two paths that apparently represented our choices in life. I have since discovered that the painting is called 'The Broad and Narrow Way'. It originated in Germany in approximately 1862, and it illustrates the text of Matthew 7:13-14: '...wide is the gate, and broad is the way, that leadeth to destruction ... narrow is the way which leadeth unto life, and few there be that find it.' Of course, when I was twelve years old I knew nothing of this, I only knew that my sisters and I were terrorised by that picture on the wall and it never escaped our eyes.

On one of the paths in the picture we saw a group of men and women enjoying life; they were walking, socializing, and dancing happily. They drank and laughed, looked healthy, well dressed and were looking generally happy. The other path showed another type of people behaving very differently. They looked extremely poor, they drank water from a well and walked over difficult paths and narrow steps, carrying shoulder bundles like tramps. My mother explained that the picture was illustrating a test for life and if you were able to pass all the tests of the narrow path you would be chosen by God and go to Heaven, while the rich people who were enjoying life on the broad path would go to Hell. The path to Hell had raging fires, many devils, images of people being attacked on the road, and even a man hanging from a window. The path to Heaven wasn't much better, with difficult terrain, steep inclines, many obstacles and I think there was a lion that tried to eat people as well. With fear my sisters and I would analyse the painting and frighten each other with comments. We tried desperately to decipher some of the words that were evidently trying to indoctrinate us, whilst we were busy trying to avoid even looking at 'the Picture'.

Because of that picture and its religious nonsense, my sisters were afraid to go out dancing and I was afraid to go to sleep. I may never wake up again … I may burn in hell … I may be eaten by that terrible lion … and I was even afraid to have a glass of wine then – but, thank God, not any more. Not that my mother and father cared very much about it – in fact I believe they totally ignored the picture, and most of the time they didn't even notice it was still hanging there.

My parents told me that when they were young there were lots of parties in the valley and they used to dance until the early hours of the morning with the music coming out of the Victrola phonograph. When my father was drunk, he used to say that he had been a great dancer when he was young. He gave dancing lessons in our house, and the earlier non-conformist Welsh people were very happy people, they danced all the time, had many parties and played football.

My father was not sure, but he believed that it was during the 1930s that the Methodist-Calvinist religious branch made a first appearance in the valley from Europe and the United States and they changed the happy system of the Welsh Patagonians with their new religion. This new rigorous doctrine apparently became unbearable and many stopped going to chapel altogether, including me. Therefore, it is possible that the picture on the wall was given to my mother by one of these Methodist ministers. I can still remember clearly some preachers coming to our home to drink tea, and to my annoyance eating all the cakes. Whatever the truth is, that picture has been bothering me since the first time I saw it, and after so many years I can still see those paths on 'the Picture' clearly. I was obviously unconvinced by my mother's explanation and I must have decided at a very young age that I would check out both paths in life, to see what would happen.

— 3 —

CHAPEL

EVERY Sunday I woke up with a mixed feeling of being between heaven and hell. To begin with, I had to wake up early to feed the pigs while my mother milked the cows and my father took care of the horses. Also I had to open the sluice gates for the water to flow into the alfalfa paddocks, and then chop wood with the axe to light the fire in the wood-burning stove. After that I had to fetch buckets of water from the irrigation canal, and then if everything was done according to plan, we could have breakfast with lots of jam.

By the time breakfast ended, the water in the saucepans on top of the stove would be warm enough to do the washing up – that included everything in the kitchen and every part of our bodies. My mother with her massive hands would wash my hair and face until I was red with rage. I kept quiet because I knew if I cried or complained she would slap me. Everything had to be done fast and with military precision because chapel was awaiting our arrival. I whinged all the way to chapel as I thought I was entering the gates of hell.

Part of our routine every Sunday morning was to drive to chapel with one horse and five or six members of the Griffiths family in the back of the four-wheeled trap. My mother was going to the chapel to sing, my father to complain about the singing, and the rest of the family to dream about those beautiful villages with nice Welsh names … one was called Jerusalem, the other Bethlehem … and so on. There were many places that had 'lem' and 'hem' at the end. And then there was Israel – that was the biggest village of all in Wales!

As a result of all this mayhem, until I was 20 years old and came to Wales, I believed that Jesus was Welsh.

Troops of farmers arrived at chapel in their dusty Sunday elegance. They appeared in majestic silence from all corners of the valley, driving black one-horse traps shining in the sun. They tethered their horses to the fence post and headed to the big door of the chapel. They shook hands and had a smoke before sitting down to hear a preacher reading the Bible, while an old woman was noisily warming up the old and out of tune harmonium with the foot pedals.

Those weather-beaten farmers were wearing their best and only suits, but for one reason or another, these old suits were too small or too big on them and probably came in the *Mimosa* ship over 100 years ago with the first settlers. As their suits were to be worn at weddings, chapels and funerals only, they were kept in good condition and scented with moth balls. Only the Indians came to chapel with the same working clothes as always, with their gaucho boots smelling of freshly cut hay and horse sweat.

The minister was always wearing a suit with a tie around his neck. He spoke with an incomprehensibly guttural and nasal accent. My mother said, 'He is a very nice little man from north Wales who probably has a potato in his throat.' The minister didn't have much hair on his round head and his round face was so white that I felt sure he had forgotten to have a wash after making 'the' bread. He gave me a tiny piece of his bread while he was mumbling something, and then he disappeared amongst the rest of the kids, as he was so small. I asked my mother why the minister gave me that piece of bread and why it was so small. She explained, without looking at me, that the bread was made by someone called Jesus Christ. Then she explained that Jesus was inside the bread and that I had just eaten his body. I didn't believe one word of what my mother said because the bread tasted just like any other bread but I did nearly throw up.

Later the little man and his helpers distributed glasses of wine of a ridiculously miniature size, and some of the men had difficulty in holding them between their dry and cracked farmers' fingers. When they'd worked out how to hold the miserable chapel glasses between two fingers, the rest was easy – a sudden swig by throwing back the head and the stuff was travelling at high speed into the darkness of the intestine. That was much easier than the bread and, again, I asked my mother 'What was that?' She said, 'That was the blood of Christ inside the wine.' Well, it would make sense, because the bread was very dry and everyone wore a dramatic expression, the tension was growing and the jaws were having a terrible fight with that little bread without crust. Now I was thinking, 'What will they offer for the third course?' because although the quantities were very mean, the taste was okay. I could imagine eating the brains of the poor man with a spoon, or perhaps they made brawn with his feet and nose like we did with the pigs at home. But no, nothing more came from the body of Christ, or from any other body for that matter. We stood up, put on our coats and sang *Hen Wlad fy Nhadau* (Land of My Fathers) and went back to the silence of the desert.

Every Sunday it was my father's day to cook and my mother always invited some of the other respectable cannibals who were hanging around the chapel yard to have lunch with us. The horses were trotting very fast on their way home, leaving clouds of dust on a horizon full of the magical silhouettes of hats and not much else. So, after a good wash in the irrigation canal, we began to talk about food because of the miniscule *hors d'oeuvre* in the chapel. I made a fire under the trees and my father put an iron stake in the ground close by with 15 kilos of meat on it. The young girls, and the old ones, were preparing salads, cakes and rice pudding while the young boys, and the old ones, were drinking wine by the fire, telling stories and falling off their stools with laughter when anybody mentioned the little preacher from Wales with a potato in his throat. And my cousin, Aidel Griffiths, said that the little priest couldn't speak a word of Spanish. 'That shows,' he said, 'if you don't go to school, you don't get educated.' One Indian shouted, 'I speak Tehuelche, Welsh and Spanish, and I never went to school.'

The argument about education was getting a bit heated, until my father corrected us all. He believed that the problem of education was the war in Wales. We asked why they had a war, but my father didn't know that – he just knew there had been more than a thousand years of war. Our neighbour, Captain Glyn Dŵr, left one leg in Europe my father said, and he was Welsh. But he reckoned that Italy was worse. They were dying there one on top of the other and they were buried one on top of the other, too. And then there was Russia … that was bad too. Then there was Japan and that was worse. He took a bottle of *salmuera*[2] and poured it all round the cooking lamb, saying that the Welsh people

2   *salmuera* – an Argentine sauce for adding to meat made of garlic, salt, water and herbs

came to Patagonia because there was no food in the old country and that we should never go back there. Looking at the sizzling lamb, he said, we will never starve here. Then he took another bottle containing red wine and he drank it all. He said that the lamb was ready to eat and then he sang a Welsh song. It was a happy song with ridiculous words and a Cossack rhythm, called *Sospan Fach* (The Little Saucepan).

The party lasted all the afternoon and part of the night. We ate most of the lamb, all the cakes, and many tins of peaches in syrup. A special treat was fresh sliced tomatoes with thick cream and sugar. The dogs ate most of the rice pudding, while the fittest males were still going strong with the red wine. Most of the kids threw up in a hysterical convulsion of hallucinations. The old women were not very impressed with this theatrical performance, but they coped well, as most of them were quite drunk too and they had to go back to chapel at six o'clock. It was usually just the women who went to the evening service because the men were too inebriated. But for all of us that was a good day. The sad part was that we had to wait seven more days to have another Sunday.

— 4 —

FAMILY

THE colonization of Patagonia by the Welsh people began in the middle of the southern hemisphere's wintertime on the shores of Puerto Madryn, on 28th July 1865, with a collection of 152 religious and intellectual rebels. My family's ancestors were not amongst those, although twenty years later they were persuaded to leave Wales and go to the promised land. The Tehuelche Indians saved the 152, or whatever was left of them, from starvation by exchanging many horses, *guanacos*[3], ostriches, armadillos, pumas or wild cats for a few ounces of bread. As bread was unknown to the indigenous population before the Welsh arrived, it became a highly sought-after commodity and the local unit of barter. All exchanges were made in Welsh, and the Indians learnt that '*bara-bara*' (which means 'bread-bread') was the key to this new local trade. The word finally became a great nuisance to the Welsh, because the Indians would arrive at any time of day or night, constantly chanting '*bara-bara*' and nothing else!

The desert was full of food; the problem for the Welsh was how to get it. The schools in Bangor and Aberystwyth never taught the Welsh to use the *boleadora*, or the *tragüil*[4]. They never taught them how to cope with hunger, in the same way as the Indians cope, by doing nothing at all until the weather or the night was good enough for hunting. They didn't know how to smell the wild animals, they didn't know how to be quiet. Their children were to become experts at the hunting game but then they were too small and, apart from crying, they couldn't do much more. Freedom was available but at a high price, and many questions arose such as: 'Is this the meaning of freedom?' They were free to wander in the desert speaking Welsh, they were free to practise their religion on the top of any

3   *guanaco* – one of the four species of south American camelids, the others being the llama, alpaca and vicuña

4   *tragüil* – a weapon made of a leather thong with one heavy stone ball on the end, used by the Indians to kill pumas

hill, like the Indians, but they were already indoctrinated by the traditions they inherited from Wales. So they built a few chapels and an invisible barrier and decided to stick together for a while, praying for their Celtic God to send another boat full of people from Wales. Somewhere on one of these boats were my great-grandfathers. One from Merthyr Tydfil – he knew a lot about coal – another from Bethesda and he knew a lot about slate quarries. Another was from Llanuwchllyn – this one was good with horses. The other one is a bit of a mystery. He came from the United States in a boat with a certain Captain Rogers. His surname was Mariani, he was born in Austria and rumours say that they were both pirates. They sank their boat off the Atlantic coast of Chubut and they settled in the heart of the Welsh colony.

These great-grandfathers arrived on this faraway coast because for more than a thousand years Wales and the Welsh had been under the thumb of English landlords. Even today some believe that these landlords are still squeezing the wealth out of the land. The English, using the Welsh workforce as serfs, divided the Welsh countryside into huge estates. Most of them began to work for the English companies at the age of ten, in coal mines and quarries, and by the time they were forty they were dead from pneumoconiosis, coal dust, and the appalling work conditions. Patagonia offered a better life than the workers had in the coal mines in south Wales. In some coal and steel mining areas, there were as many as seventeen workers living in a two-bedroomed terraced house by the end of the 19th century. The few Welsh who used to own a bit of land were so heavily taxed they had to emigrate or live on the edge of starvation. The English rulers even taxed the quantity of light that entered through windows and tried everything they could to kill off the Welsh language. Apart from the political reason, the reason why the English wanted to kill the Welsh language – which alongside the Basque language is one of the oldest in Europe – was that they could neither understand nor pronounce it.

No one in my family seems to know much about my Austrian grandfather with the Italian surname. Interestingly, a Frenchman with an Italian surname, Auguste Mariani, was one of the first to use cocaine in commercial quantities in the 1800s. He invented a cocktail with wine and cocaine, Mariani Wine, and it is said that it was a hell of a nice drink which made everyone very happy. Pope Leo XIII even awarded a gold medal to Mariani Wine 'in recognition of benefits received' from the tonic. This drink was very well known all around Europe where posters advertised the wine as 'capturing the vibrant spirit of the *Belle Époque*'. Of course, the cocaine ingredient, like so many other pleasures, eventually became illegal. But not before Coca-Cola followed the path of my possible ancestors for a while, until it also became illegal to sell a soft drink with cocaine as its special ingredient.

It is a bit suspicious that the people of the Welsh colony in Patagonia don't want to talk about the Mariani. The chapel that I used in my youth was built on land donated by the Mariani in Bryn Crwn. They were good farmers, and like anybody else in the area, they spoke Welsh. So, where did this idea of being pirates come from? Were the Welsh Patagonians involved in something dodgy down there, apart from the colonization business? In the 18th and 19th centuries the English were making a huge amount of money selling all the opium the Chinese and the Indians could produce, so is it possible that the Welsh chapel-going angels were doing something similar in South America?

The idea could have materialized because the greatest pirates of all time were Welsh – such as Black Bart Roberts (who managed to scupper 400 ships, mainly Spanish). Roberts was born near Haverfordwest and was a close friend of Hywel Davies, another Welsh pirate who was killed by the Portuguese. Roberts became the commander of Davies' ships, and attacked and killed the Portuguese, honouring Davies by stealing the treasure. Captain Roberts fled with a magnificent fortune, the biggest in the history of 'the pirates of the Caribbean'. And of course, another famous pirate was Captain Morgan, who eventually became governor of Jamaica at the age of 45 (sent by Oliver Cromwell – another descendant of a Welshman, Morgan Williams) after an illustrious career as a pirate. His name stands with pride in all the pubs of the world on the bottles of Captain Morgan Rum.

The reinforcement of the new arrivals brought prosperity of every kind to the colony. This wave of colonists was not so motivated by religious fanaticism. They had been forced by the English corporations in Wales to live a life of extreme exploitation, poverty and dissolution. These people were hard working Welshmen from the coal mines of south Wales and the slate quarries of north Wales, including some sturdy and stocky farmers from the mountains. And thanks to this large influx the little valley of Chubut flourished. There were fresh tools for the workaholics and there were fresh women for the *desperados*. Some of these women were good quality sopranos and their descendants were good sopranos too. I remember Mary Ann particularly – she'd pee herself while hitting a high note. Those coal miners, farmers, and quarrymen were not as intellectual as the first bunch, although their rebellion against the English was the same. Their definition of hatred was very simple: we hate the English language and we hate the English people. And although I didn't know what the hell they were talking about, I was not allowed to learn a word of English.

The first ever court case in the Welsh colony was to do with an argument over the Welsh language. A group of English sailors, who had arrived by boat at the port in Rawson, entered a local bar and ordered drinks in English. The Welsh refused to serve them and a massive fight broke out between the English sailors and the Welsh settlers. One of the Welsh knocked out an English sailor, so his captain intervened and the case was prepared, ready to go to court. There hadn't been a court case in the colony yet, because it was quite difficult to prepare a legal case in the desert. So the captain agreed to an out-of-court settlement with the leader of the colony, suggesting the sailor be dealt with back in England. The Welsh leader gave the captain a message to take back with him, saying, 'We haven't travelled 8,000 miles in order to speak Welsh freely, only to be obliged to speak English when you arrive in our local bar.'

All this was good news for me, as I didn't want to learn English anyway. But my family was determined that instead I should learn to tame horses for work on the farm, learn to fence in a straight line, learn to clean the irrigation canals, learn to kill cows, lambs and pigs, and learn to sing and to write poetry. And also to make sausages. I was okay with most of these things but the annual killing of a full-grown pig was a nasty job – the first time I had to do this, he didn't want to die. I was plunging the full length of my knife into his heart but half an hour later he was still squealing at the top of his voice. As a farmer, whatever I thought about it was irrelevant, it had to be done. It was forbidden to knock him out with the sledge hammer; all the blood had to drain from the veins for the meat to be edible.

Laziness was not a respectable word and you had to be alert at all times. The normal surprises were a whip across the ears, a bucket of cold water at five o'clock in the morning, or being lifted up with a solid kick in the arse. Of all these sweet family traditions, the bucket of cold water was, I believe, the worst. You could have been dreaming about the Garden of Eden when 'whoosh …!' After that, of course, I would jump in the air, knocking my head on the wall and being totally disorientated in the dark of the winter morning, with temperatures of around eight or ten below zero. It was difficult to see the work horses in the dark, but I had to feed them before I could prepare a *maté*[5] or a cup of coffee for myself and, whilst I was hurriedly drinking this, my father was preparing all the gear. Within a few minutes he would be standing at the back of the sledge waiting for me, with all the horses ready to go. The freezing morning told me that I was awake and my eyes could see in the dark by now. Another day had started and it was exactly the same as yesterday.

....

5   *maté* – the indigenous herbal tea of Argentina

— 5 —

Grandfather

I was about seven years old when my grandfather William Gerlan Griffiths died and, like the rest of the family, I cried.

My memories of him are a misty, wide, panoramic picture. He was a respected man, the oldest, and therefore the head of the entire family. I was afraid of him and saw something of the devil in his eyes. I don't remember speaking to him ever, but now that he was dead I wanted to know him. It was too late, he was cold in his coffin and people were preparing to carry him away to the nearby hills to be buried, and that was the end of that particular Griffiths.

His farm at that time was a paradise to me; it produced everything the family needed. There were paddocks of alfalfa, and fields with wheat undulating in the wind, and an orchard with all types of fruits hanging heavily from the exotic trees. In the far corner of the farmyard a cellar was always full of meat, butter, cream and milk in big jars. Horses, sheep, cows, pigs and dozens of chickens could be seen wandering lazily around the farm, and there was also a tame parrot which used to swear at the visitors in Welsh.

By the 1920s my great-grandfather had made a large amount of money by producing and selling chickpeas and decided he had to have a Model T Ford when these cars were first imported into Argentina. The whole family celebrated this new achievement with many cups of tea, although this time his whim was short-lived. He bought two of the cars, but because no one had ever seen one and he couldn't drive himself, he gave one to each of his two daughters. One of these daughters was the wife of my grandfather, but neither of them could drive the car either, so it stood under the tamarisk trees for many years. My grandfather was reasonably well off in the area; the best working horses, wagons and farm equipment belonged to him, as did the only Model T Ford now. Once a week someone would wash it thoroughly with soap, but apart from that, the novelty car was left unmolested for years under the trees. Finally my father learned to drive it, with great difficulty, when he was about eight years old. His first trip in it was on a Sunday morning to chapel with all the Griffiths family trembling on top, including my temperamental grandfather, who obviously arrived late at chapel that day. It was faster to go by horse after all!

The Model T didn't have gear levers, only pedals to change from first gear to 'direct gear', which was the equivalent of second, third and fourth gears all together. It also didn't have a petrol pump, so the petrol had to get to the carburettor from the tank by gravity, and any slopes or hills had to be climbed backwards with the car in reverse. To make things worse, the car had to use the same tracks as the horses and carts and all the horses in the area were afraid of that monster machine which vomited smoke and disturbed the silence of the desert with its horrific noise. The horses ran for their lives, bucking and throwing their riders into the mud. So whenever the Model T driver and the horse riders spotted each other in the distance, someone had to lower the wire fences temporarily for the horses to make a detour through other people's farms. After some bumpy rides up and down the colony, the Model T Ford came to a halt finally under a weeping willow tree. From then on, the Model T – which was the equivalent of a

Rolls Royce today – was used by just the chickens for them to sleep in and lay their eggs.

I heard stories of my grandfather and his brother Johnny being wild characters in the valley, and one year, after an exceptionally good harvest, the two brothers decided to buy two barrels containing 400 litres of wine. They got drunk for a week and nearly died of intoxication. My grandfather stopped drinking after that and became very religious and reserved, and my father told me that he didn't want to work any more on the farm either. All the work had to be done by his sons – 'the boys' – and he had five of them. His temper became unbearable and at any opportunity he would whip my father's backside. The 'boys' got fed up with the behaviour of the old Griffiths so they all married local girls and moved out of the farm. A young Indian named Mr Penny came to replace my father and his brothers as a farm-hand, and in a short time Mr Penny was adored by my grandfather and the neighbours, especially because he learned to speak Welsh fluently and sang hymns in the chapel of Bryn Crwn, shining with his white wide smile.

After the funeral of my grandfather the Indian Penny disappeared and we never saw him again. The activity on the farm became very messy and the local judge was walking incessantly up and down through the fields, marking out divisions and boundaries. All my family was there too, and uncles and aunts with their dogs. They were drinking tea and *maté* all day and moving the furniture. The whole house became a chaotic site, I couldn't find anything, and they were pushing me around like an orphan lamb. They divided the farm with authority and even the horses and chickens became aware of their separation. The smell of death was spreading, people were landing like vultures and dismantling the carcass into pieces, and it didn't take very long for the legacy of my grandfather, which had taken eighty years to ripen, to be turned into an unrecognizable catastrophe. The weeping willows were sad and the air carried the smell of death into the barns and fields. Old William Gerlan Griffiths had accomplished his mission and he was gone. It was the sad end of an era and I knew nothing would be the same again. Although, somehow, I felt it was a perfect time for me to grow up fast and explore my world.

— 6 —

LIVING THE DREAM

THE Welsh people didn't have it easy at all, colonizing Patagonia, and although I don't have the slightest ambition to colonize anything, it hasn't been very easy for me, either. In fact, I think the problems of life have been a bit of a nuisance sometimes. But, anyhow, the place where my ancestors chose to establish themselves was dry, windy, rough and inhospitable and I believe it must have been quite monotonous in those days because there was no one else there apart from some not very reassuring and wild-looking Indians. I am sure that the Indians laughed a lot seeing the new white arrivals in suits, dragging their suitcases into the desert. It must have been the best pantomime the Indian kids had ever seen. They couldn't talk to each other because on one side of the line there were 152 Welsh-speaking Welsh, and on the other side there were I-don't-know-how-many Indians, speaking Tehuelche. I can imagine the Tehuelches, very innocently inviting the Welsh for a party, and the distrustful Welsh saying something back like, 'Terribly sorry, we're a bit busy today – bugger off.'

God didn't try to help the Welsh either, because as soon as these *gringos*[6] began to build a house (or probably a chapel first), there would be a flash-flood and, 'whoosh,' everything came down again. The poor souls had nowhere else to go because they had one-way tickets, so they had no choice other than to accept things the way they were. After all, Patagonia was apparently the Promised Land. They got that from the Bible of course and those poor souls were easy to cheat. The Promised Land … promised by whom? Soon they found out that the Promised Land was as demoralizing as all the promises that God had made before in those cruel black Welsh valleys of coal. But now? They were on the shores of Puerto Madryn with that one-way ticket that had just expired.

Further on through the desert was a river with lush brown but drinkable water. The capricious twisted river became their salvation; yet so nearly their death. Floods were a nuisance which inundated the whole valley of Chubut. But as a child I was looking forward to seeing the river full of water, up to the very top, carrying trees and dead animals on the surface like deformed balloons. Everyone was so concerned, seeing the water rising to the last millimetre of the riverbank, and when there was no more hope of stopping God's whim, we all fled to the nearby hills with the horses and cows, dogs and cats, with tables and buckets to milk the cows. My mother was collecting pillows and throwing

6   *gringos* – foreigners

me over her shoulder like a bag of knitting wool. It was too late to catch the chickens and the turkeys. Some of the baby calves were already on the wagons with the three horses tied nervously, ready to go like hell at the command of my father. I was shivering with excitement but none of us kids was allowed to move or to talk. We were as stiff as soldiers on parade. We were afraid and cold, the dogs were barking noisily and jumping to the top of the wagons with the calves, and down again. My mother whipped the mare in the four-wheeled trap and off we went, trotting quickly towards the white clay hills.

The 'mansion' which awaited us on the hills looked as though it had been in conflict with itself for a long time. It was an abandoned shed, but a busy shed at that, because someone was keeping goats there. The smell of cats' pee was unbearable. But nobody complained. In a few hours we transformed the place. We brushed all the goat shit out of the door, laid mattresses everywhere and lit the fire in the disused fireplace. The aroma of that smoke filling the room has never left my mind. It was an incredible sight and smell. There was so much smoke inside the room that we couldn't see each other. The chimney was obviously blocked by birds nesting inside and then, just to make matters worse, the inside of the chimney caught fire as well. A huge tongue of flame with sparks and millions of little lights flew high into the sky. My father was bringing the big wagon with the milking cows following behind because inside it were their calves. The dogs were herding the sheep and other horses to my father's whistles. My father saw the pandemonium in the chimney and didn't say anything. We were all alive and smiling, with cats and dogs inside the new home.

The new home was a paradisiacal refuge, very close to the white clay hills. They were a wonderful place to play and collect wood from the bushes for my mother, and to snare hares for lunch. We got very fit climbing all the hills and were incredibly happy because the school was under water right up to the roof. We would have at least three months of holidays.

A woman gave birth to a baby during the floods and it was a problem to find the right name for the poor thing. A clever old man came to the parents' rescue and said, 'Why don't you call him "flood" in Spanish?' So they did, and his name for a while was 'Inundación ap Morgan'. My mother told me that the judge, who was also a councillor and a priest, came to see the Morgan family and the baby Inundación, to see if the family could change his name because the entire valley was laughing at the poor 'Flood ap Morgan' baby. Apparently they did, by cutting half of the name out, so he became Siôn ap Morgan. This was a bit ironic because, by law, every child born in Argentina from the 1940s on was obliged to bear a Spanish forename (or a name easily pronounced in Spanish). This ruled out most Welsh names, and explains why so many Patagonians have names such as Eugenio Griffiths, Pedro Jones, Diego Jenkins, Carlos Williams, Mario Lewis, Margarita Davies, and so on! My favourite combination has always been Dolores de Concha Edwards, which translates from the Argentine Spanish as 'Pain in the cunt Edwards'. Before the forename law was passed the Welsh were already being tongue-in-cheek as one of my grandfathers was called

Isaac Newton Davies, another was Winston Churchill Roberts, and one little farm was called Hyde Park.

The day after our arrival at our new home, my father woke me up very early and said, 'Hurry up, come and see this.' The valley was gone and, instead, the sea was right there in front of me. I had never experienced any floods before and it was frightening. I could make out our farm in the distance; part of the house, the roof, and the surrounding trees could be seen, the rest was under water. My father and mother were calm – of course, they had seen these flash-floods before, and they were old enough to have plenty of patience. They were made of a different substance from me. They never despaired or lost their tempers in situations like that. They never asked each other, 'What shall we do today, then?' They just went on with their lives as if an invisible being was telling them what to do – making bread, slapping the kids, feeding the animals, or whistling nonchalantly everywhere.

One day someone arrived with a boat and four oars to take us back to the abandoned valley. We went. For me, it was the first time that I had had a chance to rock in a boat. The heavy wooden craft was slowly traversing the valley's flooded landscape on top of the fences. It was wonderful, dramatic and sad, to see the entire valley submerged in the sludge of swirling brown water which, in the heavy silence, was transporting the stacks of straw with chickens and cats on top. Dead cows and dead sheep were everywhere, floating and turning with every whim of the wind, half buried in the constantly moving little waves.

We were heading towards our farm to collect whatever was useful, especially the chickens which by now were either dead or very wet. I couldn't swim then, and the trip was fraught with danger for me, but nobody cared about that. The excitement of the situation filled us with physical and spiritual power and, although the rowers were exhausted in a sweaty, nervous way, we managed to navigate the submerged farm. We picked up many chickens from the trees, and turkeys too. My lovely tame ducks had disappeared and probably the little devils were very happy with the aftermath of the deluge, a very special present from God that destroyed all the Welsh dressers with their blue and white china cups and plates.

The floods were a tragedy, but tragedies are sometimes necessary in many ways. They pull people together, as in war, and it is the only time that everybody becomes a socialist, defending together whatever there is to defend and eating together whatever there is to eat. I am not in favour of floods, however necessary they can be, but I must say that the people were much nicer then. Even the police were helping. In fact, it was a huge family which, on reflection, I really miss. The water stayed with us for a long time and, although we were much thinner, we didn't die. My mother entertained us by making us sing and when we didn't want to sing she would slap us in the face with her big hands. Then we sang, very seriously.

Eventually the muddy brown water began to say goodbye, but it took all the time in the world to retreat gently into the far away sea, leaving behind a thick layer of chocolate clay, that enriched the whole valley with minerals which came from the far away Andes. Was that the real present from the Gods to the Welsh settlers? Now we could plough the farm, now we could plant the potatoes, carrots and melons, now the flowers would begin to open once more, and the bees busy would be. The willows would be heavy with flocks of doves bending their branches, and the falcons would fly like bullets through the gaps in the poplars. Humans would begin to look fatter all round, and the children of the valley would carry on playing and annoying everybody with their tricks. The wild sons of the Patagonian valley would continue to grow in their isolated nest, without knowing that they were born in the healthiest place on earth.

At least these floods were natural and didn't last long, soon disappearing back into the sea. Once, near Bala in north Wales was a village called Treweryn. But in 1965 the English wanted water to wash their socks, so they constructed a dam and flooded the Treweryn valley, leaving the little village submerged by the water. They didn't ask the Welsh their opinion or permission, they just did it. And this happened in what is supposed to be a free and democratic country, so perhaps the isolated nest of the valley of Chubut was a better place for democracy to be put into practice.

In 1902 Chile nearly declared war on Argentina over the land that covers most of the Andean lake district of Patagonia. The Chilean argument was that the land on which rivers and lakes flow into Chile should be theirs. Argentina disagreed. War was inevitable, until the Welsh Patagonians stepped in and said, 'We have been in Patagonia since 1865 and if we can't be a free Welsh nation in South America, we shall belong to Argentina, not to Chile.' This was done in the village of Trevelin, in a democratic way via a referendum, with a unanimous vote by the Welsh in favour of Argentina.

Argentina had made a big effort to help the Welsh settlers to establish themselves in Patagonia. The government had given them land, stock, farm equipment and building materials. Also, the Welsh would be free – for the time being anyway – to use their own language, laws and culture. After that little disagreement between Argentina and Chile, and at the request of those two countries, King Edward VII of Britain stepped in and his appointed referee approved the decision that the frontier should be drawn across the highest peaks of the Andes, so war never materialized. Thanks to the Welsh again, a vast area of the Patagonian Andes, which for many contains the most astonishing views in the whole world, belongs now to Argentina.

— 7 —

ITALIANS IN PATAGONIA

IN order to see the most astonishing views in the whole world it was decided that a railway should be built from the Welsh colony in the east to the Andes in the west. But to practise a bit first a railway would be built from Trelew (which was just a rail staging-post at that time) to the 'port' of Madryn (which was just a natural harbour at that time). So, from 1889 when the railway was begun, many Italians arrived in the Chubut valley as labourers to build the 40-mile railway line that was to unite Trelew with Madryn, therefore opening up Madryn as a port to export farm products. This rail track was a great success for the Welsh. Now they could go to Porth Madryn by rail in a few hours, and some went on Sundays. From Madryn they could go on holiday to Buenos Aires by boat, and some did that as well, and some never returned.

The next whim was an ambitious one: to unite Trelew with Cwm Hyfryd or Esquel in the Andes. This project was to lay tracks across 400 miles of very rough country – rocky, stony and totally deserted land. Several bridges had to be built over the river Chubut and tunnels had to be dug for the little train to pass through. After about 100 miles of rail had been laid, they stopped to think seriously about it and nothing has moved since. Because they stopped the construction in the middle of nowhere, the poor little train had no reason to go there. So someone started to dig up the freshly laid railway track and sell it as scrap metal.

Now the problem was that many Italians were then without a job. They wanted to stay with the Welsh in the Welsh settlement, so they stayed. They sang alongside the Welsh and they married the Welsh Patagonian girls. As most of these Italians were from northern Italy and therefore of Celtic extraction, they integrated nicely into the Welsh community. Only a few years after their arrival they were better off economically than the Welsh. They sang all day long and sang louder than the Welsh. Also they worked extremely hard. Even on Sundays, when the Welsh were praying, the Italians were making money somewhere. Some Welsh religious fanatics were not very happy with these 'Italianos' but they had to accept them as they were so friendly and ready to help anyone at any time.

I remember one Italian man arriving at my father's farm. He had been walking all night and had got lost. My mother had been cooking some wood pigeons and they were still warm inside the wood-burning stove when this half-starving Italian stepped into our home. The Italian devoured the pigeons, leaving nothing for the dogs, not even the bones. I had never seen anything like that before. I thought he had the teeth of a lion. After that flesh and bone meal, my father asked him which country he preferred – meaning Italy or Argentina – to which he replied, 'My country is where I can eat.' He stayed on the farm that night, drinking wine and talking to my father all night long. I was half asleep under the table, on a sheepskin as a mattress, and I vaguely recall some of their conversation, which was something to do with the war in Europe. My father couldn't follow that conversation because he didn't know much about why the people in Europe were having a war.

The Italian was a strongly built man, about 90 kilos in weight, but he described how during his imprisonment in a concentration camp he weighed only 30 kilos. He was just bones and, in desperation, he had eaten his shoes. My father couldn't comprehend that but both of them became very good friends. This exotic Italian with strange stories taught me some Italian words that I learnt with pride. He used to call me 'il bambino', the little one, and as my mother was a fine soprano, he took any opportunity to sing with her while my father jumped on his horse and went for more wine. The Italian spoke hardly any Spanish so he learned the Spanish that we understood comfortably in the community, well mixed with Welsh.

Some years later the Italian, with a name like Boccini I think, became a successful farmer, and while harvesting the alfalfa he broke a bolt on his harvesting machine. The word for this machine in the Welsh colony was 'el ripar'. So Boccini took a bus to Buenos Aires to get the spare part that was not available in the valley. When he finally found the place that sold the part, no one understood him, because Boccini wanted a bolt for 'el ripar'. He didn't know that the Welsh had adopted the word 'ripar' from 'reaper' in the English language and had introduced it into the farming vocabulary. When he came back from Buenos Aires, he invited us for a party under a tree on his farm to celebrate the arrival of the bolt for 'el ripar'. He asked my father, between glasses of wine, why the people here called it 'ripar', when in Buenos Aires 'el ripar' was called *guadanadora*, *cortadora*, *cegadora* or *cosechadora*? My father didn't have a clue what our Italian friend was talking about.

— 8 —

Music

My family became aware of my interest in music and sometimes they would help me to hit the right note but not without a temperamental disagreement of the Do-Re-Me-Fa-So-La-Ti-Do system. My father would be seated on one of the beds with his hands on his knees, locking any possible movement. His neck would shrink between his shoulders and his eyes were busy drilling holes into the wooden floor around his feet. In that peculiar position, he would free his cracked, double bass voice, frightening the cats. By contrast, my mother could hit some top soprano notes whilst walking, cleaning, cooking and kicking the chickens out of the kitchen.

In a nice way they were always interfering in one way or another with whatever I wanted to do alone. They couldn't understand my way of writing songs. My father said that this kind of writing seemed to come from a long time ago … something to do with the Druids. 'Who the hell were the Druids?' I asked, and he looked me in the eyes for a few seconds, without saying anything. Then he turned his head to the window. One of the racehorses was loose, eating my mother's flowers.

I became very intrigued by all these things that I didn't know about, and my parents were very irritated by so many questions that they couldn't answer. So they bought me a dictionary. That was a wonderful book, packed with all kinds of words. Most of them were new to me, they were clean and fresh. I was no longer shooting doves at siesta time with the twelve-bore, I was reading my book, and at night my eyes were getting very tired after hours of reading in the light of the little paraffin lamp. After finishing my book many times, I would open it again on any page and it was magical – there were new words inside every time. I was sure that my *duende*[7] was putting in new words while I was sleeping because my little book was getting bigger.

Now that I was 'well educated' and I could sing and play the guitar, I decided to investigate the closest village – that was Gaiman. Gaiman was one of the most important stopping places for the nomadic Tehuelches, long before the obscure and beautiful name Patagonia came to bother our ears. The meaning of Gaiman in the Tehuelche language is apparently

7   *duende* – invisible impish spirit (around a room or place) / magical quality (of a singer, for example)

something to do with a stone. It could be true because I remember two massive boulders opposite each other at the entrance to the village. The only roads came from the south and from the west and both passed through these unique boulders. In Welsh, 'cae man' means 'narrow enclosure', and when I was a child I wondered if this had something to do with the narrow road in 'the Picture'.

I never found out why the roads squeezed through the narrow gap between the boulders when there was so much flat and clean land around it, or why the new white sons of the desert decided to blow the boulders up with dynamite. My father told me that he could not recall any accidents around those huge stones. The only accident that he remembered in the village involved two Model T Fords. In 1922, at one corner, the drivers, who were usually so polite to each other and always used their horns, forgot to use them and crashed into each other. It was the one and only crash in the village and after the smash they didn't know what to do. One day, very close to the boulders, my father didn't know what to do either and would die as the result of an accident. But that was later.

By the time I was around twelve, school had finished forever for me, and the chapel didn't smell as fresh as that little girlfriend I used to meet by the river. The whole valley would become a large bed after lunch, when the farmers would forget their ambitions for two hours of sleepy siesta. That was always the perfect time for me to escape to the river, relaxing under a romantic shower of silence between that shy 'hello' and the timorous 'goodbye', although that silence had somehow a different meaning to anything I had experienced before. And when nobody was waiting for me any more, I was still going to the same place because I had discovered a new type of music. It was not the music of the chapel, or the music of a funeral, it was the sound of branches in the river creating a symphony, beautifully orchestrated, and beautifully performed by the most talented birds and insects. Those were my friends now, I knew it. They were singing all the time and for no reason at all. But it was for that reason that I bought a guitar and learned to play. They accepted me into their orchestra and I spent many summers and many siesta hours experiencing the whispering of the silence. I was composing songs for the birds and I was composing songs for the trees. One of the dark willows was dead but in my song he was a cradle, all green and young, with hundreds of songs. The beavers taught me how to swim through the mirage of different dimensions. And the dreamer embraced his *duende* and together they began to fly.

By the time I reached the age of fifteen, my strides were longer than the villagers' and the people in the tranquil village were nervous. They took a breath, and analysed me thoroughly, from the viewpoint of the better-painted, red-tiled school. My school never learned that Germany had something to do with it. I joined a little mixed choir and as I had never seen so many girls before, I fell in love with all of them. I met other guitarists in the village and we decided to form a folk group. I loved my new friends. Benito Jones had a lot of sense and he was a good bass. Mario Lewis had a deep voice too, and he had a talented way of imitating people and animals. My favourite was the imitation of a male pig that had just finished making love. Mario would slacken his long legs a bit, then he would slacken his whole body, then he would fix his eyes on a non-existent point in the air with a ridiculous comic manner. His human pig was in silence, and that made us laugh.

Hector Williams had a sweet tenor voice but he didn't last long; the Evangelist Church had other plans for him. Armando Ferreira had an extraordinary sense of percussion, so he played his drums. Carlos Dante Ferrari was a good poet and together we composed over 100 songs and, of course, by that time The Beatles had begun to jump around on stages around the world, and although we couldn't understand a single word of their songs, we thought they were good. The *Yellow Submarine* theme became quite popular in the desert, which was a bit ironic. Our group was born. We called it 'The Voices of Chubut' and we travelled up and down the country in an aeroplane with very clean seats. We always looked at each other with big eyes at take-off, then we would knock down one or two glasses of whisky, have a quick look at the stewardess' legs, and applaud in the excitement of landing safely. We didn't have time for anything else while the courageous machine was going through all kinds of catabatic winds in the southern Patagonian Andes, freezing our acting skills, and creating pandemonium, at a very high altitude.

The weather also created pandemonium with my guitar. It had a problem with the dust in the dry season, as it would crack and lose its sweet sound. I asked my music tutor what I should do about it, and he advised me to put a handful of damp wheat or barley inside the guitar. That was a good method of keeping it in good form. The dust would stick to the grain, leaving the porous wood clean. When I arrived in

Britain for the first time with my guitar containing wheat, the customs officers at Heathrow airport found it and were sniffing the grains, looking at me suspiciously. I don't know what they told me because I couldn't understand any English, but they took the wheat away.

Our folk band lasted four years, no more. We began to chase the few available girls, and somehow we didn't have time to practise our songs. As soon as the sun had disappeared in those late afternoons the boys would disappear as well, to the back of the hills, where the Indians and the rest of the poor people lived. In that area it was quite easy to find girlfriends although you had to be a bit careful about the sharp knives in the dark and the intolerable gossip of the nice chapel people. Love began to show its powerful weapon and we were just like any other zombies at its mercy. My father's rather agricultural expression was that 'One fanny can pull more than a pair of oxen,' and now I began to believe him! I was losing interest in the farm and at the same time I was getting a bit fed up of the sentimentalism of love songs, the gossip, the bullshit of people with broken hearts and the narrow society moving slowly through the only street of my village. It was time to do something about it, so I went far away and joined the Navy.

— 9 —

The Military Experience

THE lorry taking me to the Navy took many days to arrive at the big city of Buenos Aires. It was a slow, big lorry dragging its trailer in unbelievably slow motion. When I could see some long hills coming up ahead, I would jump out of the lorry, and walk by its side for a while. It never managed to pass me on the hills. I told the story of my life to the driver and that took about one hour. He agreed with everything I said. So I realized that I was going to swallow a few days of silence, but that was not too difficult. I began to drift, like the lorry and its driver, and I threw myself into a sack packed very tidily with my memories. Some letters, many voices … hundreds of them, I could hear them individually, and the lorry couldn't make enough noise with its engine to distract me. It was an extraordinarily interesting toy to play with – as soon as I switched off, these memories with pictures appeared in front of my eyes. I was enjoying this and I began to give life to them somewhere in my head.

The spirit of Old Fuentes joined me for a ride in the lorry many times, and I really enjoyed his company once again. It had been a long time since I was a young child, but I still remembered him well as he lived in our house. He had died when I was about five but even in those early few years I had grown very fond of him and I thought he was a better person than any of my family. Old Fuentes and Mr Roberts decided to hunt down an Indian who had gone mad, cutting out horses' tongues, eating them raw, and leaving the poor animals to suffer an agonizing death. Mr Roberts used Old Fuentes as a guide to find the madman in the desert and he, Roberts, killed him. They promised each other to keep that a total secret. But one day Mr Roberts was drunk and he told the story in a bar, and then somebody reported him to the police.

Old Fuentes was a Tehuelche Indian, a huge man, single, without property or commitments of any kind. Mr Roberts was his friend and he was married with children, so Old

Fuentes went to the police and held himself responsible for killing the mad Indian. The police believed him, of course, and they sent him to Ushuaia, in Tierra del Fuego, for 25 years with a ball of iron chained to his leg. He was already an old man when he went and he was the same old man when he came back 25 years later. He died in our house when I was still a kid. Sometimes I thought that he was my grandfather. He was a sincere friend to my father and to many other Welsh people in the area but he was a Tehuelche and so nobody saved him, nobody in the colony stood up for him.

That is a sad story my father used to say, and there are many more sad stories too. The people of the colony were nice people but they were not angels. Many of the Welsh Patagonians left the settlement in the early stages of the colony and joined other groups in the desert. Some of those groups were very famous in the United States but they couldn't live there for some reason. So they chose Patagonia and, like the Welsh, they built their homes in the same province – but in the west, in the area of Cholila. Amongst them were Butch Cassidy, the Sundance Kid, and also a woman; she was a teacher by the name of Etta Place. They were good farmers who dressed very elegantly. Even their horses were always in impeccable condition.

I had plenty of time to dream about those nice people who lived 700 kilometres away in a big ranch in the Andes. I decided that, one day, I would visit them on an elegant horse and they would give me a job. But then the lorry driver spoke. We were passing through a flat part of the desert and wherever I looked there was nothing to see, just the normal scrubland of the pampas, very nice for about two seconds.

The driver said, 'Look, look,' and I looked and he said again, 'look, look, look, the guanacos!'

I saw the guanacos staring at us with indifference, and I said, 'Yes, I see them, so what?' So he explained the strange thing that had happened to his friend. This friend used to race cars and one night he went with his fast car to see his girlfriend, without knowing that his girlfriend was travelling to see him in the opposite direction. 'The tragedy happened around here,' he said, 'on this straight part of the road and with no traffic at all. At the precise moment that these two lovers were approaching each other at high speed, a guanaco decided to cross the road. Both cars hit the guanaco and the lovers embraced themselves in a terrific accident. The day after, a lorry driver found the wreckage. The two lovers were very close to each other with parts of the guanaco strewn over them.' I was shaking a bit after hearing about such a strange coincidence; it seemed an impossible place to have an accident.

Ten hours later we stopped for a meal, and Buenos Aires was not much closer, but we did arrive eventually. The sprawling, humid city was very cold, and although I was used to the cold weather of Patagonia, this was a dirty, damp day. I knew it was the middle of winter, and I knew there was nothing nice about it. In the morning I went to knock at the door of the devil. There were thousands of young boys already crammed inside a huge shed and, like me, they were quite nervous. Everything looked so similar to shearing time in the *estancias*[8] of Patagonia. Relaxing against the wall of the shed were about twenty quiet middle-aged men,

8   *estancia* – farm or ranch

dressed in grand clothes, with pieces of metal hanging from their shoulders. They were like the owners of the *estancia*. Shouting and running up and down the shed were lots of younger men – there was nothing grand about their way of dressing but they were very fit, stamping loudly with their heavy leather boots, and their faces didn't invite you to ask any questions. Those were the sheepdogs of the *estancia* and, of course, we were their sheep!

They told us to take all our clothes off, and we stood there naked, trying to avoid looking at each other by gazing at the ceiling of the shed instead. We then passed through a rigorous physical test. They opened our mouths and looked very slowly at our teeth, like I used to do on the farm to check the age of the horses. But these people knew our ages very well, because we had given our birth certificates to them. After that they looked at our arses, touching them with some kind of instrument, and again I couldn't understand why this was so important to them. I began to doubt about my decision to join the Navy but it was difficult to concentrate because now these guys were playing with my testicles. Somehow, we all managed to pass through the examination, with a feeling of extreme vulnerability. They opened the wide door and we trotted, giggling, to an outdoor corral.

The day after that high-handed examination they put us on a flat boat that resembled a floating sledge pushing the waves apart in the mouth of the River Plate. We were heading towards the island of Martín García where more disorientated Argentine cadets were waiting for us. We were around 8,000 young dreamers wondering what on earth had made us decide to join the Navy. The island was a dump of a place in the middle of the river, close to Uruguay. It used to be the prison for the rebels of the Argentine Government – even General Juan Domingo Perón went to a little dungeon out there. We were supposed to study the sea and the boats and so on, in order to become a captain or something like that one day, but there was no boat.

The food was excellent but, apart from that, everything else was senseless. We were spending hours sitting down in a damp concrete yard, apparently for no reason at all. I don't know if these Marines were mad or insane but they sent me several times to guard an empty water tank with a rifle without bullets. The damp soon took hold and we all had terrible influenza. The yard was green with our phlegm. It was really bad and stupid, and the romanticism of seeing myself sailing around the world in a beautiful white boat in a white uniform died in me that minute. I wanted to leave immediately but it took a few months of hell before I succeeded in persuading the Navy to let me go back to the farm.

All the Navy officers began to appear ugly and stupid to me. It's possible they had a hearing problem because whenever I complained about something no one listened. It was very simple. I didn't want to see any more Marines. I didn't want to talk about Marines. And I didn't want to be amongst Marines. So four *desperadoes* and I decided to swim the River Plate and to escape to Uruguay. But after studying the river for a while, and after someone saying that it was full of piranhas and it would be just a suicidal trip, we decided not to try. It was a heartbreaking feeling seeing all these boats cruising smoothly through the River Plate whilst we were stuck like pumpkins on that God-forsaken island.

Most of the high ranking Marines were an ignorant bunch, rough and seemingly uneducated. They were hard on us, and on themselves, and I didn't know how to tackle them with my problem. If we didn't polish our shoes correctly they would slap us in the face. If we didn't shave correctly, they would stare at us for a long time in the eyes without blinking – very disturbing – and we had to go and shave again, while the others were having breakfast. If we didn't do the exercises as they wanted, they would hit us with the butts of their rifles and make us jump around the yard in a squatting position, like frogs, until we dropped in agony. I chose one of the tortures. I stopped shaving and caused a mini revolution between the high ranking prats and the poor cadets. But, to everyone's surprise, it worked. A few more joined the bearded rebellion of not shaving, until after many disagreements the Generals said 'Okay, okay, okay,' and eventually they gave us shore leave, for us never to return. I had become a kind of leader of a pack of young lambs. They embraced me with happiness and we celebrated with laughter on our way back to Buenos Aires. There was a great sense of freedom and it was clear that joining the Navy was not the right path for me to follow. That road was much too narrow. I said goodbye to my revolutionary friends and began the long ride back to Patagonia.

I was very sad on my return train journey. I remembered the tears of my mother and father when I left the farm. I was the youngest of three natural sisters and one brother, plus four adopted children, therefore I was the only companion that they'd had left. The others had married and gone, and my parents were getting old in their solitude. The tears in my father's eyes burst out once again at my arrival home, and we couldn't talk. It was an incredible feeling, one I find hard to describe and, even now, the long journey with its shivering momentum feels like a rope with many knots inside my throat. It ties my neck and stops me from falling over forever into that sad past.

The farm returned to normality for a while, but soon after my father died in a tractor accident and I was left alone with my mother. It was very difficult for me, at that age, managing the farm without my father. Not long after that though, I applied for a scholarship to study at a college in Wales, and it was awarded to me. Coleg Harlech in north Wales offers one scholarship each year for a resident of Patagonia to study Welsh, and to help develop cultural connections between the two countries. My mother thought it was a great idea and we agreed to sell the farm. She decided to make extended visits to her various daughters who were scattered across Patagonia, but before leaving she helped me prepare my suitcase for Wales, with perfectly ironed shirts and a tie. She had always dreamed of going to Wales, so saw this as her opportunity, and she didn't want to stop me going first. So in 1972 I left, and a year later she came to visit me, and realized her dream during a hugely enjoyable six-month stay.

— 10 —

ARRIVING IN WALES

A fast train took me and my guitar from London to Cardiff, the capital of Wales. People were running in and out of the station and I didn't know what I was doing. I was blind with happiness and emotion in the middle of the throng. I was in Wales, I was sure of that – or was it a dream? Yes, it could be a dream, and the more I thought about it, the more I convinced myself that I was just dreaming. I could see into the future, I could see myself in the dream, and I could smell curious smells.

A man approached me and said something – I didn't understand him. The same man said something to me again, and I didn't understand him that time, either. Maybe the man told me that I was not dreaming at all and that Wales was as real as it could be, who knows? Then I thought I should say something polite to him, as he was still looking at me, so I polished my Welsh and I asked him 'Where is Llanuwchllyn?' But the man didn't want to tell me that, he just disappeared. Not realizing that the man had no idea what I was saying, I thought he must be a bit thick! I left Cardiff station and decided to walk for a while, to see what kind of interesting Welsh people were living here and to speak the language of my great-grandfathers in their own country. More than 100 years had passed since they left Wales for Patagonia and I was the first of my family to return.

I was still very emotional walking through Cardiff city, yet very content with myself. The hoppy fermentation from a nearby brewery was sticking to my face with a strange smell, humid and heavy – not very pleasant at all. I asked some young lads where I could find a hotel. They looked at me but they didn't answer my question. I asked the same question to a woman. She smiled at me but she didn't stop. Neither did she answer my question. I was getting really fed up and frustrated by now – I wasn't asking anything difficult, I just wanted a simple hotel. So, my first half hour in Wales, after that hundred-year interval, had turned into a nightmare. I couldn't understand anyone and, worse, they couldn't understand me. I blamed my mother, my father, my sisters and brother, aunties, uncles, teachers and all the neighbours, for not teaching me the correct Welsh. The owner of the hotel that I finally found without asking anybody spoke some Spanish and Italian. He was a very good man but I never got his name right. We were chatting away very nicely in a mixture of Spanish and Italian. He said that he couldn't speak any Welsh, but neither could the rest of the people in Cardiff. That was why no one could understand me. He said that because Cardiff was so close to the English border, everybody spoke English, and Welsh was non-existent.

I couldn't believe it! I had travelled 10,000 kilometres to speak Welsh and now I couldn't, because nobody else could! I was totally disorientated. I didn't know a word of the English language and so, to be a bit more out of balance, I went to drink my first few Welsh beers in the centre of town. It was about ten in the evening, and I thought it was a bit early to go out but I wanted to wash down my frustration. As I was crossing a narrow street, I noticed that many people were vomiting everywhere. Some people were eating chips out of newspapers and then vomiting the chips as well, while they were laughing. That was an incredible sight, and nobody seemed to care. I entered the first bar I could find and it took approximately 30 minutes to get a beer. The place was packed and there were not enough people serving. Everybody was drunk and, a few minutes later, they rang a bell and threw us out, before I could finish my big glass of brown, warm beer with a very nice taste. At first I thought there was a fire in the pub – the alarm, the shouting, pushing people out – but no, that was the law.

Something was totally upside down in this country – why were they closing the pubs so early on a Saturday night, especially when the place was full of people and the barman was making good money? It was a very stupid system indeed. In Argentina we would have let them carry on all night if they had money to pay for their drinks.

On the way back to my hotel, I crossed the same streets and people were still eating chips and vomiting. It was difficult not to walk all over the chips and the vomit. In the poor street light the chips looked like big sticky slugs and I was jumping around trying to avoid that dreadful mess. Early the next morning, I walked back to the train station, passing through the same little street to take a photograph of it, so I could show part of Great Britain to my friends back home. A miniature lorry with two round brushes was pushing, brushing and swallowing the vomit with chips. I wanted to speak Welsh, so I took the first train to the west.

The noisy old train was galloping quite quickly towards the west of Wales. I had the address of a contact called Tom in the village of Kidwelly. I knew that Kidwelly was in the west of Wales somewhere, but where? I stumbled up and down the train with difficulty and shyness. I am sure people thought I was totally drunk but I wasn't, which was a shame because by now I was very annoyed with myself and my daft idea of coming to Wales. Even in the train no one could speak Welsh and that 'Sorry, sorry' I'd learned in Cardiff the night before didn't help at all. Just before the town of Llanelli, and as I was trying to get some sense out of these Welsh people, one man said to me in Welsh, 'I speak Welsh, what the hell is the matter with you?' I gave him a big smile and I explained that I had come from Patagonia and that I couldn't speak English and that I didn't know where Kidwelly was. He was very knowledgeable, so he knew where Kidwelly was.

It was a Sunday afternoon when I stepped down from the 'galloping' train at the village station. The village of Kidwelly was quiet and lifeless. A huge, beautiful and monstrous old Norman castle dominated the river bank, and a modern Renault garage belonging to Tom's family dominated the upper, more undulating part of the village. Lower down the hill a church dominated the entire village on that Sunday afternoon with songs. The sopranos inside the church were in good spirits. They were howling and screaming their love to God like anywhere else in the world, but of course, they were howling in Welsh in west Wales, and that made a difference to me. All the stories, all the romanticism, all the years that had gone by, the struggle to survive both here and in Patagonia, got hold of some emotion inside me in that tiny village on that Sunday afternoon. I was tired. I smoked one of my last cigarettes from Argentina and waited outside my host's house until the church had firmly closed the doors of God and Tom headed back home for tea.

When he saw me, he said in Welsh, 'Wel, wel, wel,' – which in English means 'Well, well, well'. 'Come on in and have a cup of tea,' he said, 'but take your shoes off, I've bought a new carpet!' I looked at my shoes and they were perfectly clean – I hadn't been in the corral with the dung of cows and horses for a long time. I didn't know what the old boy's problem was but I took my shoes off in order to please the white carpet. I thought that the first lesson to learn here is not to be too Patagonian, so I said 'yes' to everything he offered me, and that included a small sandwich with some transparent ham inside, two biscuits and a cup of tea. That was dinner, without shoes on a white carpet. Sundays were certainly going to be different here.

Tom taught me some south-west-Walian Welsh words and drove me to a house where the Fisher family lived. That, apparently, was going to be the house in which I could stay for a few weeks. Mrs Fisher showed me the house and in one of the bedrooms, where I was supposed to sleep, was a boy called Simon in the other twin bed. He was about twelve years old but was 'reading' magazines that seemed to have only pictures of girls in them. I had never seen that kind of magazine before! Around ten years later we met again on a film set, when both of us were actors for Welsh television. Another ten years later in this recurring connection he came to ride horses on my ranch in Cholila, and because we tend to meet only once a decade we're still friends.

— 11 —

HEADING NORTH TO MEET MY RELATIVES

THE experience in Kidwelly, with its southern accent and many cups of tea, had been worthwhile. I learned so many remarkable Welsh words that I was sure didn't exist in any possible dictionary but I was happy to use them. I was mutating my image and beginning to look like a respectable Welshman. Distant relatives of mine were waiting for me in north Wales, so I hitched a ride north. The driver of the first car was explaining the history of Wales while eating sweets. He was bombarding me with 5,000 years of history – it was all a bit too much for me. The Celts, the Romans, the Saxons, the Vikings, the Normans, the Scandinavians, the Flemish invasions and wars, and so on … the only thing that made real sense at that moment was the introduction of grapevines to this country by the Romans.

He explained that the Romans built the roads in Wales and I was sure that he was right. I could imagine all the Italian designers and legionnaires plastered by the road side, and the commander-in-chief in his chariot, trying to design the superb road on the back of a barrel of wine, definitely the worse for wear. I couldn't find any other explanation for the badly built roads. Unless Julius Caesar was still annoyed about the Celts having destroyed and burned down Rome – not once, but twice! I was used to travelling in Patagonia for many thousands of miles without a single bend in the road. Here, there was bend after bend after bend. I was getting dizzy and sick and the driver just wouldn't shut up. After being a bit sick on 'the road', I began to feel extremely hungry. I could have eaten half a lamb, with no problem at all, but no, the driver gave me a sweet.

The small village of Llanuwchllyn overlooking Bala Lake was somehow eerie in the dusk. There was not a soul to be seen anywhere. But the welcome was very warm at my family's farm on the hill overlooking the lake, and they filled me with tea, cakes and questions which were very difficult to answer because I couldn't understand them. The people of north Wales speak with a peculiar nasal utterance, a unique way of making sounds, which at times seems incomprehensible and amusing to an unaccustomed ear. From this farm on the hill I could see 'Dolfawr', the farm that had once belonged to my great-grandfather, the farm that he left behind when he emigrated to Patagonia. It was a beautiful old stone building, situated at the end of the lake, at the foot of the Aran Mountain. I couldn't believe that anyone would want to leave this place, to go to an unknown wilderness at the far end of the world. I went to bed that night thinking that his desire to move must have been very strong.

In the morning, after more cups of tea, we prepared to go to Yr Hen Gapel (the Old Chapel) in Llanuwchllyn. I was looking forward to going, because it was the chapel that my great-grandfathers used to attend. In fact, the leader of the Welsh colony of Patagonia was a preacher in that chapel more than a century ago. His name was Michael Daniel Jones. He is buried there, with a big stone on top, in case he ever escapes and starts with the drama all over again. During the service, I could feel the power from the pulpit, the power that Michael Daniel Jones would have had over those farmers, that now, I was part of. Yes, it was the same chapel, with the same hymns, the same smell of emptiness, the same Bibles, the same commitment to God.

During my stay with my relatives in Llanuwchllyn I got into the habit of accompanying my aunt to chapel on Sundays, and on one occasion I was invited to say a few words and to sing a song to the congregation. So one Sunday I went to sing and play the guitar in the old chapel where Michael D. Jones used to pray at my great-grandfather. My uncle Trefor in his best suit was driving me and my auntie Elisabeth to the chapel of Mr Jones, but for a reason unknown to me, Trefor went to a different chapel one mile away. I didn't know what to sing for my 'recital'. I didn't know any religious songs with the guitar, so I sang a tango. The acoustics were wonderful in that chapel, it had an echo similar to a swimming pool or bathroom, so my little tango went very well indeed. The congregation applauded fervently and all of them congratulated me. The priest was the last one to shake my hand and congratulate me with his serious-cavernous face, adding that I should translate the song from Argentine Spanish into Welsh. 'By the way,' he asked, 'what was the meaning of the words?' So I replied that the song was about a man who found his wife in bed with another man, and he killed them both, and then went to a bar and drank champagne for hours and hours, saying that today was the last day of his life because after drinking another bottle of champagne he would cut his own throat. The priest with the long nose was listening to my translation and his face was changing colour, then he said, 'Mmm ... perhaps it's not a good idea to translate that song into Welsh after all!'

Michael D. Jones had a dream – a solid, well-planned dream, with all the necessary elements of success. The people who had influenced him most were two Jews – Jesus Christ and Karl Marx. Having the concepts of these two formidable men as a guide, the future of the Welsh colony in Patagonia should have been a total success – and it's true that it was for a period of time. But the perfect organization, the success of the colony in such difficult conditions, was to be the root of its decay. It seems possible that there was a conspiracy between Britain and Argentina against the Welsh colony in

Patagonia. The Welsh were strong in Patagonia, with their own laws, their own methods of education, their own social and cultural power, which made them the most successful settlers in the whole of the American continent – with their economic system creating miracles and winning prizes (including Firsts) in Chicago and in Paris with their produce. People were jealous and concerned about this small, well-organized new Welsh nation with its own national emblem and its own monetary system.

Patagonia is a big piece of land, roughly forty times the size of Wales, and it was empty of white people before the arrival of the Welsh, even though it was claimed by Chile, by England and by Argentina. The British were already in the Falkland Islands, the Chileans were already crossing the Andes and Argentina had all its soldiers fighting the Brazilians, the Paraguayans and the Bolivians in the north. Even though it had assisted the colony, it has been said that the Argentine government was mistrustful of the idea of the Welsh colonizing Patagonia; after all, the Welsh were British, and the British were already all over the South Atlantic. The Falkland Islands, South Georgia and the Sandwich Islands were in British hands, and rumours of the British claiming Patagonia for the Crown were of great concern for the Argentines.

Although this is understandable from the point of view of the Argentines, it is also ironic, for after the Welsh obtained permission from the Argentine government to settle in the little valley of Chubut in 1865, Argentina leased millions of acres of the Patagonian plateau to the Southern Argentine Land Company, a British company based in London.

Although the company was dissolved in 1986, in those 100 years of British rule the no man's land of Patagonia was like an invisible British colony. Most of that land now belongs to the Italian company Benetton.

These vast *estancias* produced an enormous quantity of meat and wool for the British market and, as the railways in the whole of Argentina were built by the British, some of the narrow gauge tracks cut straight through their land, and the British were able to move their product swiftly when other ranches were using mule trains. The British were the best ranchers at that time, well disciplined, clean, tidy and fair. Many of their managers were ex-British Army from the numerous colonies around the world. These managers were tough guys of the no-nonsense type, but the Indians didn't like them very much. You had to work!

While the Tehuelche Indians were living a nomadic life throughout Patagonia, they soon found out that catching a sheep was easier than running after a guanaco all day long and it was more tender to eat. One of those robust Tehuelche could easily devour one or two lambs per day, so as the ranchers found it almost impossible to retain any lambs, something would have to be done. The Europeans threatened Argentina that they would not send any more colonists if the government didn't remove the native people from the land, a demand which would prove catastrophic for the Tehuelche people.

Juan Manuel de Rosas, a totalitarian dictator and governor in the region of Buenos Aires, was not a very rosy person. He was a farmer, with half a million head of cattle to entertain him on the great pampas. But that was not enough; being a raging totalitarian, power was a tremendous aphrodisiac and nothing would stand in his way. He created the 'Mazorca', a vicious paramilitary force, in order to kill anyone who opposed him, and of course, among those who fell into that category were the Indians of Argentina's Wild West. In 1833, he mounted his war horse and with his Gestapo-type paramilitary friends, was directed by the government to wipe out the 'savages' from the pampas. He killed so many Indians that he eventually tired of it; he returned to Buenos Aires and was informed that the Jesuits were helping the Indians. He declared war on the Jesuits and they were all killed or deported. He believed that he had wiped out all the Indians, and Argentina was safe to be colonized by Europeans. He was wrong. Many Indians escaped the massacre and found, for a while, a safe haven in north-west Patagonia, where the evil Señor Rosas was nowhere to be seen.

Rosas had other problems to worry about. There were many other feudalists like him fighting for power in the territory of Buenos Aires, and bit by bit Rosas found himself unwanted and isolated until finally, in a massive revolt, he was deposed and exiled from the country. Juan Manuel de Rosas ended his days on a little farm in Hampshire, England.

Now that Rosas was gone, Patagonia had to manage on its own while the Indians were having a great party, which didn't last long – the powerful landlords organized themselves and employed gauchos and European mercenaries to hunt down the indigenous people. The Indians were too heavy to be carried dead on horseback back to the ranches, so the hunters just cut off their ears and testicles as those bits were easy to transport in saddle bags. The hunters got paid good money as well as bonuses of wine and whisky, depending on how many they killed.

Around 1870 another human monster appeared on the scene in the powerful Buenos Aires army élite: this man was General Alejo Argentino Roca Paz. This tough, arrogant, and ambitious man was called later on in his life 'the King of the Desert' because he really managed to wipe out most Indians, or anyone who he thought looked like an Indian, in the infamous desert campaign.

General Roca was designated for a new dirty job, the same job that Señor Rosas couldn't complete. General Roca was seemingly capable of carrying out any atrocity, and his excitement was unstoppable at the prospect of commanding the biggest genocide of all time in the Argentine Republic. He and his soldiers killed thousands of Indians regardless of age or sex and, from time to time, in order to save bullets, he commanded his men to slit the throats of captured Indians. Some of the most docile Tehuelche tribes were captured and sent to a kind of reservation, where they could roam miserably on the unwanted dry land in the centre of Patagonia.

When the other race of Indians, the Araucanos who lived in the western mountains, heard about the truce between the Tehuelches and Christians, they went wild, and at any opportunity they would attack the few Tehuelche who were left alive by Roca, so the poor Tehuelche were decimated on all flanks. Today it is difficult to find a pure Tehuelche, as the magnificent, indigenous old race of gigantic people has perished and vanished for ever from the Patagonian pampas.

General Roca received five million hectares of prime land from the government as part of his payment for a job

well done! This land was distributed among a handful of
his friends as a gift for helping him in the dirty desert war
campaign. I feel incredibly sad about it all, as the Tehuelche
were the people who helped the Welsh to survive and to
establish themselves successfully in the valley of Chubut.
After the Indian holocaust Roca became the first president
of the Argentine Republic to visit Patagonia and to hammer,
with his military determination, the first and last nail in the
colony's coffin. On one occasion he visited an English rancher
in the colony, and asked him if he had any Argentines on
the ranch. The Englishman said yes. 'Well,' said Roca, 'bring
them here, I would like to congratulate them for being
Argentines.' The Englishman called his two daughters who
were about seven years old, and the two little blonde girls
came out, trembling with shyness. The Englishman said,
'There you are Sir, the rest are one Italian, one Basque and
a two Chileans.' Roca wasn't happy with the outcome of his
visit to that ranch and with his face looking like a dry rock
he mounted his horse and went back to his beloved Buenos
Aires. Nobody saw him again in Patagonia.

After that impressive visit by the General, the dream
of Michael D. Jones was crushed, and the *débris* of this
nightmare began to bother him. In desperation, he used
most of his wife's wealth to support the little settlement but
it was already too late. The Argentine flag was flapping in
the wind, alongside the Welsh one. The new flag was larger
and it came with a determination to stay. The young Welsh
boys were in no mood to be obliged to join the Argentine
army. The dream of their freedom and the logical fantasies

of the creation of a new Welsh nation in South America had disappeared for ever.

Back in Llanuwchllyn, after visiting the chapel where the dream of Michael D. Jones was born, I met so many of the Jones family in north Wales that I asked Auntie Mary if we were related to Tom Jones.

'Which Tom Jones?' she asked.

I said, 'The singer.'

She said, 'Which singer? they all sing in Wales'.

To my surprise, she worked out what I was on about, and she said, 'Oh, the one who sings Green, Green, Green, Green Grass something?'

And I said, 'Yes.'

She said, 'No,' and then she said, 'no, no, no,' while throwing herself back in the armchair, with her legs in the air, laughing. 'That Tom Jones comes from the south,' she said, and her expression was as if he came from the south of Siberia. So, Tom Jones wasn't related to us but Rockefeller was, because he had married one of the girls from Llanuwchllyn, and although they weren't singers, they lived in the United States, with lots of money. I had no idea who this Rockefeller fellow was. Auntie Mary was always full of life, but was quite eccentric, and her house in north Wales was packed with photographs, brass artifacts, and a very beautiful old piano with shining wood. One day I asked, 'Who plays the piano?'

'No one,' she said very seriously, 'we just use it to put the family photographs on top.'

The cups of tea and cakes with a kind of false cream on top became quite indigestible and I had a taste of hiraeth (nostalgic longing) for the first time. I began to visualize a big chunk of horse meat being cooked on the open fire, with plenty of *salmuera*, giving life to the crispy aroma of the smoked meat wafting through the branches on the wind and landing in the whispering meadows of the stream. There was nothing as romantic as that in the green, green, green, green grass around here, so I set off from Llanuwchllyn, to see what could happen next.

— 12 —

COLEG HARLECH

I had arrived in Wales with the scholarship to attend college in Harlech; so that's where I went. The college was a tall, modern building by the sea, close to an old library, a modern theatre, a tiny post office and a massive castle. There wasn't much more to see in the village but I could sense more, especially at night around the castle. I was concerned about those feelings, and I was a bit uneasy about them, and I never discovered why.

There were about 115 students in the college but only around ten of them spoke Welsh. One could speak Spanish – he could say 'señoritas', 'fiesta' and '*Guantanamera*'. He told me that he had been all around the world, and many other places too, but never to Patagonia. He was so curious about my homeland that he invited me to drink many gallons of beer in the village pub. We met many other heavy drinkers already trying to push the bar away with their huge beer bellies while saying, 'Ahh, so this is the Patagonian kid? Here, come and drink this!' I couldn't possibly disappoint my great-grandfathers, so I went for it! Hours later, the bar was very peaceful with a noisy yet relaxed ambience. The pints of warm beer came from every direction until our table was awash with glasses. Some were full, some were half-full, and many were empty with cigarettes inside. It was quite an ugly sight but in many ways it was very nice, too, with no inhibitions of any kind, and everybody was incredibly friendly. We forgot to talk about Patagonia after all – instead, we talked about beer and my friend kept interrupting with the word 'señoritas' all the time. 'Río de Janeiro, señoritas, ohh, mama mia, Buenos Aires, señoritas, ohh mama mia, Cuba, señoritas, ohh, molto bene ...' He began to mix his broad knowledge of Spanish with Italian, while kissing the points of his five fingers. I said to one of the Celts, 'Don't you think we are drinking too much?'

'Oh no,' he replied, 'we can drink this stuff just like milk.'

And I thought, 'What a bloody liar, he would never be able to drink twenty pints of milk just like that!'

Suddenly, the pub transformed itself into a chapel and everybody was singing hymns at the tops of their voices – it was really fantastic. There were tenors, basses and first voices, in perfect harmony, without a conductor or a priest around. It was difficult to believe that so many drunken people could be so well disciplined. We stood up and sang the Welsh national anthem, *Hen Wlad fy Nhadau*, with passion and power, with a furious rage of national identity. I was enjoying this new discovery. Wales was not only in the green grass and inside the cups of tea – 90% of Wales was inside the pubs, discussing literature, politics, history, poetry, music and so on – and that became my university. The college was not important any more and, probably for that reason, it took hours to find it that night. The impressive mediaeval castle was in deep dark silence now; the proud lumps of stone were in ruins, frightened by our presence. It couldn't fight the Celts any more. It was tired of standing there without a roof in its decaying silhouette on top of the rocks. We marched with laughter through the steep hills – we were alive, the castle was in ruins, forgotten and dead.

The name of my tutor was Dafydd Elis Thomas – I didn't know any more than that about him. He had a clear and fluent way of speaking and had the ability to slide through the most difficult tongue-twisting Welsh words with the speed and grace of a master skier. He became very aware during the first week of college that I was not as conventional and middle class as most of the other students. In fact, I didn't belong to any class at all and I was probably disorientating him. He wouldn't teach me music, because he was not a music teacher, so I chose literature instead; firstly, because I knew the word, and secondly because it was a well respected subject to study in Welsh. And with a bit of flair, I carried the word 'literature' all around the college and up and down in the lift, proud of what I was doing, although no one, including myself, knew what that was exactly.

My tutor was aware that something was going on but he respected my philosophy of freedom and was not interested in my private life inside or outside the college. He devoted many hours of his life to waiting for me in the classroom, and I devoted many hours of my precious life waiting for him, too. It was a kind of telepathic pact, without either of us being aware of it at that time. But that was fine by me. The few times we met in the classroom, there were many gaps of beautiful silence – he would look at me while I was looking through the window at the little robin in the garden and although the robin wasn't as majestic as a condor, he had the same sense of freedom as I did. My tutor was aware of that.

In one of the lectures, Dafydd said that Snowdon was the highest mountain in Wales. It reached an altitude of 1,085 metres ... and I thought about it ... then he thought about it and he said, 'Well, that's not a lot for you in South America, is it?'

And I said 'The Andes reach an altitude of 6,960 metres and are still growing.'

'Well, there we are then,' he said, 'see you next week, perhaps?' And he disappeared into his mountains inside his car. I met my tutor again many years later. He hadn't changed his witty sense of humour but in the meantime he had become a Lord.

As so few students spoke Welsh, and I didn't speak English, I was not totally enjoying my life at Coleg Harlech and the daily routine was quite monotonous as well. To one side of the college was the sea that ended in Greenland and to the other side was the Snowdonia mountain range. Just like the sea, nothing happened there, either. On top of that I had to learn dramatically more Welsh than I thought I needed and I was getting fed up with the chore. It was one thing to speak the Welsh language on the streets or in the pub, quite another to make any sense of it while writing it down. I knew that Welsh and the Basque languages are the most ancient in Europe but I didn't know that the complexities of the language would be so complicated for me. But anyhow, at least in Coleg Harlech I learned to say Patagonia in four ways:

Patagonia, o Batagonia, ym Mhatagonia, and a Phatagonia. With the help of my Spanish-Welsh dictionary I did work my way through some excellent books on Welsh literature and history in the college library though, and this information began to shape my knowledge of the land of my forefathers.

It is a miracle that Wales has kept its own language alive for so many years, against all odds. The debates about the Welsh language at Coleg Harlech were interminable. I remember spending most of one afternoon, between cups of tea and joints of marijuana, trying to find out what was the Welsh word for 'entrepreneur', until someone spoiled the intellectual moment by saying 'We don't need it in north Wales, anyway!'

One old farmer in south-west Wales, in the Preseli mountains, told me that he couldn't understand a man from Caernarfon. Both of them were born in Wales, and Welsh was their mother tongue, but they had to speak in English in order to communicate with each other. And they were born only 100 miles apart! Probably that's why it had been so difficult for the Welsh Language Society and the Welsh nationalist movement to get their message across; few people understood what they were talking about. Although most of the Welsh clergy were almost tap-dancing on the pulpit in order to get the message across, most people in Wales thought it was more interesting to go to the pub.

Whether I was going to or coming back from the pub, the Warden of the college used to give me a hard time. He was a different type of man from my tutor and he would catch me in the most awkward places, in the lift or in the narrow passages. I was sure he had been a trapper when he was young. He noticed that I was missing too many lectures and he was always asking me 'Why, my boy?' I always said that I'd been lost somewhere but he never believed me, although it was true sometimes – I was lost in the middle of a big bed, in the heart of the Snowdonia mountains.

The weather was showing its attitude of willingness in the cold early spring, touching my face with its shy sunny skin erupting in hills of hopes. My year of college was coming to an end and we performed a farewell concert in the modern theatre. My mother, Eirwen, was in Wales at that time and she was in the audience. She went on stage to say a few words and to sing a song in her soprano voice. She received incredible applause with a particular song which was unknown in Wales. Apparently her father composed this music in Patagonia and now that song has been immortalized by a Welsh folk group called 'Ar Log'. The song is called Leisa Fach, which means 'little Lisa'.

I never said 'adios' to my tutor, the Principal, or to the 'trapper', because I couldn't find them. The college was quite empty, except for one room which was full of people laughing, singing and smoking marijuana, and in that paranormal chaotic ambience I did manage to say goodbye.

— 13 —

LAND OF MY FATHERS

'Land of my Fathers! As far as I'm concerned, my fathers can keep it.'
— Dylan Thomas, in *The Three Weird Sisters* (1948)

AFTER the concert in Harlech Theatre, some of our innumerable family in Llanuwchllyn took care of my mother for a week whilst I explored further the land of my fathers: this land of myths and legends, Romans and Celts, Arthur and Merlin, romance and passion. The land of my ancestors and relatives, of saints and songs, that I had learned something about at college; this land of two languages, Welsh and English, where I spoke only one of them.

During my last weeks at college, a director from the BBC's Light Entertainment department phoned and invited me to participate in a television music show in Cardiff. I took several local buses and arrived at Bangor train station where I boarded the Holyhead-London train and finally, after a multitude of stops and train changes, I arrived once more at Cardiff Central station. When I arrived for the first time at the same station a year previously, the only English words I knew were those I had heard on local radio in Patagonia, but they were all from Beatles' and Rolling Stones songs and I didn't even know what they meant. Strangely, *Hey Jude … Yesterday, all my troubles seemed so far away* … and *I Wanna Hold Your Hand* … weren't a great help in getting around Cardiff.

The interview, singing and guitar playing at the BBC studios went very well, but unfortunately, as I had never been on television before I didn't know the technicalities of repeat takes, waiting around or camera work, and the unbearably strong lights and loud music were making me nervous. In the process of filming, the temperature in the studio rose to dangerous levels and, all in all, my first appearance on television was a very sweaty experience. The programme was called *Disc a Dawn*, a Welsh language pop music show, and I played only folk music. In an interview for the weekly Welsh newspaper *Y Cymro* I said with raw honesty that I deeply detest the noise of disco, which didn't sound very polite about the show, but to the surprise of many people (including me), the invitation was repeated and I appeared on the show again and again.

Even though these shows were in the Welsh language, I realized that without English my ability to move freely in Cardiff was restricted, so I headed back to north Wales, where at least I could make myself understood in one language, and I grabbed every opportunity to bury myself in a Welsh-English dictionary. Most of my friends in Harlech belonged to Welsh Nationalist movements, and firmly resisted my attempts to learn English. They encouraged me to remain 'atypical' as they had never met anyone before who could speak Welsh and Spanish, but not English! I saw my teacher once having a rest in the tea room and, to demonstrate my progress in English, stammered loudly *I can't get no satisfaction* – and he laughed!

Soon after those first television shows, and to my great satisfaction, many doors of opportunity were opened to me, as if by magic. I had become a kind of celebrity and people commented on my red poncho and gave exaggerated compliments on the way I was playing guitar, calling me 'the gaucho flamenco player'! I wasn't sure what they meant most of time as I've never played flamenco, but whatever they thought about my South American style of playing guitar and singing, it was clear that something was working. Welsh newspapers and magazines published photographs of this exotic gaucho who played a guitar, wore a poncho and couldn't speak English. Most people encouraged my optimism and were delighted to be my friend; others were jealous or mildly cynical.

My mother had reconnected joyfully with numerous relatives throughout Wales, but mostly in Llanuwchllyn and Bala. She spoke Welsh perfectly and her language was so pure that not many people believed she was born in Patagonia or that this was her first trip to Wales. Her ability to lift people's hearts and make everyone sing along with her was quite extraordinary. Without a word of English she could socialize and communicate with most people and felt perfectly at home wherever she went. This is a rare achievement for anyone who has never travelled outside Argentina before and, in fact, people were so delighted to have her company that she spent most of her time in Wales going from one party to another – drinking tea, of course!

My mother returned to Patagonia after spending over six months in Wales, and her departure left me feeling nostalgic about the farm I had left behind in Patagonia. I decided to look for farm work in Wales between television shows, and I began by going to Anglesey to work on a large farm in Aberffraw that belonged to Iolo Owen. The lambing season was getting close and Mr Owen had thousands of ewes likely to have difficulty giving birth naturally. Iolo had developed a new breed of sheep, the Easy Care Breed, and consequently was awarded an MBE for his contribution to agriculture. But the problem he had that year was that many small Welsh Mountain ewes had been crossed with Iolo's huge new breed rams, so the new lambs were simply too big for the mothers to give birth without help. So for the first time in my life my job as a farmer was to assist the ewes by 'pulling' the lambs. I really enjoyed that work tremendously as it was a pleasure to be in the fresh air on a farm that bordered the south coastline of Anglesey. Added to that, I even had a horse to accompany me on the routine checking of the vast farm, and shopping in Aberffraw on horseback was always a lovely day out.

The long lambing season in Aberffraw came to an end and I went to see my family in Llanuwchllyn, where the shearing of the little Welsh Mountain sheep had begun. Naturally I joined in immediately and we went from farm to farm, shearing and baling wool. The area we worked was from Bala to Dinas Mawddwy, where my relatives have their lovely ancient farms and had lived for many generations in those beautiful old houses: 'Nant y Barcud', 'Tan y Bwlch', 'Braichceunant', 'Rhos y Gwalia', 'Gelli Grin' and others that I don't remember the names of. But I do remember the farmhouse meals provided by my aunts and cousins with huge portions of ham, chunks of various kinds of cheeses, bread and butter, and pickled onions.

At Tan y Bwlch, while we were having a break under a tree with a cup of tea and a roll-up cigarette, a horse was looking at us from a field.

'Lovely horse,' I said to my uncle.

'Yes, very pretty,' he said gruffly, 'but he's very wild and nasty too. No one can ride him.'

To me the horse looked tame and I wanted to show off my horsemanship, so I asked uncle Treb, 'Do you mind if I try?'

'Do what you want,' my uncle said, 'but be careful.'

Some young lads helped me to catch the horse and I used a rope to improvise the reins and a bit by tying it around his nose and mouth, then jumped on his bare back. After two seconds on the horse I was back on the ground with a bump on my head and the side of my ribs bleeding. Everyone came to help me, but with a rush of adrenaline I felt furious. A gaucho like me had made a fool of himself in front of all his family! I cut a branch from a nearby tree and jumped back on the horse, which innocently looked as if it had done nothing wrong. This time I prepared myself well by tightening my legs around the horse like a lobster with his claws. I used the branch as a whip, and with all my strength I gave him a good and long hiding, until I was tired and the horse was trembling with frothy sweat pouring out of him. I never saw that horse again, but one of the farmers told me that he never again tried to buck, and that his children were riding him at full gallop over the hills of Tan y Bwlch.

In those days I was in great demand and combined physical farm work with singing and television work. I became an expert in taking buses and trains back and forward to Cardiff studios from remote farms in north Wales. An adorable producer and director named Rhydderch Jones offered me many jobs on television programmes and a monumental amount of beer in the BBC club, where the real 'show' was always on. I had learned a few more English words, and now that people seemed to understand me slightly better they appeared much nicer. On one occasion, while filming a concert for Rhydderch in Newport, west Wales, I had to arrive on horseback onto the stage. The horse came prancing through the big doors of the barn and stopped in front of the live audience. Rhydderch was half asleep lying on the floor, but when he saw me arrive on the horse he shouted, 'ACTION!'

The spectators exploded with laughter and I couldn't stop giggling while trying to sing a serious song.

— 14 —

AFTER NORTH WALES

AFTER spending about a year on farms in north Wales, and the lambing season had ended once again, my Gypsy soul was pushing me to travel in search of adventure. I had to decide once again whether to take the high road or the low road. I had survived well in north Wales speaking Welsh on the farms and with my family, but venturing south more permanently and being forced to use more English turned out to be an adventure in itself.

The first lift I hitched took me as far as Harlech. I climbed the hill once more up to the imposing castle then walked on the winding coast road to the nearest holiday town of Barmouth in search of a plan. Plan A was to find a job with my guitar in a pub or hotel; the problem with that was that they couldn't pay me any money, but they could provide me with beer and so I got drunk and starved most nights. I searched for a plan B, and I came up with a not-so-glamorous idea and offered myself as a waiter to some coffee shops alongside the road. Not much happened. My English was so bad that no one could understand me.

Running low, morally and financially, I walked through beautiful countryside in the company of rough looking sheep. Someone had painted their heads blue and red, and in fact they looked like those punk girls I saw on one of my visits to London. The villages, built with brownish-grey stones and somehow attractive, depressed me – Dolgellau, Machynlleth and a handful of hamlets where only the locals knew how to pronounce their names.

In Aberystwyth my luck changed. I was accepted as a cleaner and waiter in a small Welsh-Italian restaurant. I couldn't sleep that night, as the thought of me working in Wales for the first time in a serious job kept me awake, but at ten o'clock the following morning I was ready and extremely excited. I washed plates, cleaned tables and floors, then turned the hanging sign to OPEN. Troops of ladies arrived for their morning teas and toast with orange marmalade, and one large lady ordered spaghetti bolognese. As I carried the hot plate with hot spaghetti and hot sauce on top, I stumbled on a loose bit of carpet and ended flat on the floor. The plate of pasta ended up on the prominent bosom of the fat lady, and the 'nice cup of hot tea' emptied itself in her lap. She began to scream and I panicked. I got a serviette and tried to clean her dress, but it got worse. She continued screaming louder and louder. The alarmed owner trotted over looking like a wild boar, shouting at me; he grabbed me by my shoulder, lifted me up into the air and threw me into the street.

I walked down hill, depressed and wet in the midday rainy street of Aberystwyth. I looked back in case the wild boar was following me, but I couldn't see anyone. I ended up in a pub of course, and with every pint of beer I was getting even more disappointed about myself, and a carnival of vicious devils inside my head was telling me I was a failure, and the idea of becoming a restaurateur in Aberystwyth was gone forever. In one pub I met a sea captain called Glen Davies who invited himself to be my manager. We drove to his house in Cardigan one late afternoon and from there to a birthday party in the nearby Preseli Mountains that lasted one week of drinking, singing and eating peanuts. Glen apparently knew the way to convince people that I was an international and superb artist, so he got me many jobs as a singer, mostly in small pubs and clubs where money was scarce and people were indifferent to my music. This wasn't working out as I had hoped, so I abandoned my 'manager' to his own devices and returned to Aberystwyth to find my daily bread (and hopefully daily wine).

Although I wanted to die and be remembered as a total failure, my luck quickly turned and came to impress me. A man with a square face and dirty boots said 'hello' and invited me for a beer and a chat. He was the manager of a garage in the centre of the town, and said I could work with him if I wanted to. I sobered up in an instant and said YES! 'Okay, come at seven then,' he replied! And at seven in the morning I was there, trying to make sense of his instructions, which included his offer to lend me a room above the garage where I could stay, and it had a bath! After I had deposited my bag and guitar in the room and examined the bath I began to investigate the fuel-smelling greasy area of the garage. This garage was in fact just two old fashioned petrol pumps and my job was to take care of those pumps all day long … a piece of cake!

I hadn't worked in a garage before so everything was new territory to me, even the boredom. The busiest part of the day was always in the morning when I had to be alert and work fast, and I had to master the language of the petrol station: 'Mornin' … fill it up please … cheerio.' I took a full

week to learn that. All the customers had an account with the
manager of the garage, so my job was easy enough – lift the
hose, put it in the tank and wait until the tank was full.

By the end of three months I had become a robot, a foreign
Welsh robot. The job was so tedious that I was composing
songs in my head while serving petrol, and I sang some of
those songs on a local Aberystwyth radio station. On one of
my trips away from the town I went to Blaenau Ffestiniog
and recorded a 4-track EP (extended play record) of my own
songs on the Sain label. This was one of the highlights of my
time in Aberystwyth, which was usually uneventful.

On one monotonous afternoon, and while I was eating
repugnant sweet biscuits, a car pulled in to the pumps driven
by the elderly gentleman who came every day for one or two
gallons of petrol. I did the same thing as hundreds of times
before – took the rubber cap off the tank, lifted the hose and
inserted it into the tank, and then asked the driver, 'How
much?' But before I had the chance to ask the old gentleman
'how much?' he drove off, dragging the petrol pump behind
him. Petrol was pouring out of the broken pump and into
the street, causing a rather entertaining pandemonium that
could have been a set for a film in the calm street of Aber-
bloody-rystwyth. Fire brigades, ambulances and the police
arrived at the scene in minutes and I had never seen the place
as busy as that. They poured buckets of sand over the leaking
petrol and washed the street, pavement and inside the garage
thoroughly with water and foam. The square-faced manager
was in a rage with sweat, shouting and swearing at everyone.
He looked at me with mad eyes and shouted … 'pack your
bags and go!'

I did exactly that. Red with embarrassment I went upstairs, got my guitar, the plastic bag with my clothes, and in the blink of an eye I was hitching a lift to south Wales, glad to leave behind a place which had never impressed me very much anyway.

I headed south, to the ugly side of the coal mining valleys of south Wales. Everything was grey and black. The furious, monstrous grey lorries were following each other like ants, carrying on their backs the precious and heavy loads of black gold. The drivers too were quite black with dirt, and as furious and wild as their lorries. There was mile after mile of the same type of house on each side of the road – I imagined that only one architect had been employed to design these houses and he hadn't concentrated very much to produce such a miracle – they were all the same. The cafés and ice cream enterprises were owned by Italians and were all known as 'the greasy spoon', even though they had traditional Italian names. Some of the Italians owned small picturesque ice cream vans which crawled slowly up the hillsides like giant snails, selling cold ice cream and cold drinks in the cold Welsh weather, and blasting out the music of the *Greensleeves* theme, reputedly composed by the Tudor king Henry VIII who came from the Tudur family in Wales.

I wandered around many clubs and pubs in the valleys searching for work with my guitar but it was all in vain – all the greasy spoon cafés and rugby clubs were already booked by someone called Max Boyce. He was the new singer in fashion, and not even Pink Floyd could touch him in the valleys. Rugby was at its best in Wales in the Seventies, so it was quite impossible to get involved in any other subject outside rugby songs, rugby drinking, rugby tours, and rugby machismo. Anyway, I didn't play rugby, I played guitar. Many journalists, scholars and authors talk of South America as the land of machismo; it is quite ironic that those gossip lovers clearly haven't visited the south Wales valleys yet!

There was nothing soft about life in the valleys, from the time of the Industrial Revolution and the iron works coming to Merthyr Tydfil in 1765, to the present time. The town of Merthyr was not only famous for leading the world in the manufacture of iron, but also for the appalling conditions in which its people lived and worked. And then famous because Buffalo Bill came with his circus from the United States with Indians and Cowboys with their guns to frighten the Welsh. After iron, the mighty coal was discovered, making Wales the best producer and the biggest exporter of this dirty mineral, engulfing with lies the biggest times of penury that Wales ever saw. I didn't know that, years later, in 1997, I would play the part of Sitting Bull in a film version of Buffalo Bill's 'Wild West Show' visit to Merthyr Tydfil.

Money began to attract other Britons to live among the Welsh from every corner of the country. The Welsh never thought that their culture and language, as well as their own lives, would be jeopardized by the paltry wages that the highly profitable companies were offering. The picks and shovels were in full swing, digging away their own destiny below the mountains, workers filling their lungs with dusty wages that ended in the toilets of rugby clubs and pubs in the long drinking sessions on the long-awaited Saturdays. God was happy with this; Sunday was just next door to the club, and the big chapel with a preacher inside would brush away all their sins in only two hours. But I was sad about the horses which worked and lived underground, in total darkness for many weeks at a time.

When I went to explore these tunnels and stables so deep underground, I nearly cried from the indescribable feeling that took hold of me. I could understand my grandfathers much better now; I would have done exactly the same as them, and buggered off somewhere far away from that incomprehensible environment. Possibly the only good thing to come out of Margaret Thatcher's closing of the coal mines during the great strike of the Eighties is that people and horses are no longer working and dying underground in the dark. I couldn't do very much about that when I visited the mines, so I walked to a roundabout to hitch a lift somewhere else.

Somewhere else ended up being Tredegar. Aneurin Bevan was born in Tredegar, south Wales, and because he was not very bright at school, he went to work on the tips at the coal mines at an early age. Soon he discovered the reality of the mines, the stark poverty, the lack of decent housing, the maltreatment of the workers by the owners, and he rebelled against them, organizing strikes and so on. He didn't last long there – he was kicked out or made redundant – and he was very often without a job. He became an insatiable reader, and among his beloved books were some of Karl Marx's; he was very influenced by them. From then on he became a busy man, organizing strikes, talking freely to the people in the streets about the appalling conditions in the mines, and eventually went into politics.

Soon afterwards he had a huge following. People in the south Wales valleys adored this new hero. He was a miner;

he was one of them; they were marching and protesting together. He didn't have two faces like the owners of the coal mines, and of course he made a lot of enemies as well. The greatest among these enemies was Winston Churchill. Aneurin Bevan became Health Minister in 1945 and, during this period, Churchill called him 'the minister of disease', to which Aneurin replied, 'Now then, there is a man suffering from petrified adolescence.' But because he was a well respected socialist, he managed to guide the National Health Service Act through Parliament in 1946 for England and Wales. In 1947 and 1948 the Act was extended to Scotland and Northern Ireland. So, thanks to him, Britain today enjoys a free National Health Service. Previously, when the Civil War had broken out in Spain a decade earlier, Bevan tried to persuade the British government to send troops to the Iberian peninsula in order to stop the spread of fascism by General Franco in Spain, Mussolini in Italy and Adolf Hitler in Germany. But the British parliament laughed at his silly ideas. In the event, the fascists spread like wildfire and the Second World War exploded, killing 50 million people.

If Bevan's ideas during the Spanish Civil War had been adopted, perhaps the later war in Europe might have been avoided. Instead, many Welsh people went to Spain, and they joined the Resistance but these brave poor souls were farmers and coal miners, not soldiers of any kind. Even the excellent English writer Laurie Lee went, never having handled a gun in his life. There was not much they could do against Franco's right wing mercenaries, mostly from the Spanish territories in North Africa. The atrocities that Spain suffered during the Civil War were indescribable, but the rest of the world seemed not to have Bevan's foresight. Aneurin Bevan deserves to be remembered as the greatest Welshman of all time.

The next day I was still on the road and didn't care very much where I was going, or whether the path was narrow or wide. The road was teaching me a lot more than any college or school had done so far, and I knew that I was there for a reason. There was more to see, to learn, to understand, to suffer and to be aware of, by throwing myself into whatever the stubborn road wanted to show me. I was quite ready for it now ... I was not prepared to be let down by any grandfathers of mine, so if the next lorry wanted to go to the end of the world, that was fine by me. But I was not so lucky. A lorry took me back to the city of Cardiff and I was stuck there for a week. Although Cardiff is the capital of Wales, it is not a very large city, but I had the feeling of being in New York. The influence of north Wales in my mind was evident. I was shy and mistrustful. I felt like Crocodile Dundee that evening, wandering around the city. It was Saturday night and every street was full of people. These people were rough-looking and obviously were totally and utterly drunk. I felt uneasy and wanted to go back to north Wales.

The possibility of getting a job as a singer and guitarist was as grim there as in the tiny villages of the coal mining valleys, and the money they were offering me was as bad as the 'sophisticated' food which they served in rugby clubs and pubs, where chips were always the highlight of the menu. Then I heard the distinctive sound of a Paraguayan harp being played in La Fontana de Trevi restaurant, and I went in like a shot. I introduced myself to the Italian owner and asked if he would let me play some South American songs for a plate of food. He agreed. I was introduced to Fausto Franco, the Paraguayan harpist. Fausto was world-famous; he had played with Los Paraguayos and with Luis Alberto del Paraná. Luis Alberto was better known than Elvis Presley in South America. I tuned my guitar to his pitch, we exchanged a few words about songs, and we went to the tiny stage to perform. Surprisingly, it went very well. People were clapping and shouting 'encore, encore'. That is a rare achievement in a high-class restaurant.

The owner brought us champagne and we drank it all in one go. I walked around the restaurant from table to table serenading with my guitar and at each table I drank glasses of wine. It was a fantastic fiesta night; we played, we sang, we danced, we drank everything and that night I was definitely on the wide path of life and I didn't care if I was going to Hell. I don't remember how the fiesta ended.

Much later that night I walked through a park with a river running through it. I thought this was a good place to be and lay down to sleep under a tree. I was happy and felt like a prince, I had money in my pocket and my belly was full of cannelloni and wine. I put my guitar with its soft cover as a pillow and I covered myself with my light red and black poncho. But I couldn't sleep.

The night was serene and packed with the scent of trees and grass, a perfect night to meditate, to think about who I was and what I wanted to do in life. I thought that I could be an artist quite easily, I could become famous one day if I wanted it. In fact, I could be like Tom Jones or Mick Jagger or someone like that. But also I thought, the life of an artist is

not always good and glamorous. An artist has to keep moving
from town to town, from one hotel to the next, or in my case
from one tree in a park to another tree in another park.
Also, I felt good in the mornings and not so good at night. A
musician has to work at night and sleep during the day and I
am absolutely hopeless at late nights. The spirit in my voice is
perfect in the early hours of the morning and probably for that
reason I have never been very popular in my neighbourhood.
I may have been a rooster in my previous life.

I remember performing in a rugby club somewhere
in Wales, and although I thought I was singing brilliantly,
nobody clapped. I tried all types of songs, I tried singing
in all the languages I knew, I tried some jokes, but nothing
worked. I thought I must be really bad or the audience was as
unappreciative as a bunch of armadillos. But when a concert
is good, it is difficult for an artist to find anything in the word
to describe that buzz of satisfaction. It seems that your body
is on fire, or that you have gone to another dimension where
people are nice to you, they give you alcohol and drugs, they
invite you to have cups of tea at their homes, they feed you,
they kiss you, and an abundance of girls follows you as if you
are a tropical flower bursting with pollen.

Somewhere in the middle of those thoughts I must have
fallen asleep, happy with the freedom of an aristocratic
tramp. And now I was dreaming. I was in the immensity
of the wild pampas of Argentina on a clear cosmic night,
where millions of horses came galloping with their manes on
fire. Then, somehow I was a dolphin swimming with grace
in a warm ocean, and suddenly I was me again, lying on a
cushion of butterflies. Surely, that was paradise. What a load

•

of bollocks! I was not in paradise at all, I was in Wales and it was raining! The cold tears of hell took me by surprise, I didn't know exactly where I was, and as I was drenched to the bones, confused and disoriented, I got hold of my guitar and stood up. The park was now a lagoon with no signs of any path to follow, so I zig-zagged through trees and bushes in a dark and miserable state.

Finally I was back in town, with lights beckoning, and desperately searching for a cantina, a shop or somewhere I could buy a cup of warm coffee. But of course, I was in Wales and everything was closed. I headed to the train station and said good morning to a man with sleepy eyes who seemed reluctant to serve me a cup of coffee. Once again, which way to go? I took the first train that came along, and followed its path to the west.

I continued to drift towards the west of the fictitious nation, on the train that passes through Llanelli, Caerfyrddyn ('Carmarthen' for the English, 'Moridunum' for the Romans), Aberdaugleddau, and so on. At Carmarthen, the birthplace of Merlin the wizard according to legend, I disembarked and after a few pints ended up joining a local foxhunt. There were over twenty horsemen and probably forty hounds riding in the area of Talley. I sat and wondered if this was where *tally-ho*! with the hunting horn was first used. The people who appeared to be the most important were riding very large horses, 17 hands high! They wore helmets on their heads, tightly-fitting bright red coats and creamy white trousers, which left little to the imagination – like ballet dancers. But some of these people were quite fat, and including the fat women, the circus was really a pantomime. The man who had invited me to the hunting pantomime lent me a horse, a stubborn Welsh mountain pony, low and fat like his owner, but with plenty of life to disobey me when he wanted to. My friend took a flask of whisky from the inside pocket of his jacket and offered it to me, saying, 'C'mon, it's good for the cold.' I asked him, 'How many foxes are we going to kill?' and he said 'I'll be very surprised if we catch one.'

Two hours later he was as fed up as I was. We left the horses at a farm and he telephoned for a lift to the pub. The pub was called 'Y Ceffyl Du' – The Black Horse – in the town of Carmarthen. Some of the members of the hunting crowd were already there and the rest arrived a few hours later, quite miffed because they couldn't catch any foxes and because it was very cold. Soon enough, we were warm in our heads, and we began to sing and to forget how the foxes had won and had probably enjoyed the theatrical performance, at least on that day.

Later I left the Ceffyl Du pub and I criss-crossed Carmarthen town in search of the bus station. I couldn't find it, so I asked around: 'Do you know where the bus station is?'

'Yes, I know,' said the man I had stopped.

'Can you tell me where it is?'

'Yes, I can.'

I realized that in Carmarthen if you want to get at least close to the bus station, you should say something like: 'Would you be so kind as to tell me where the ***** bus station is, please?' Preferably in Welsh, of course! By the time I had worked out that what he wanted to hear was simply, 'Where's the bus station?' I was in danger of missing the bus altogether.

Somehow, and only just, I found the place called 'Gorsaf Bws' even though it didn't have a sign or a bus shelter, just a few old people standing miserably in the grey drizzle-breeze. I don't know if I was disappointed by then, or had given up being disappointed, but after spending almost an hour searching for the bus station, I discovered there were no buses going to the place where I wanted to go anyway. I thumbed a lift again. The driver told me to put on a seat belt, but the belt buckle didn't want to stay in the holder, so I lassoed myself and we departed at high speed to the west, me feeling claustrophobic and hot with a rope around my neck.

— 15 —

ST DAVIDS

As I continued on my way to the west, not very happy and with a terrible hangover, I stopped in a pub in Haverfordwest and had a few of the famous 'hair of the dog' drinks – vodka, etc. When I began to think clearly, I realized that if I didn't get a job soon I was going to be in a terrible financial mess – and I was, because not even here was there a job for a lost Patagonian. I decided to take what I thought was the only road to north Wales. A driver stopped and I dived inside the lovely car. With authority, the driver obliged me to put on another very uncomfortable seat belt and then he asked, 'Where are you going, young man?' I said, 'Anywhere in the north will do fine.' And he said, 'The north? This road is going to St Davids in the west, not to the north.' Bloody hell!

Of course, at that time, all the road signs in Wales were in English and I didn't understand them. (Most road signs in Wales are bilingual now, thanks to the Welsh Language Society which defaced the English signs and confused the English tourists.) At that time, I thought that if we continued any further west, we'd end up in Canada. 'Have you been to St Davids before?' asked the respectable old driver. 'Have you seen the cathedral before? Have you been in the Bishop's Palace before? Or to Solva? Or on Ramsey Island?'

I said, 'No.'

'Well, well, well, well,' he said (which in Welsh means 'Wel, wel, wel, wel'), 'you're going today then, because that's where I'm going and because there's no other road to anywhere else from here, you see!'

I realized that I had no choice of road at all at this point (wide or narrow, good or evil) and gave myself up for lost. This wouldn't be the first or the last time that I got lost in Wales but that little mistake led to me staying in St Davids for ten years longer than I'd planned.

By that time we had arrived at the mighty St Davids and the kindly driver continued to surprise me with his eloquence, chatting away like a very well trained parrot. This friendly parrot told me that St Davids was the land of saints and also it was, he said, the smallest city in Great Britain. I could see that as we arrived and I groaned to myself, 'Oh, no.' I just couldn't believe my bad luck. Why the hell I had assumed that all the roads were going to north Wales, I will never know. The driver said, 'Oh, you'll enjoy it here ... see the sea? It's like an island here in the middle of nowhere, it's beautiful, isn't it, my boy? You should take photographs of the cathedral, and show them to your friends when you go back to Argentina. This place is full of history, my boy.' I thought that he would make history if he invited me to have a plate of chips, I was so hungry. Instead, he dumped me at the entrance of the smallest city in Great Britain and said, 'It was very nice to meet you.' I stood there, in front of the Grove Hotel with my guitar, thinking that the driver hadn't met me – I'd met him – he did all the driving, all the talking with his luxurious explanations – I had only said 'Oh' from time to time.

If I couldn't find any kind of work in Cardiff, Swansea, Carmarthen or Haverfordwest, where at least there were plenty of people, then I had no chance here. The village was in silence, except for a few crows entertaining themselves and performing a macabre welcome, perched on top of the only group of trees at the entrance to the city. I was alone in a foreign country, with the wintry weather telling me that Christmas was not far off. The decorations on that group of 'Christmas' trees were unique and perfect for me, with shining black crows inspiring me to touch the land of the dead saints.

I entered the only pub, The Farmer's Arms. A ghostly feeling of unwelcome was encouraging my thoughts and I followed my legs through the standing clouds of smoke until they stopped at the bar, where some people were talking in deep voices. In Welsh I asked for a pint of beer – and the reaction was as if I had dropped an atomic bomb. The owner, Mr Richards, said, 'North-Walian, eh?'

I said, 'No, Patagonian,' and it was as if I had dropped another atomic bomb in front of their noses. The pub was in silence and I was quite enjoying it. Some of the everyday customers were leaning over their pints to see how many legs a Patagonian had. A man by the name of Trefor gave me a cigarette and I said, 'Diolch' (thanks), and he said, 'Croeso' (welcome). He didn't say much else that afternoon.

Whilst drinking my pint in silence I could hear someone playing the harmonica in one of the other rooms, so I went to investigate. The man was dressed like a cowboy, but not quite – he was wearing a big sombrero, moustache, and an open shirt, with some long chest hairs sticking out of it, Mexican-Hollywood style, and he was drinking tequila. I asked where he was from, and he said, 'Solva, where the fuck you from?' I thought that the welcome was getting better by the second and I felt at home for the first time in Wales. I was surrounded by a sense of individualism. They were very nice people but they didn't care a damn about anyone and I knew I was going to love this.

I arranged to meet Mr Trefor Martin a few weeks after our brief and silent encounter. This time I was prepared for a long chat with him, as someone told me he knew a lot about the history of St Davids, and as I was in the process of – so far – liking the toy-village, I was ready for a long and pleasant afternoon. Of course, the only place suitable for that would be the smoky Farmers Arms pub.

We filled our bellies with beers, ciders and God knows what else in a lovely, dreamy atmosphere. Our conversation was serious, lively, and Mr Martin could speak after all! In a very deep voice Trefor told me the story of the area, and it was obvious to me that the whole region had been intoxicated by religion for many centuries, especially after the arrival of Christianity. Trefor told me there is no hard evidence about the existence of St David. It seems that the famous Saint who is the patron of Wales might never have existed at all. It may have been a well-created myth, a well-constructed cunning plan, in order to enslave people within the confinements of the Bishop's Palace. The powerful doctrine of the Saints made the Palace an attractive place for pilgrims who came by the thousands to pray, work, study and die. The whole area is littered with human bones. There were so many dead pilgrims that even the boat owners were furiously rowing the decomposing dead bodies from the mainland to be buried across the strait on Ramsey Island. That is not a myth. I learned a lot from Trefor.

Again the word 'work' was not an attractive subject but I was still searching and somebody sent me to the Warpool Court Hotel, the only three-star hotel in the area, which belonged to the Lloyd brothers. Apparently something was going on there and as I was walking up the drive, lined with trees and flowers, two men were standing there trying to do something with the fence. The tallest man, with a totalitarian attitude said, 'Can I help you, Sir?' This was the last hotel in town and no one had called me 'Sir' before, so I polished my poor English, and I replied, 'Yes, I want to work.' The taller man looked at the other and then came close to the fence. He looked at me with a lot of mistrust, whilst firing all kinds of serious questions at me with his very well trained manners – all tight and sharp and slightly out of place, like the strings of an old guitar. I was listening very carefully to the slender twist of his tongue and the thrusting waterfall of words he was delivering to me, with the whim of a child. I was a new toy for him and the game was going to be a long one.

'What is your name, Sir? Where have you come from, Sir? How old are you, Sir? Who sent you here, Sir? What qualifications have you got, Sir? Which university did you attend, Sir?' He turned to his fencing friend, and said between his teeth in Welsh, 'Who the hell is this one?' Then I interrupted, saying that I could speak Welsh, too. Well, he nearly fainted. He couldn't believe his ears, and it was obvious that his confused brain couldn't cope with the simple fact that I spoke Welsh. His eyes were like two well-cooked fried eggs by now. As he was coming out of his trance, he asked with a trembling politeness, 'Would you join us for a meal, Sir?' I was delighted with the way I said 'Yes'.

The table was full of food and I was not sure what to do with it because I was so hungry – and also because I was the centre of attraction. He introduced me to some builders, gardeners, cooks, washing-up boys, and many young maids who were running and giggling around the hotel. One of the builders was a farmer. His name was Derek Rees and he spoke better Welsh than I did with a curious accent. Slowly that spontaneous and voluminous meal was turning into a party, with jokes, lots of healthy laughter and with a strong sense of madness about it. Soon I realized that the fencer was the owner of the hotel, and the conductor of the madness that now I was proud to be part of. His name was Dai. He stood up and shouted, 'Reit boys, fuck the work and bring the sherry in!'

Many two-litre bottles of Spanish sherry were standing on the table, inspiring awe in the face of the grim attitude of winter. The first cork went out, and all hell broke loose. The afternoon was sorry I'd arrived! I was the match waiting to set the volcano on fire and the explosion erupted in a myriad of songs and stories. I knew most of the hymns, and some of the folk songs, but there were some wonderfully rude songs too called 'limericks'. Although I didn't know them, they were highly entertaining with their well constructed lines and rhymes, many made up on the spot.

Derek Rees and I became good friends. We shared many similar interests in life. He, like me, was born on a farm and was good with horses. In Britain today it's difficult to find good natural riders, in my opinion. Most riders here look like someone has put an iron bar through their spine, and they cannot bend. They look far too stiff and unnatural while riding. And when they trot, it's like they are making love to an invisible being, with very strange movements, pushing from the stirrups, up and down. They don't seem to have any control of their horses, and it takes many metres to stop them, which is very different to my experience of riding. It's a great pity as the horses are a magnificent cross breed here. Derek and I spoke only Welsh together, firstly because Welsh was the natural tongue for Derek, and secondly because I could speak hardly any English. Spanish was out of the question, although Derek could say rabanito (horse radish). Apart from working at Warpool Court Hotel, we used to go around Pembrokeshire helping other people as well, mending their bathrooms and other parts of their houses. Once, while we were putting a new roof on a house in Haverfordwest, the owner said to us, 'I don't understand how you boys can put the roof on in Welsh!' And Derek didn't say anything more than, 'Well!'

I met all of Derek's family, including his grandfather who was about ninety years old. At that age he went to court for the first time while he was still working on his farm. Apparently he had fallen out with one of his neighbours and in the dispute the ninety-year-old man hit his neighbour in the face. So in court the judge asked him, 'Now, can you tell us, why did you hit this poor man in the face?' To which the old man replied to the judge, 'Because he is a fucking bastard.' The judge didn't put the ninety-year-old man in jail but instead told him not to hit the neighbours for a while. Not long after that I went to his funeral to sing some Welsh hymns.

Many years later a friend of mine asked me if I could help him with a court appearance. He was Gareth Phillips from Solva, just outside St Davids. Apparently it was not his fault, but he had punched someone, and had broken the guy's jaw. The police were not very happy with that, so the court was likely to sentence Gareth to a year in jail. I wrote a letter to the judge, saying that Gareth was a good bloke and that I was offering him a job on my ranch in Patagonia. On the day of the trial in Swansea, the giggling judge said, 'Mr Phillips, tell me which you would prefer – a year in Swansea jail or deportation to Patagonia?' That day everybody laughed a lot because they still remember that judges used to send outlaws and criminals far away, and Patagonia was the ultimate sentence.

The sherry continued to flow very nicely that first afternoon in the Warpool Court Hotel and I am sure we created the most noisy and messy choir that ever existed in Wales. I played the guitar and sang all the songs I knew and some were repeated over and over again. *Guantanamera* was the favourite and, after twenty times, everybody was singing it in a very funny Spanish.

In the morning, everybody was saying 'Good morning' in Welsh to me, but for the rest of the day they were stuck with the words 'Si, señor' and 'Guantanamera'. I finished the fencing and the next job was to build some extra bedrooms for the hotel. When we finished all that, we were invited to participate in the owner's next whim. Now he wanted a heated swimming pool, with a roof, and a boiler room, and two separate changing rooms, one for men and one for women. We did all that too and when it was finished, and the water was heated inside, the swimming pool stood out as the main attraction of the whole building. David, the owner, took all his clothes off and jumped into the middle of it. Throughout the summer season, this swimming pool was the local centre of attraction, not so much for the guests in the hotel, but for the farmers, carpenters, builders and potato pickers. They would flock to wash their feet in it and at night after a few good drinks, everyone was willing to show their bodies in the dark of the swimming pool, and to run naked through the well-kept lawns of the hotel.

The hotel started to look very busy, the swimming pool was working well, even at night, but the bar was getting too small. So we built another one. People were coming from all parts of Wales, and even from London, to stay at the Warpool Court Hotel. Something was going on there, people were inquisitive to find out more about this remote corner of the world, where apparently anything could happen. I'm sure they weren't disappointed, because they kept coming back with their families, showing off their brand new cars and their brand new wives. Everyone was invited to contribute to festivities and perform to the best of their ability, in any circumstances and in any form. The musicians were always at the top of the list but there were other events, like drinking competitions and storytelling. That made some people happy and others sick. Many locals could swallow a pint of beer in less than two seconds and they could vomit in less than that again, before reaching the toilets. I remember some of the more fussy guests complained a lot about the chaos on those nights, but getting no response.

Alan Jenkins was one of the locals who could play the banjo and the guitar beautifully. He could sing every kind of song imaginable, from blues, jazz, folk, pop, to rock 'n' roll. They all seemed to suit his voice somehow, through the endless hours that we spent entertaining everybody. He was the owl of the nights and the skylark of the mornings. During the day he would transform himself into any kind of bird, although I believe the cuckoo was his favourite – not for the monotonous tune this bird performs, but for the number of nests Alan regularly visited.

After only a few weeks of being in St Davids, people began to treat me as part of their own family, a unique position at this point in my life. It had never happened before, not even in my own village in Patagonia, or in many hundreds of places I have visited since then. The older people were delighted to speak to me in Welsh, which was a natural and normal thing to do, but the kids (who didn't speak Welsh) were totally confused. They couldn't make much sense of it while they were talking to me because I couldn't hold a conversation in English and that disorientated them totally.

So in order for them to have a good laugh at me, they had to teach me their own kind of English and, by doing so, I had to reverse my age and transport myself into a kind of primary school once again. It was great fun to be a pupil and a teacher at the same time and in a short period there were more kids in St Davids who knew the geography of Patagonia than probably anywhere else in Great Britain.

Throughout that first summer in Pembrokeshire I got into the routine of getting up very early in the mornings, normally about five o'clock. There were a few reasons for that, of course – one was to feed my horse, which I had bought from a local farm, another was to jump on her bare back and have a good gallop around St Davids before the monstrous invasion of tourists began to drag their feet with sandals through any of the three streets, always with colourful plastic bags and the rotten smell of suntan lotion. All this could easily frighten any normal horse and spoil her forever, especially when young, in the first weeks of training. But the understanding between man and horse in the early hours of the morning is unique for people who work with horses, feeding the instinct of survival and companionship, instead of transforming these magnificent animals into pets for profit. I met many people in Britain who, for some stupid reason, molest horses by rubbing the palm of their hand in the poor horse's nose. If any of those people did the same to me, I'm sure I would react in a very nasty way, probably with a slap.

One day, returning to St Davids from the hills of Carn Penberry and Carn Llidi on my beautiful palomino mare that I had named Lleucu, I decided to call into the chemist's shop of the village, to buy some athlete's foot powder. My feet were getting very smelly with so much humidity and through wearing wellingtons all the time. I didn't know the word for 'athlete's foot powder' at that time, so I tried to translate from the Spanish, but that didn't work. I pointed at my wellingtons, but that didn't work, either. The three ladies in the chemist's were scratching their heads, trying to work out what was wrong with my wellingtons, apart from being full of mud. I wanted to take my socks off and show them, but I was too shy to do that in front of these nice ladies. So, because Welsh is a very familial language, I said, 'Mae 'da fi madarch yn tyfi ar fy nhraed.' That translates as: 'I've got mushrooms growing on my feet,' and – what a miracle! – they understood that perfectly. The three ladies rushed round the shop to fetch some cream and powders. A day later, everybody in the village knew that some kind of mushroom was growing on the Patagonian's feet!

Leading Lleucu, I walked from the shop back to the Warpool Court Hotel, where I could let her loose in the field, and where I could lose myself in my 'hacienda'. This was a very small, private but desirable accommodation that I had found for myself in the hotel grounds, and where I was living very happily whilst working at the hotel. When I began working for David Lloyd he had offered me a room in a caravan where I could sleep. This caravan was placed with a few others in a field close to the main house, and it had four small compartments with just enough space to put a bed in each one. On my first night I squeezed my guitar and bag into the room and settled down on the bed to sleep, but soon realized I had disturbing neighbours on each side of my little room. On the left a roaring snore was blasting through the wall all night, and on the right someone was vigorously rocking the whole trailer as if murdering a rhinoceros. After two damp, cold and sleepless nights I abandoned the caravan and began searching for a more homely place to stretch out and rest.

I found it in a secluded corner of the same field, but well away from the caravans. Completely covered with ivy and brambles was an abandoned tower-shaped building, camouflaged by trees, overgrown weeds and neglected fruit bushes. It caught my eye and seemed an ideal place for a Patagonian to disappear without trace as no one from the hotel ever ventured into this long-forgotten corner. Without disturbing the camouflage I investigated and discovered that just inside the perimeter wall of the grounds were some small stone outbuildings and abandoned greenhouses adjoining the walled garden. One of the buildings was a square stone tower, two storeys high, that I later found out was a pumphouse originally built to service the gardens, greenhouses and orchard. It was solidly built as part of the perimeter wall but the doors and windows had rotted and blown away long ago in the salty sea wind. What remained was just an opening to the ground level, and a set of exterior stone steps leading to the non-existent 'door' on the upper level. Inside the first floor was a single stone room, about three metres square, with a rough wooden floor, and a window opening with no glass left. The tower must have been quite decorative originally, as the window had brick arches and there were black bricks creating a hidden pattern amongst the stones beneath the ivy, but now someone else's folly was to become my whim.

After investigating I immediately fetched my mattress from the caravan and threw it onto the tower floor, releasing a cloud of dust from the clutches of the spiders, and named the place 'La Hacienda'.

A family of swallows was nesting in the corner of the low ceiling, and a donkey with the face of having been retired for the last hundred years had made the ground floor room his home. I accepted their company and thought I was invisible, as they seemed oblivious to my intrusion. My guitar and the few items I had scattered around the room didn't disturb them, and the blanket I stretched over the 'door' didn't block their passage. It was beautiful to see the swallows coming and going through the window-less hole in the wall to feed their adorable chicks, whilst I was practising the guitar. From my mattress bed I could see a row of sweet chestnut trees through the window, and I descended the stone steps each morning to the welcome of the neglected fruit trees that were as happy as I was with the undisturbed peace.

The peace didn't last long when the locals discovered where 'La Hacienda' was. David Lloyd was incredulous when he was told the Patagonian was living in the garden wall rather than his beautiful caravan, but he overlooked evicting me. Instead, the fruit trees provided a canopy for quite a few lively barbeques and impromptu parties, and many of my friends stayed overnight on the tower floor rather than face the walk back to St Davids or Solva after a few beers. Friends came and went like the swallows via a gap in the wall and the back lane that I also used as my private shortcut to the beach. That summer in La Hacienda at Warpool Court Hotel I was probably the happiest person in the whole of St Davids.

My days in St Davids were immensely interesting. All doors, windows and gates were somehow open to me. The people were my new family now. I could work in the hotel, in farms, stables, or by giving concerts with my guitar and, as well as working hard, they taught me to play hard, too. That was their way and I had to adapt to it in any language or in any circumstances, with the horses or with the boats, with the tractors or with the cars, with the singing, partying, or fighting. Many times I felt a bit run down – but that was a small price to pay in comparison to the huge amount of pleasure and laughter I was getting out of most situations. On one occasion I met a family of Scottish Gypsies in a bar, a lovely family with plenty of kids of all sizes and ages. We spent many hours on a rainy afternoon playing the guitar and singing with these nomads named Isaacs (and it is possible that was their real name). At one point a drunken man who was also from Scotland came to the pub in search of a fight. He challenged everybody but no one seemed to be interested in fighting that day. They were all too involved in music and relaxed conversation. But the drunk insisted, until Mr Isaac stood up and said, 'Okay, I'll fight you for £20.' The drunk didn't like the sound of that £20, so he opened his eyes very wide and then stumbled out of the pub with his tail between his legs.

The Isaacs invited me to drink tea and cider in their caravans, which I couldn't refuse as their hospitality was as open and sincere as the life they were living. They taught me how to pick potatoes in order to make good money very fast and, although it was a back-breaking job, I enjoyed every second of it, being out in the fields all day quite dirty and

with plenty of sun and plenty of rain as well. The owner of
the potato farm was Merfyn and after the harvest of the early
potatoes finished, he invited me to stay and continue working
on the farm if I wanted. He said that he could provide me
with a caravan to stay in, in order for me to take care of his
farm. 'I'd love to do that,' I said. 'Okay, you're on then, but I
hope you're not afraid of spirits,' he said. 'Clegyr Boia' was
the name of the farm – *clegyr* meaning 'rock', and Boia was an
Irish magician, landlord and pirate whose home had been on
that spot at least 1,500 years ago. But now, for the time being,
it was my home.

Merfyn was damned right about the spirits, or the spirit
of Clegyr Boia at least. I was never really afraid of this spirit
but I must confess that I was very aware of his presence
around his rock, especially in one particular spot in front
of the beautiful old farmhouse which, for some reason, was
empty. Boia was kicked out of his home with the arrival of
Christianity. The local version of events was that the magic
of the Christians was too much for Boia so he decided to
bugger off somewhere, and he hasn't been found since.

Saint David built a magnificent palace with a wall around
it. Whoever Saint David was, he must have been a man of
incredible influence and power, whose Bishop's Palace is
still attracting people today to see the ruins of an interesting
architecture, built with real blood in order to strengthen the
mortar to bond the stones. I always jumped over the walls
and had a great time catching rabbits inside the grounds at
four or five in the morning before the place was open. The
fantasies I could create there, when alone in the early hours
of the morning, were unique pieces of spiritual garbage. I

loved it, I loved all the challenges which the place was so determined to offer me. I didn't understand what was going on there but I always adored it. I composed songs at night in the Palace and I composed songs on Boia's rock. The romanticized dramas in those compositions were similar but somehow it was easier to drift into an unknown dimension in the Palace and I saw the immortal dance of the serpents in the stream telling me something of the past.

The spirits of Boia and Saint David were helping me to compose a lot of songs which, from time to time, I would continue to perform on the BBC, HTV and S4C Welsh television channels. They were paying me very good money for these interpretations so I used to pray to Boia and Saint David for more inspiration, so I could perform again on these programmes and receive more fat cheques, in order to spend at least three days in the pub in the great company of local people. Then it would be back to pick potatoes until the next TV or radio performance. One invitation was a bit different – I was invited by Cwmni Theatr Cymru to play the part of a Patagonian prince in their next pantomime. I hadn't worked in theatre before, so this was a new adventure. I spent three months touring theatres in Wales in this musical pantomime called 'Afagddu' and probably the best part for me was the touring and working with other musicians.

When the pantomime closed I took part in the company's next production, 'Harping Around'. This was a combination of music, dance, and telling the history of Wales. From this show I learned that the word 'Welsh' derives from 'waelisc', an old Saxon expression meaning 'foreigners'. The old Celtic language was call Brythonic, hence the word 'Britain', and according to the historians, words like London, Paris and Rome descend from Brythonic roots. For another three months we performed this show in Bangor and Betws-y-Coed, mainly for summer tourists. I also accepted other invitations to perform at concerts, birthdays and wedding parties, mostly held in impressive halls.

One night, after finishing the show in Betws-y-Coed, and as I was walking back to my hotel, a gentleman who had been at the concert stopped me and invited me to sing on St David's Day at the Royal Albert Hall. The next St David's Day was about eight months away so I thanked him by saying, 'Yes, sure, no problem,' but without asking where this venue was exactly. Typically, I soon lost the invitation details. I didn't worry too much because by now I was getting used to singing in many different halls and one more wouldn't make much difference. The contract with Cwmni Theatr Cymru ended and I returned to my 'second home', St Davids.

After another winter of hotel and wet farm work, the spring arrived along with daffodils and flags in the streets. The smallest city in the UK was full of activity, especially at the Warpool Court Hotel, with the owner making plans for the forthcoming St David's Day celebrations. He asked me if I would perform at their concert in the evening.

'Sure. When is it?' I asked.

'March the first – St David's Day – next Monday,' he replied.

Suddenly I remembered about the invitation I had received at Betws-y-Coed to perform at the Royal Albert Hall.

'Sorry, Dai, I think I need to be somewhere else that day.'

'Where?'

'The Royal Albert Hall. Do you know where it is?'

'It's in bloody London – are you sure you're supposed to be there?'

'London? I thought it was in Caernarfon. Are you sure it's in London?'

'Yes, of course I'm sure. It's not in Caernarfon, it's in London, man.'

'Ohh … do you know the address?'

'No, I don't know the address. It's a big place. Ask a taxi driver when you get there.'

With no other information to go on, early in the morning on the first of March I headed towards London. David had recommended that I ask a taxi driver in London, so I did. The driver knew exactly where the place was but until I arrived there I never imagined that the Royal Albert Hall was a huge, opulent theatre with the most spectacular balconies and an interminable stage, with a dangerously superb sound system, and where all the superstars in the world had performed, in the same situation in which I now found myself. It was just as well that I did turn up, because my name was printed on the billing for a huge concert organized by the London Welsh Society to celebrate St David's Day. How could I tell my friends in Patagonia about this exclusive experience? They would be jealous or proud or, more likely, they wouldn't believe me at all.

My contribution to the concert was very well received, which was unusual of course, because I sang in Spanish and Welsh, wearing a big north-Argentine poncho with bright red and black colours. The response of the public was extraordinary, better than in the pubs in Wales, and better than anywhere else I'd played so far. I felt great after the performance, and very excited by the experience, but the organizers were very poor, apparently, and they couldn't pay me very much, so that was that. Late that night I decided to leave London and find my way back to Wales. As I didn't have much money and the train fare was very expensive, I hitched a lift at a roundabout. A lorry stopped as soon as I put my thumb up, and I made myself comfortable in the passenger seat in the warm cabin of the lorry. Immediately the driver and I began to chat away as if we had known each other for a long time, while a ferocious rain was hitting the windscreen. The driver found it amusing that I was from Patagonia but I sensed he didn't believe me when I told him I had just finished a concert at the Royal Albert Hall.

Somewhere on the motorway, the driver stopped for a rest and invited me for an extraordinary English breakfast in the motorway cafe. He chose an enormous and succulent meal of sausages, bacon, black pudding, beans, mushrooms, potatoes and bread, all fried in pork fat, and alongside the warm plate of breakfast a mug with tea, and more bread with butter and jam. The driver was such an interesting person, but unfortunately he was heading towards Manchester. Slowly he drove his lorry from the car park and continued on his way in the opposite direction to Wales.

I moved to a position on the sliproad and tried to hitch to the west, but this time no one stopped and I got drenched to the bones while waiting for a lift. I walked back to the cafeteria thinking it would be better to find a place indoors to sleep for a few hours and then try hitching again in the morning. But every time I tried to sleep in a chair, someone woke me up, and eventually I was told I was not permitted to sleep inside the building. I was herded outside where I got soaking wet once again. I wanted to sleep, and after searching around I finally found a caravan parked alongside a row of trees. I crawled underneath it and settled down to sleep where it was nice and dry, but I had hardly been there for five minutes when the caravan pulled away, leaving me lying on the ground in the middle of the car park with my head on my guitar case.

It took me about a week to get back to Pembrokeshire. I wasn't in a hurry, and I always hate travelling in a rush anyway. So I took my time visiting small villages, medium sized villages and larger villages in Oxfordshire and Gloucestershire, and somehow I arrived in the city of Bath, a beautiful place which the Romans had created with their skilful designs. The well-kept Roman bath ruins invited me to belong to a lost era of stylish grandeur, and the temptation to be like a Roman took hold of me. I was feeling good there, and I imagined being up to my neck in clean, warm water with amazing people, talking about new ideas, new designs, new trade, and new countries to invade, planning new towns with newly designed baths in an orgy of pleasure and fantasy. But right now, 2,000 years later, I couldn't even have a wash because the baths were closed and I was concerned that, if I took my shoes off, the Roman pillars would collapse in agony. So I decided to help keep the history of whatever is left of the Romans and hit the road to the west.

When I arrived back in St Davids I went to visit my friends at the Warpool Court Hotel and, to my (lack of) surprise, they were having a party! This was a big party, with lots of important people like bank managers and so on, so everyone was trying to impress each other by wearing their best suits. The women were wearing long dresses, which somehow made them look taller than they really were. There were plenty of red lips, and earrings and necklaces hanging from their bodies, so they resembled African tribeswomen. I knew them well but it took a long time to recognize them, and as I arrived looking like a tired tramp, they stared at me as if I was a toad from another pond. However, after a few solid hours of drinking, nobody was able to judge anybody by the quality of their suits and the *ratatouille* became a lot more interesting.

In that turmoil I saw my friend Lyn wearing a Mexican poncho and a very expensive North American cowboy hat. He was looking incredibly smart. When he saw me he shouted across the dining room, '*Eh, amigo, porqué no, eh?*' He told me that he was learning Spanish. He also told me that he didn't know more words than that. He had learned *porqué no?* from a dictionary, which means 'why not?' I never met anybody trying to learn the beginning of a foreign language like that before but it makes sense – 'why not?'

I decided to put on my poncho and a big sombrero, too, so now we were two Mexicans singing and dancing around, inside and outside the hotel. After hours and hours of playing the guitar, singing, entertaining, and Lyn performing miracles with his harmonica, we decided to call it a night. It had passed four in the morning and we'd been at it for almost eight hours. It was difficult to even talk, let alone attempt a single note. Noticing that my Welsh-Mexican friend was half asleep in a chair, I suggested we look for a room somewhere in the hotel. We tried all the doors until we found one which was unlocked. We entered the room and put the lights on. To our surprise we saw two old ladies sitting upright in one double bed, looking at us with big disorientated eyes. I closed the door and we ran through the passage, until finally we found an empty room. In the morning, Lyn reminded me of that unusual incident. I thought I'd dreamt it, but he told me that he had seen them as well although, he said, 'It could have been the ghost, but it's strange because there were two, and the ghost in this hotel is only one lady, and we weren't drunk enough to be seeing double.'

The mystery was solved when we went down the stairs into the reception area, where Dai, the owner, was looking very serious with a very serious hangover. He called us forward and without looking at us too much in case he burst into laughter said, 'Good morning boys. Two old ladies have complained in this hotel in the last ten minutes. Apparently two wild Mexicans were inside their room last night and turned the lights on. Now, Mr Perkins and Mr Griffiths, do you have any idea who these Mexicans are?' We stood there with the sombreros, the ponchos and the big moustaches, trying to think how on earth we could get out of this one. But, thank God, he just smiled at us and said, 'Don't worry too much boys, I've done that a hundred times myself.'

That year was one of the hottest summers ever and I worked with a family of Gypsies who had come to pick the crop of early Pembrokeshire potatoes in May and June. The back-breaking job made us all very fit and healthy looking with the wind and sun beating down on the fields of the Pembrokeshire coastline. While sharing their picnic of sausages, tea and cider I asked them where they were heading next. They told me they usually went to Evesham to pick fruit in July and August, then Hereford to pick hops in September, but this year they were thinking of going to France to pick grapes. The word 'France' stuck in my mind, and I must have mentioned it quite a few times to my friends in the pub.

— 16 —

BONJOUR LA FRANCE!

By the end of August, the Welsh summer of 1976 was coming to an end and we were already complaining about the eight months of miserable winter that we had to face from now on when, in the middle of that depressing conversation, Derek Rees said, 'Why don't we all go to southern France, to pick grapes, or something like that?'

I said, 'Yeah, why not?' and Lyn said, 'Porque no, eh?'

So we decided to transform Derek's old Ford truck into a comfortable van, with a roof. We got hold of hammers and nails and many pieces of wood and the job was done. We threw in some mattresses and pillows, sombreros and ponchos, guitars and harmonicas and a few boxes full of food and a few hours later we were travelling at high speed along the motorway towards the port of Dover. The members of this suspicious contingent were Derek Rees, his wife Carol and their young son Steve – they were in the front of the van – and in the back was Lyn playing his harmonica, and me, thinking, 'What the hell am I doing here?' We looked like Gypsies but I doubt if we were as organized as they are.

Once in France, we passed through many villages, picked many grapes, drank many gallons of wine, and ate beautiful meals, rich in garlic and herbs. I will never forget the smell of French cooking, even the breakfasts on the farms were so special, with lots of different kinds of cheeses and patés, with drinking chocolate, teas, and strong coffee and a bottle of wine to wash it all down. We were about sixty workers, and after an interesting breakfast it was time for a bit of work. That was at eight in the morning, and at ten we stopped for a picnic. At 12.30 pm we stopped again for a huge lunch and went back to work at two in the afternoon, stopping at 4 pm for another picnic, and finished the day at 6 pm.

After finishing work we rushed for the showers, and that was probably the busiest time of the day. Everybody was running to get there first, although we had plenty of time. The evenings consisted of a splendid three-course dinner with all the wine we could have dreamt of in front of our eyes. I couldn't believe that I was getting paid on top of all this and, as if that wasn't enough, we demanded a party every night. The owners of the magnificent Château de Mombousquet at St Emilion were Messieurs Allan and Daniel Querre. They joined in these parties and as both of them sang and played the guitar, all the workers tried to show off as much as they could, with acting, singing and drinking, as well as fighting competitions. Now all of these healthy activities have been destroyed by the introduction of machines to pick the juicy grapes, and by the stupidity of some of the workers who used to complain that the work was too hard, and the food wasn't good enough. I couldn't believe it!

My friends went back to Wales after the harvest finished but I thought I'd stay a bit longer in order to get to know the French people better, and to learn their beautiful language. So I did – for a year. The southern Alps of the French territory were my favourite part, although I have to admit that I felt like settling down in many other parts of the country as well. I couldn't speak much of the language and I didn't have any family connections anywhere in France but somehow I was feeling very much a part of it, as if for some reason France was a region of Argentina, as Patagonia is.

As a musical nation, I find France very uninspiring. It is lacking good rhythms and probably because of that the radio was broadcasting songs from all over the world. It was very interesting for me to hear Astor Piazzola from Argentina, George Moustaki from Greece, Jacques Brel from Belgium, Joan Manuel Serrat from Spain, and Edith Piaf from France. Those great poets and musicians were filling me with an amazing and beautiful kind of culture. I was excited because I knew all the songs and with the radio at full volume, I was singing with them. British radio rarely played anything like that; George Moustaki was singing *Le Meteque*, Jacques Brel *Ne Me Quitte Pas*, Joan Manuel Serrat was singing *Pueblo Blanco* and *Caminante No Hay Camino*, Edith Piaf *Milord*, and Astor Piazzola was playing a very complicated composition on his *bandoneón*[9] – all those songs were on the radio in just one morning.

In the beginning, I used to laugh a lot when the French singers exaggerated their guttural 'R' as they sang, like those

9   *bandoneón* – a type of accordion, a complicated instrument
     originating in Germany

annoying parrots of Patagonia. But after a while I got quite used to it and in fact I think I like it now. As I was listening and learning through those songs the pronunciation of the French 'rrrrrr' in a bar on the banks of the River Seine, a beautiful and elegant young couple began to dance a tango. All the customers applauded this couple for a long time but for me their performance seemed very poor, amateurish, and their movements were awkward. As the tango dance was born in the docklands of Buenos Aires, the poor Parisienne couple didn't have a clue how to dance it. The girl dancer showed she had some vague idea by twisting and showing her legs quite a lot, but apart from that it was a dull performance. There is no comparison between the Argentine tango and the French tango. The French tango is stiff, theatrical and robotic in appearance. By contrast the Argentine tango is elegant, with fast, twisted, sexy movements, with a very definite rhythm and exaggerated dramatic passion. The city of Buenos Aires is full of tangos in the cafés, bars and restaurants, in the streets and discotheques. It's the folklore of the city, but in Paris it is quite difficult to find anybody who knows anything about this interesting dance, and that's why there are so many Argentine *tangueros*[10] in Paris.

Italian descendants in Argentina seem to believe the tango came from Italy. The Spanish descendants said it must have originated somewhere on the Spanish peninsula, and the 'turcos' (all Arab descendants) say it is a variation of a long-forgotten Arabic dance. Argentine people are reluctant to admit that at the beginning of the 19th century there were more black African slaves in Argentina than white colonists.

---

10   *tanguero* – someone who plays or dances the tango

As slaves, they were living like animals in corrals and huts alongside the port of Buenos Aires waiting to be distributed to somewhere in the countryside, or to be sent to the front line of wars against the Indians, the Paraguayans and the Portuguese in Brazil. The port became famous for dance and prostitution, and for some white Argentine aristocrats the novelty of having a black girl for sex and for a dance partner, became irresistible. It is well known that black African people always have been fabulous dancers and drummers, it is a natural gift well rooted in their genes, and there, in the port of Buenos Aires, this extraordinary foreign dance became a nation-wide popular phenomenon. But this 'slave' dance was taboo, and forbidden amongst the South American 'respectable white people'. It has been said that one form of tango originated as an African war dance performed by men only.

The wealthier Argentines were sending their kids to study in France, a relatively safe country with strong ties to the Argentine armed forces, where there were no restrictions about the tango or any other dance. Therefore the Argentine tango became acceptable in Paris as a dance with a male and female partner and an overnight success. The problem was how to tell the world that the tango originated in the cradle of prostitutes and slaves in Argentina. It had to be described as 'Tango Parisienne'.

I met many Gypsy musicians in France. Mostly they were jazz players – good guitarists with a great sense of rhythm, but I don't like jazz very much. In the south-east of the Pyrénées are the French-Caláns and they were playing rumbas. The rumba rhythm comes from Cuba but originated in Africa, and it has taken over the flamenco rhythm in many parts of Spain and France. They didn't know *sevillañas*[11] or *cante jondo*[12] but, nevertheless, they were all tremendously talented guitarists. I think these Gypsies should come to Wales for a while and teach the Welsh rock 'n' rollers that it's possible to play more than three and a half chords on the guitar!

At Saintes-Maries-de-la-Mer, in the month of May, there is a festival. This is a lively and religious gathering of about 15,000 Gypsies coming together in a spectacular array with their colourful rituals and artifacts. They have their white Carmargue horses and a strong belief in the dark Virgin Mary who, they believe, escaped the Roman persecution in Israel. Together with two other white 'Marys', they settled down in Château du Rennes, in the heart of the Pyrénées mountains.

When I went to Château du Rennes, I felt very peaceful and I don't know if it was something to do with the place, the Virgin Mary(s) or with those glasses of local wine which the English lady in charge of the place gave me at nine o'clock in the morning. But, anyway, it doesn't matter; the fact that I was there was good enough. I was enchanted by the place and its people, and if there is any truth in the mystery of Jesus Christ's mother, she must have been a very clever woman to choose a place like this to live. The Gypsies know all about these things but, of course, they keep it to themselves. Although, once a year, they carry the dark Virgin Mary through the streets of Saintes-Maries-de-la-Mer and then they all walk into the Mediterranean sea in a frenzy of horses, children young and old, and priests carrying crosses bedecked with flowers. They stop when the water reaches their necks, then

11   *sevillañas* – a type of folk music and dance of the region of Seville
12   *cante jondo* – serious, deep vocal flamenco

they all go to the bars for a good chat, with music and beer. It was an opportune time for me to join them.

Most of the musicians were playing rumbas and some were trying the more difficult paths of the Flamenco, but only the Andalucían Gypsies were comfortable with this kind of complicated and tragic composition. They were putting their hearts into it, in a powerful emotional manner that only they, the Andalucíans, knew how to do. Many Gypsies fled over the Pyrénées, avoiding General Franco's massacres, and the French Republic gave them shelter and another language. Soon they were better off in France than in Spain but slowly the deep culture of the Andalucíans in France began to fade away, lost in a foreign language. The extreme discipline of the Flamenco guitar is now rare amongst the French Gypsies but the rumbas are very much alive in the south, especially amongst the young people. Some of them have gone around the globe playing these rumbas beautifully, with extremely virtuoso guitarists.

I feel very much indebted to the Gypsies, or Romanies, or the people from north-west India, or whatever we choose to call them, because not only have they managed to keep their culture alive against all odds but the cultures of many other countries too – regions, languages, races and religions – they adopt all of these without any apparent effort. They create and perform music and poetry more passionately than anyone else I have seen, with their raw, coarse and wild ability to adapt to any circumstances. Thanks to them, today we can appreciate many professionals using the Spanish guitar, with Spanish compositions that have been composed previously by 'illiterate' Gypsies, memorized and passed on from father to son. Like the ancient Celts, the Gypsies didn't have a written language, it was all in the memory. I know a Gypsy family in Patagonia who can memorize every telephone number they come across yet I have a huge problem remembering my own!

Historians say that the Gypsies introduced the violin to Wales, and promoted its acceptance amongst the gentry; there are certainly many people today playing fiddle around the place. The Welsh triple harp was very much kept alive by the Welsh Gypsies, and the Roberts family was a typical example. John Roberts and his nine sons were playing the triple harp so amazingly that Queen Victoria asked them to play for her at Palé Hall, near Bala, in 1889. That was a very successful presentation. Also, the Welsh Gypsies spoke three languages fluently and naturally – Romani, Welsh and English – a rare achievement considering the number of days those people probably spent at school. Charles, the Prince of Wales, still has problems with the pronunciation and the mutations of the Welsh language, as have I, but I believe that he must have had better opportunities and facilities than the Gypsies to do something about it.

The Gypsies in France are trilingual today – Romani, French and Catalán – and this, along with music, contributes to the culture of the country. France is not a very big country but its multi-cultural population, with hundreds of completely different regions with their variety of foods and climates, makes it seem much larger. You can work out which region you are in just by tasting its extraordinary array of cheeses. They vary so much, from Alsace to Aquitaine, or from Normandy to Aix en Provence. I found myself traversing the west coast of the Atlantic and going north from the Pyrénées through wonderful farmland, sampling excellent red Bordeaux wine from Gironde and, even better, cognac from Charente and the white wine from Nantes. By the time I arrived in the centre of Brittany and accepted one hundred glasses of *chouchen*[13], I was in an unstable haze of hallucinations.

— 17 —

BRITTANY

OUR historical Welsh cousins in Brittany were blowing the *bombard*[14] as noisily as they could, in a monotonous and painful manner, when I arrived at the village of Pulawen. This trumpet-type instrument really could blow away all the walls of Jericho, and that story in the Bible could have been true after all. My ears couldn't believe what I was putting them through, as they'd never experienced this sort of traumatic torture before – and haven't since. That human gathering is called *Fez Nos* in the Breton language ('Happy Night' in English, 'Noson Lawen' in Welsh), and it consists of everybody holding hands and trotting around the place, a bit like dressage with Andalucían horses, but not as elegant.

The Bretons were trotting, or dancing, with their grandfathers and grandmothers, and with all their kids as well. They'd form a big circle and then move backwards and forwards, while shouting and drinking *chouchen*. This *chouchen* is a sweet mediaeval kind of aperitif, like mead, and today they drink it as an aperitif all day long. It is quite

....

13   *chouchen* – a form of mead popular in Brittany
14   *bombard* – a reed instrument similar to the oboe

pleasant if you like that type of thing. I drank plenty of it, in order to see if the mighty music would get a bit sweeter, but it didn't. I went to bed early that evening but I couldn't sleep. An enormous drum had gone totally mad inside my head and I promised myself never to set foot in a *Fez Nos* again for the rest of my life. But in less than twenty-four hours I was invited by some youngsters to participate again in a *Fez Nos*. As I entered the big, noisy town hall once again, I thought that the madness of the Breton people had begun to affect me. I was following the dancers without having a clue what I was doing. I was entranced by the *Fez Nos*, the Bretons, the *chouchen* and by the craziness of those '*bombards*'. I left the Celt-Iberians while they were still sweating with wild excitement.

In the large town of Rennes – or maybe it was Nantes – on one of those pleasant Breton afternoons, I met up with an intellectual-looking type, part hippy. He was wearing some wicked spectacles with lenses so thick that he looked like an owl. He told me he was not in fact Breton, but French. He hated the French Republic so much that he had become a Breton overnight, just like that. He had changed his French name to a Breton one and sadly I can't remember either of them now. I just remember that, as in Argentina with Welsh names, the government in France had made it illegal to give a child a Breton name. But, the man said, he had learned the Breton language and decided to settle down on the outskirts of Rennes to write books and to live the life of a hermit. He was probably quite safe in his burrow. The smell he was distributing freely around the Breton countryside revealed that the place he was living in didn't have any water for washing – either that or water was an alien element to this intellectual tramp.

This man, apart from bothering my nostrils, was a good sort, a knowledgeable and self-elected Breton who had taken the trouble of learning this ancient language, probably better than many true Bretons. The Bretons were originally Welsh people from Britain, he told me. They escaped the barbarous invaders and settled around this area and in parts of Galicia in Spain. However, the Iberians settled down here long before the Welsh Celts and there are plenty of sites to reveal that – for example, all the stone circles and standing stones are Iberian. Even Stonehenge in Britain was allegedly begun by Iberian people – the Celts just took over the Iberian culture, like the English took over the Welsh culture, or the Aztecs took over the Mayan culture, or the Incas took over the Aymará culture.

'And there we are,' he said, 'we are constantly on the move, conquering new areas to settle down, killing a few cultures on our way. We aren't different from any other race on this mad planet. Just look at the Welsh, they even conquered Patagonia. Are we fucking mad or what? Did you know that Perón was Breton?'

I thought he was really taking the piss out of me by now. 'Yes,' he continued, 'his forefathers went to Patagonia from Brittany, and there are plenty of Peróns still living around here.'

'Well, well, I never thought about that,' I said. 'I know that Juan Domingo Perón had family connections in Patagonia and, in fact, in the same province as me in Chubut, because someone once told me that Perón's mother was a Tehuelche Indian (and there are a few Peróns around the village of Camarones today), but I never knew that he was of Celtic extraction.'

'Oh, yes,' he said, 'that's why he is immortal.'

In that rather smelly and relaxed ambience he stood up, turned, and began to walk with determination. In seconds he had vanished in the multitude, leaving behind a highway of odour that made the Breton flies very excited, and I didn't know whether to believe him or not. But he'd made me think. This man with two names, who had come from nowhere, constantly reminded me of Merlin, the Welsh wizard. As I put my rucksack on my shoulders, I wished I had a ton of magic mushrooms to eat for dinner that night, so I could become one of them, or simply a Welsh-Iberian-Patagonian-Frenchman, with a Breton *bombard* playing hell with the Devil.

I didn't know that Juan Domingo Perón was a descendant of these Breton people and still don't know if he had any connection at all with the Celts. In fact, I know very little about the history of that man because when I heard that Sr Perón was the President of the Argentine Republic I was only about four years old and I didn't have much interest in politics then.

Señor Perón wanted to rid the country of all the Freemasons and also the Rotarians. They were reproducing a lot, filling the Jockey Club with the upper class citizens of Buenos Aires, leaving Señor Perón without a chair to sit on. Now, with Evita Perón it was different – she was a strong woman of Basque descent and also Perón's wife. She was one of the first women in the world to become Vice-President of a country. The people of Argentina adored her and she became more popular than the President. She died very young, apparently of cancer, but rumours say that she was assassinated with some kind of drug. We will never know the truth now that she has gone, but somehow she is still immortal, and Argentina has never recovered from that tragic death. The lucky ones who had the honour of meeting her will never forget how caring and open-hearted she was to everybody. It is weird how many famous, infamous or intelligent people died so young – Mozart, Princess Diana, Carlos Gardel, Dylan Thomas, Che Guevara, Alexander the Great and Evita Perón as well. It looks like destiny is busy choosing them one by one, sending them all to a special place.

— 18 —

THE SOUTHERN ALPS

I left the Atlantic shore of the Breton coastland and headed to the magnificent Alpine area, not far from Aix-en-Provence in the Département of Var, and only over some hills from the small village of Meounes. In the early Eighties I found a welcome and work at Planestel Claylade, a smallholding with an owner from the region of Alsace, named Michel. After about a week of my being there, he realized that I probably knew more about farming than he did, so he asked me if I would like to take care of the farm while he went to Paris on business. I accepted the proposal with some surprise, as we didn't know each other very well yet and, although the farm didn't require too much attention at that time of the year, it was a big responsibility for me to take care of anything in the French language.

The telephone was the worst part. I was trying to write down all the messages in French but it was quite difficult, and when Michel returned he was angry because he couldn't make any sense of my writing. And when he realized that most of the messages were from women, he went completely mad, asking me how they sounded, what kind of accent they had, and how old did I think they were? I said that all of them sounded alright but he wasn't convinced.

We became good friends and I really enjoyed a good deal of freedom on the farm. I also enjoyed his excellent cuisine, and probably the only time we disagreed was when buying newspapers. He always had to buy the right-wing papers. I grew tired of the same style of writing and the same critiques about third world countries and third world French citizens. 'I don't like communist newspapers,' he said, 'but my holidays in Moscow were very nice, because in Russia nobody is allowed to steal your money.' He didn't like England because there were 'too many Lords there'.

One night the telephone rang. He shouted, 'C'est pour toi René, c'est un Anglais, c'est pour toi, c'est pour toi.' This English telephone call turned out to be in Welsh. Some people in Wales wanted to make a film which was to feature a gaucho, a real gaucho who could use the *boleadora* on horseback. So far they had had a terrible problem in finding one. So the telephone call was from Endaf Emlyn, director of a company called Gaucho Films, who was also the director of his film called *Gaucho*, and he wanted a gaucho. Until today, I have no idea how he tracked me down to this farm in southern France.

Gaucho Films invited me for a meeting in Wales to talk about Endaf's latest idea. I flew to Cardiff and after three pints of beer in the pub, the meeting was over. We talked a lot about gauchos and horses, about *boleadoras* and the Spanish language. In his film he wanted to use the word 'box' in Spanish, but later he changed his mind because I told him the word 'box' in Spanish is 'caja' and 'caja' in Welsh means 'shit'. We shook hands on the way out of the Halfway pub and he went off with a smile on his face.

— 19 —

FILMING *GAUCHO*

THE next morning, I went to Gaucho Films' office to sign a contract to act in the film as a Welsh-Patagonian gaucho and to talk more about gauchos and *boleadoras*. They'd billed me as the star of the film, without asking me too much if I wanted to be an actor. The make-up girl said that I had a good face – did she know anything about gauchos, or what? I was trembling with ignorance and excitement at the thought of being a Patagonian Clint Eastwood but Endaf calmed me down by saying, 'What is an actor anyway? You know how to use the *boleadora* – that's what's important.'

It must have been important for Equity, the actors' union, because they gave me an Equity card as a result. I carried it all around Cardiff but these Equity guys changed my surname. I didn't know, but apparently a woman in Scotland had already registered the name Renée Griffiths with Equity. So from that day on I became Eugenio René Gruffydd for film and television work, and there's been confusion about my real name ever since.

We, the 'actors' and crew, took an aeroplane to south-east Spain in August 1983, to the town of Almería. There we had a full half-day of relaxation by the swimming pool of the hotel, paid for by this new-born company. Endaf told us that it was extremely important to relax before starting to act the next morning, but for some unknown reason we all got drunk that night and the next morning we were all very nervous.

I'd been told that our *Gaucho* film had a budget of around £300,000. At that time it sounded phenomenal, but when I mentioned this to an American producer who was staying in the same hotel as we were, in Almeria, he laughed his socks off and was sure that I was joking, saying that £300,000 wouldn't be enough money to pay a single actor. By now I was feeling ashamed to have mentioned our *Gaucho* film at all, but because I had never been involved in filming before I thought £300,000 was an extraordinary amount. The budget for his film was ten million American dollars! Ten million dollars? I was sure he was joking now.

Feeling a bit downgraded by our *Gaucho* budget, I made an effort to change the conversation, but I couldn't. He told me that he didn't care if his film was a hit or not, or if they sold it at all. I couldn't understand the logic in that, but when he said that the only important thing in a film is the budget, and not whether the film is good or bad, I realized that this must be what happens all around the world. The American producer was a nice man, down to earth and very sharp, but when I told him that Hollywood was called Griffithtown originally, he laughed. I began to tell him the story of Welsh descendant David Wark Llewelyn Griffith who established Hollywood and revolutionized the motion picture industry as a director during the silent movie era. He took his sunglasses off and looked at me very seriously. He didn't say anything but I was sure he thought I was on drugs or utterly mad. I'm related to the Rockefellers I said, so I could be related to D. W. Griffiths too! He put his sunglasses back on, and made himself comfortable on the sun bed. I thought it would be better for me to go to the bar and leave him there to roast alone as he didn't believe a word of what I said.

In the morning we went to meet our Spanish crew, which consisted of two funny horses, one funny trap and two funny Spanish lads. I took one look at the horses and thought 'Oh my God!' The carthorse was too small and thin to pull a cart, or any type of trap, and during shooting the actors had to push the trap several times, in order to help the poor old horse to trot at the right pace, so he could at least be in the picture a bit.

My horse was supposed to be a gaucho horse. A kind of *criollo*[15], or a quarter horse, or a Welsh cob would have been fine but a tall nervous thoroughbred mix, trained badly for the *rejoneo*[16] was not in my mind at all. Its colour was a dirty white and its tail was almost non-existent. The wardrobe girl said she could extend his tail by adding something to it and I was sure she could, but I didn't allow her to do it. The designers told me that they could paint it black if I wanted but I said forget it, let's try to find another horse somewhere.

15 *criollo* – a mixed-breed horse in South America, descended from horses brought by the conquistadores
16 *rejoneo* – bull fighting on horseback

The location for the film was the desert, close to the small village of Tavernas, between Almería and Mojacar. Hollywood has used this location in hundreds of films, and all of the greatest stars in western films have been there, sweating – Charles Bronson, Clint Eastwood and the rest – and now me, without a horse. These huge companies created a place for filming in the desert and, because it hadn't previously existed, obviously it had no name. Someone came up with a spectacular idea and called it Mini Hollywood but with a difference in the pronunciation … so it's called Mini Chollywood ('ch' as in Scottish *loch*, or as in *ch*appy *ch*olidays). I did find a horse by the end of the day. He was called 'Jota'. Again, the 'j' is pronounced as in *ch*appy *ch*olidays, but this time it's correct.

By now it was the second day and whereas the first day hadn't been too convincing, the second day was not convincing at all. When we arrived in the desert that morning, it was already hot, and by the middle of the day the sun was really showing off in all his pride as Master of the Universe. It was a beautiful and sincere star, making changes to the colour of our skins, but we all detested him because we were sick with diarrhoea and stomach upsets. We didn't know this but, apparently, there was a bug in the area. They called that disturbing feeling 'Spanish tummy'.

I told my horse Jota that we were not here for a '*ch*appy *ch*oliday', and I made a wide gaucho whip with some leather I'd found around. I showed it to him many times, as he was already spoiled by these gangs of Chollywood people. Jota understood my intentions at once and he behaved extremely well, as if we had known each other all our lives. But poor

Jota didn't know in which particular scene of the script I was going to use the whip on him and he didn't know that this Spanish tummy, or whatever it was, was really bothering us. So making him gallop like lightning over the hills in order to improvise a toilet amongst the scorpions, in that deserted area where so many famous people had been, came as a bit of a surprise to him. At least I had Jota with me, and I knew how to use him in emergencies. But I felt really sorry for the rest of the crew, especially the actresses. They didn't have a horse to disappear over the hills, like I did, so it was up to the designers to construct a kind of tent with towels and newspapers, while the rest of the cast and crew were looking in the opposite direction – especially Endaf, who was wondering how the hell he could stop this diarrhoea business. It was costing him a lot of money.

I really admired the patience of Endaf because as soon as our little problem stopped bothering us, the first cameraman collapsed in the desert. He couldn't cope with the heat, and they had to fly him back to Britain. So now although we were very healthy, we didn't have a cameraman, and although I didn't know much about filming, I imagined it would be quite difficult to make a film without a one. Panic began to thrive like the desert scorpions but, somehow, despite the time being lost and some worries, everybody was in good spirits and determined to help Endaf to finish this gaucho film so we could all go home and be very famous – but, damn, more problems arose.

Now it was the sound man's turn. He went into frenzied schizophrenic moods of laughter and emptiness. He believed that he could fly and so he went to the highest room of the hotel and scared the shit out of us because he was so determined to show us that he could. Personally, I think he was scared of heights, because he ran downstairs to the main room of the hotel and shouted that he was in love with us all – that was very nice of him – but we didn't have the time to play with love, we had to go back to the desert and shoot the film, and we went without him. He was sent to hospital for a few days and then they sent him back to Britain, a bit 'loco'. The rumours said that the sound man had eaten a big lump of Moroccan hashish for breakfast and that he was, quite simply, hallucinating and it was nothing serious to worry about.

That was excellent news, but nevertheless we were still really in the stew, without a cameraman and without a sound man. One of the Spanish Mini Chollywood crew, with plenty of 'ch' in his throat, took over as the sound recording technician and, with some help, he did very well. He didn't know what the hell was going on; he couldn't understand English or Welsh, so he simply did the job very quietly, carrying the microphone wherever it was needed.

The assistant cameraman took over as first cameraman, again very quietly and responsibly, and to my knowledge he was excellent. Without complaints or any kind of fuss, the film was rolling along very smoothly every day. We couldn't possibly disappoint ourselves or Endaf any more, so we decided to work as hard as possible, and have plenty of fun at the same time. We stuck to it and the plan worked. There were no problems from then on, apart from a few hangovers of course, but that didn't stop us having a good laugh.

The only sad moment was when the production came to an end, and everyone flew back to Wales, leaving myself and the producer behind in the airport at Almería. The last farewell came and our short-lived family disappeared behind the clouds. With our souls confused, the producer and I walked out of the airport and we also disappeared. I had rarely spoken to the producer during filming but we came to know each other better after the film had finished and we spent a week relaxing in Mojacar. We told everybody we were film-makers and in that area it was easy to play that game. We talked very wildly about the experience.

I worked on many other productions after *Gaucho* but none of them has been able to surpass the excitement and fulfillment of my first filming experience. Probably it was something to do with the horse.

— 20 —

ANDALUCÍA

OF HORSES AND TOROS AND FLAMENCO

I left Almería and the filming experience behind and decided to drift along the roads towards the south of Andalucía. The magnificent gardens of the Moorish Alhambra in Granada reminded me that I hadn't lost contact with nature yet, despite the cold-blooded extravagance of the hotels with champagne. The resin of some trees in the heat of the afternoon was floating around me like an invisible whim of butterflies. I never knew exactly where it was coming from, and I kept sniffing the bark of the trees, like a local and territorial dog. Gypsies were everywhere with their shiny dark eyes and shiny dark skin, wearing fat gold rings on their fingers and with gold teeth welded into their jaws.

Granada was the last stronghold for the Moorish invaders who lasted 700 years on the mainland of Europe and, visiting the Alhambra, I thought what a pity these Moorish tribes had left Europe as they were without doubt the masters of a wild gust of incantation, the creators of a phenomenal beauty. I like pretty things, so I go along with that. Federico García Lorca was born and assassinated in Granada, an unjustified tragedy. He was possibly the best ever poetic dramatist in the Spanish language and I adore his writings but the fascist General Franco didn't, so his Nationalist forces killed him.

I bought a cassette of flamenco music and continued southward. A roaring little lorry picked me up and I made a huge effort in that noisy cabin to listen to my cassette, until the driver said, '*Bahh, no vale nada*' (it's not worth anything). And he put on a cassette of his own choice, which to me was exactly the same as mine. By the end of the trip, and with the help of this lorry driver who sounded like a master flamenco teacher, I more or less learned the complicated differences. My cassette was made for ignorant tourists like me but he had the *canto jondo* type, and master guitarists like Manolo San Lucar and Paco de Lucía. I couldn't tell the driver that I was quite a professional guitarist, in case he took a guitar from under the tomato boxes and I made a fool of myself in front of this Andalucían who, by now, I knew was very serious about flamenco music and who knew his ground very well. Instead I began to wander in my mind to an incident in Wales.

I remembered meeting a farmer in a music shop in Aberystwyth once. He wanted to buy a flamenco music cassette from Spain, but he seemed to be totally lost. I jumped at the opportunity to help this gentleman as I realized that apparently he didn't have any knowledge of flamenco music. I asked the farmer if he would like guitar playing only, or singing as well, and his response bemused me. 'I don't know,' he said, 'it is for my horses.'

Apparently, he had been to the Royal Welsh Agricultural Show at Builth Wells, and he saw Andalucían horses dancing to a soundtrack of flamenco music. So he bought a cassette at the Royal Welsh Show and played it to his horses, but his horses didn't want to dance. He thought his horses didn't like that kind of flamenco, so he came into the Aberystwyth music shop hoping to buy the right type of Flamenco for his horses to dance to. I chose a cassette with some lively *sevillañas* rhythms and said, 'I'm sure your horses will like this one!' I said goodbye and hurried out of the shop to have a good laugh. I knew that it takes about eight years of high school training in Spain to make some horses 'dance', and the flamenco music is purely for the spectators. I was sorry I couldn't help the farmer with his reluctant dancing horses, but I thought that ignorance can produce wonderful moments, in unexpected circumstances.

We crossed Marbella and the lorry driver jolted me back to his cab, saying, '*Bahh, mira que basura, turistas,*' (look at that rubbish, tourists). He asked me if I liked bull fighting and I said that I had never been to a bull fight. He told me that on Saturday there would be a good one in Estepona and there would also be a very good *rejoneo* with the best horses of Andalucía. So I went. I have never admired something as cruel as that before. The courageous style of the *torero*[17] had an aura of power and grandeur, as the flowers, shawls and hats rained on top of him in response to his perfect killing. The carnivorous maestro walked like a jaguar in the hot sand of the arena, with pride. His sweat ran with blood in the uncontrollable ecstasy of the afternoon. A glamorous applause and an uninterrupted vociferous *Bravo!* came from every soul in the arena and all, apart from the dead bull, were shivering with excitement.

Several *toros* (bulls) came at full speed through the wide door and into the ring, throwing dust and saliva with rage, their nostrils open like the mouth of a basking shark, snorting away their disorientation. These bulls wanted to kill anything that moved, or didn't move, but each of them was killed and dragged away at full gallop by powerful mules through the same door they had entered by only a few minutes earlier. One bull was different. He came through the same door as the others, with the same intention in his mad eyes. He was powerfully built with 400 kilos of lean muscle. He was not going to give up easily, this one. The *torero* knew this better than I did, so he played with him beautifully. He did all the tricks that anyone could possibly imagine, all the turns with the synchronization of a Swiss watch, risking his life with each passage. But the *toro* was tactful and intelligent and he was not lowering his head at all. Therefore, it was quite impossible to kill him – to attempt a killing at that stage would be disastrous for the *torero*, so the play continued and the spectators were tense. He played with all the respect that the bull deserved. The spectators were jumping out of their

17   *torero* – bullfighter

seats in an explosion of *Olé!* The *torero* and the *toro* were the real heroes of the day. They were challenging each other, they were looking each other in the eyes, they respected each other, they touched each other, they were in love with each other, both of them were hypnotized by the other. But then the time arrived and one had to die.

I truly believe that the *torero* didn't want to kill this bull. It was something unique to him, probably the only love he ever had, the dream bull of any *torero*. He adored this bull and my feelings were that the bull at least should have been released into the open fields of his birthplace, to live out the rest of his life with dignity and pride. But no, the yard-long sword went through the skin of the bull's shoulders as if they were made out of butter and down into his heart. In that perfect synchronization of man and beast, the bull lowered his head and destiny was irreversible. He was obviously dead but although he was still standing on his four legs, only the instinct to survive and fight was keeping him from falling down for the last time of his spectacular life. The matador, with an emotional self-confidence, turned his back on the dying bull and raised one hand to salute the excited public. In that precise moment the bull played his last card and sent one of his horns through the heart of the unsuspecting *torero*. The 400 kilos of dead muscle crashed on top of the brave and trusty matador. The two lovers lay hot and dead in the arena, bound together in death.

After watching those serious gladiators going to hell or heaven together, I found myself uneasy and, although I could understand the writings of Federico García Lorca much better now, I was not sure if I ever wanted to see any more

bull fighting. But the next things that came into the arena
were the magnificent and incredibly well-trained Andalucían
horses. These beauties are trained for the *rejoneo*, and it is the
most elegant, dangerous and breathtaking performance with
horses that I have ever encountered. There is no comparison
in any possible way to the cruel cowboys of North America,
the uncaring gauchos of South America, the ungainly
Mongolians, or the robotic stiffness of the English riders.
These horsemen were masters in the true sense of the word
and tears sprang from my eyes with passion and emotion
like I had never experienced before. I had the pleasure of
meeting the Peralta brothers, years after, in the outskirts of
Arcos de la Frontera but that day in Estepona I didn't know
who they were, and the fact that the Peraltas were there
changed the picture of bull fighting in my mind for ever.
These *rejoneadores*[18] were controlling and commanding their
horses with the weight of their bodies, rarely touching the
reins. But this was not a little stroll in the back lanes. They
have the task of challenging and avoiding the charge of a
massive, light-footed, unpredictable bull, where one mistake
would cause the horse to lose all his intestines on the bull's
horns and for the remains of his body to be dragged at will
all around the arena.

No, this was not 'Hello darling,' from the top of a tiny
English saddle on Sunday mornings, this was a hard, 'Hello
darling,' with elegance and death. These horses could
trot backwards very fast, and gallop sideways, without a
rejoneador touching the reins. And this was not dressage,
by the way! These superb horsemen tied the reins to their

18   *rejoneadores* – bullfighters on horseback

belts and charged the bull at full gallop, the horse bravely measuring the delicacy of the distance and then, when it appeared that the worst would happen the horse threw himself to one side and immediately to the other, cheating the bull's way of thinking and avoiding by millimetres the deadly horns. And at that particular moment the *rejoneador* would deliver two tiny darts with both hands on top centre of the bull's shoulder, with an extraordinary mastery and understanding of instinct, where one relies on the other for survival, perfection, entertainment and companionship. By the end of that exhausting afternoon, I headed towards Portugal, intending to travel from there back to Wales, via the Basque country.

— 21 —

BUYING A RANCH IN PATAGONIA

BACK in Cardiff in 1987 I was irked, writing a song and an idea for a low budget Welsh television programme, work that refused to make me smile. I was drifting in my mind, back towards Andalucía and its magnificent horses, when I noticed that my knees were touching the underside of the table. When I tried to cross my legs I lifted the table up. I couldn't concentrate on the script, and I couldn't compose a sad song because I was not sad – I was irritated. Something was wrong, so I started to design – on top of this table – the table of my dreams; a table that had plenty of space underneath, a logical design, a table which wouldn't lift when I crossed my legs. It was a beautiful design but a bit difficult to sell to Welsh television.

I was so enthusiastic about the table I had designed that I decided to design a house to house my table – another masterpiece of composition, I thought, with its two octagonal blocks and its massive door facing east. I placed my table inside one of the octagonal blocks before putting on the pointed roof and then I put myself inside the house, sitting at the table with my elbows relaxing on each side. I drank a glass of very good quality wine and I didn't know what to do next. I thought that I had just one more problem to solve – where to locate the house and the table – without knowing that I was entering another journey of my life, the biggest and the most complex nightmare so far.

I forgot all about the sad song and the low budget script for the mighty S4C television in Wales and concentrated on my table and my house. The tiny problem was that I couldn't find an appropriate location to place my logical table and the house with its sixteen angles. In Wales, and probably because Wales is a kind of museum, the regulations about houses with windows and angles and doors are horrendous – there was no point even trying to get permission to build my whim here. And so I thought of composing the sad song after all.

I seriously believe that some of the worst architects today are to be found in Britain. There can't be many of them as all the houses look exactly the same – just the house names or numbers on the doors are different. So a pure Patagonian couldn't build the house of his dreams in Wales, and although my great grandfathers were Welsh and I spoke Welsh and I worked in Welsh for Welsh television, it didn't make any difference. I could have been a black African, a brown Pakistani, a white prince of Wales, or a multi-coloured garden gnome and would still have the same problem because Britain is a tough little place with not much sense of architectural freedom.

To hell with that. I decided that I would buy over a thousand acres of freedom back in Patagonia, where I could put more angles to my octagonal house if I wanted. I returned to Patagonia in 1988 and chose a little paradise in the Andean mountains with a lake, ten miles long, that was difficult to find on any map. As I was brought up on a farm in Argentina, I knew all the pros and cons of the land. I knew that if I wanted to be a good farmer I shouldn't be too traditionalist. I was prepared to plough the land with my hands, to breed cattle, sheep, horses, pigs, or whatever ... and then that 'whatever' hit me on the back of my head, and on the front: I was going to breed guanacos. 'What the hell are they?' asked my Welsh neighbours. My friends asked the same, and even my enemies had the curiosity and the courage to ask. I couldn't answer all the questions which these ignorant people were bombarding me with because, at that time, I was ignorant myself about these animals. Apart from knowing that the guanaco has four legs, I didn't know much more about it (although someone had told me that the wool, or fibre, it produces is the most expensive in the world).

It all sounds terrific, grand and sophisticated. In no time at all, most of Wales and parts of England knew that I was breeding 'millions' of guanacos. Nobody had a clue what they were talking about but they were talking very seriously. I was embarrassed by the nonsense which was spreading about this beautiful animal – for some people it was a kind of goat, for others it was a kind of kangaroo, but in fact it's a kind of camel. I was on the front pages of some national newspapers in Wales and even the *Financial Times,* that pink newspaper, found some space to talk about me and my guanacos. This stuff was getting a bit serious. I went to the pub.

I ordered a pint of brown Yorkshire beer and sat alone, thinking of my guanacos with four legs. Three hours later I was still thinking about the guanacos with four legs and getting seriously drunk. A girl who I knew in the media business came and said hello. She said, 'What about this idea of breeding guanacos, then?' In a bit of a blue mood I said, 'I'm thinking of abandoning the whole idea of breeding the guanaco, it's a bit crazy.' And she said, 'It's so damn crazy it just might work!'

I looked at her with surprise. Her name was Yvonne and I knew her from somewhere, although I couldn't remember at that time if we had worked together on some television programme or if she was a singer or a producer or a director. But she was definitely not a farmer so … well, there we are! My mood changed after her words, as I realized that I was not totally mad or, at least, that I wasn't the only person totally mad. We talked of many other things besides guanacos that night, at least that's what I remember, and she's still encouraging me today.

The ranch that I had chosen to buy had an interesting history. It had once belonged to the legendary Butch Cassidy and the Sundance Kid. They acquired most of the Cholila valley from the Argentine government in 1902 and were peaceful ranchers there until the U.S. authorities nearly caught up with them in 1908. They escaped through what is now my land into the Andes, crossing the mountains at parallel 42° and into Chile, leaving the U.S. sheriffs scratching their thoughts in Argentina. No one knows for certain what happened after that. Every outlaw enthusiast has their own theory about Butch and Sundance and sometimes you have to wonder if these guys ever existed at all.

Daniel Gibbons, a Welshman from Swansea, was working on the ranch for Butch and Iwan Jones, another Welshman, was working on the Gibbons ranch next door to Butch, now next door to mine. A dilapidated building where the Sepúlveda family now lives is the only factual remaining evidence that Butch, Sundance and Etta Place were ever living there, although the old building used to be part of the stables and storage rooms. The main house of their ranch vanished from the scene a long time ago. It was stolen by neighbours and parts of the wooden beams are holding up other houses, built in the 1930s by incoming colonists. But the gang's real hide-out was not there at all. It takes four hours more on horseback to arrive at Cassidy's real hide-out in the mountains, which is very close to the Chilean border. Butch was a very clever man, because if he had a problem in Argentina, he could just move one leg to the west and he would be in another country with different laws.

There is no visible sign in this rugged wilderness today that Butch ever had a hide-out there but a friend of mine told me that his own father burned it down because it was 'La Casa de los Bandoleros', and that these *bandolero*[19] Yankees robbed banks and killed people all around the place. The poor ignorant father didn't know that Butch and his sidekicks were gone long before *he* was even born. Today the trees and

---

19   *bandolero* – gun-carrying bandit, outlaw

the flowers of the mountains have covered up forever the mystery of these remarkable people. 'Amen' to them!

As I acclimatized into my new territory I began to enjoy these stories of '*bandoleros*', 'yankees', 'northamericans', 'pistoleros', bandidos', 'bank robbers', etc., etc., and sometimes in my imagination I was one of them. I thought that destiny had put me here in order to continue something that Butch Cassidy and the Sundance Kid had been unable to finish. So I began completing the acquisition of the ranch and, good God, what a task! The inheritors, the legal owners of the ranch, were growing like Colombian weed throughout Patagonia – an area that is bigger than France, Spain, Portugal and Britain put together – and were increasing every day. By now they numbered over twenty living souls, and were still growing. Why did these people have so many kids? I thought of the long frozen winter nights of the southern hemisphere and I got it right – there was nothing else to do.

I travelled thousands of miles and probably found most of the inheritors, scattered across the pampas, glaciers, villages and shanty towns. They were in the desert and by the seaside. Some had telephones in their houses, some had just a horse; some could put their signature on the paper, and some didn't have a clue what a signature meant. An old woman threw me out of her house with a broom in her hands, shouting that she had nothing to do with that ranch, although she was the most direct inheritor of all. She couldn't write, so it was a bit obvious that she couldn't sign this important paper. One day I helped her to put her rustic fingerprints on a document and she looked at the first signature of her life with pride. It became clear that I needed a lawyer to help me out, but as soon as I found one, I regretted it.

I don't know if there is another country in the world with more lawyers than Argentina. There are so many of them that you really wonder why. Every other person I was meeting in those days in the untidy and rather ugly town of Esquel was a lawyer, some of them looking as if they hadn't been weaned yet. In that dusty town I was looking for a superior lawyer, one who actually knew something about the law if possible, to fight the other crooked lawyers. In that area if you buy a kilo of tomatoes you need a lawyer to prove that what you've bought is correct. The situation with the ranch was getting really stupid and not easy for any Patagonian lawyer to solve. Inflation was rocketing in Argentina at 2,000% (yes, really!). Prices were changing three times a day, people were nervous, and the legal sharks knew I was carrying dollars. One lawyer told me that in Argentina a good lawyer is someone who knows exactly how to avoid the law. Could it have been Butch Cassidy who taught him that?

While I was travelling on a dusty bus and complaining about just about everything to do with Argentina, I remembered what a friend of mine had once told me. 'Argentina is a country of French architecture and Italian culture, they speak Spanish and think they are English.' It didn't make much sense to me then but now I thought it was an interesting soup which, although lacking some important ingredients, still tasted quite good!

Argentina was once the fifth richest country in the world, with a huge reserve of gold. It was the granary of the world during the Second World War, the tins of corned beef were leaving Argentina by the million and Señor Perón got very rich for a while. He began to nationalize all the foreign companies that were sucking the juice out of Argentina. The railways once belonging to the British were now in the hands of some kind of Argentine governmental corrupt gang that didn't make any money at all. The decaying wagons survived only at a slow trot with subsidies from President Perón. The bucketful of gold in the Argentine Treasury was getting low, the workers – parasites of the Perón era – demanded more wages, less work and more tango, which by now the semi-poor Perón couldn't deliver. His wife, Evita Perón, came to his rescue. She became the Vice-President and she was loved by millions of the poor citizens. She didn't last long. The military, a disease that is an epidemic in South America, hated her. Suddenly, she became ill and died. The military took over the country, kicked Perón out and an era of horrendous politics flourished in Argentina. A few decades later Perón came back to rule Argentina again but soon died, bitter and old. Nevertheless, until today, he remains the only president elected three times to run the country. After being buried for a while, someone broke into his coffin and stole his hands. The rumour was that Perón had a Swiss bank account that could be accessed only by the imprint of his hands.

I felt my own hands were tied and cut in half by all the problems I was encountering, buying the ranch. But I persevered and finally I believe that most of those semi-nomadic inheritors signed the 'magic' paper which stated that I had bought the place. All I needed now was the stock to start the breeding programme. This new start left me sleepless and exhausted but also excited by the challenge ahead.

— 22 —

BREEDING THE WILD GUANACO

THE guanaco had remained wild, challenging human whims for thousands of years, until my brother and I came along and disturbed the dust in the desert. In Argentina there is a national organization called INTA – Instituto Nacional de Tecnología Agropecuaria[20]. In other words, they are supposed to know how many legs a donkey has. And they knew it! But the guanaco was another matter and although they knew about its four legs, I couldn't get much more information than that out of them. Finally they told me not to attempt to breed the guanaco as no one ever had, no one ever would, and I would surely fail. Disappointed, I left the senseless organization wondering about this rare breed of intellectuals with curious surnames: one was called Señor Cabeza de Vaca. In English it translates as Mr Cow Head.

Despite being classified as a dangerous wild animal and an endangered species, I also began to wonder why no one had attempted to breed the guanaco before. The fibre that the guanaco produces is finer than cashmere and is therefore highly sought after by connoisseurs. The problem has always been how to get hold of supplies of the raw material. The finest Chinese White cashmere, the most valuable in the world, is 16 microns thick. Guanaco fibre is even finer, at only 14 microns. The only fibre in the world that is finer than guanaco is that of the vicuña, at 12 microns.

As the only camelid in Patagonia is the guanaco, I thought I could contribute to the economic development of

----

20 INTA – National Institute for Agricultural Technology

the region by promoting the taming and breeding of these animals for their valuable fibre. But I found that the ranchers in Patagonia are just as conservative as those anywhere else in the world. Instead of seeing an opportunity, they continued to see the thousands of guanacos that roamed wild on their land as pests. The wool market worldwide was plummeting but they clung to their traditional sheep farming in the hope that its fortunes would revive.

I could envisage guanacos being farmed and the fibre being introduced to the world market in small but exclusive quantities. Dawson International in Bradford confirmed that they had the capability of handling the raw material and told me that there were established companies in Scotland who dealt with the finest cashmere, who could weave the fibre into the most exclusive fabric. Knowing this, I approached the various development agencies in Wales, suggesting that this unique and valuable fibre could, with a little investment in the right machinery, be woven into fabric in Wales. My idea was to promote the guanaco fabric internationally as a Welsh product – with the raw material being produced in Patagonia, imported into Wales, converted into fabric in Wales, and marketed as a Welsh product. I envisaged that Wales could build an international reputation with this product in the same way that Scotland had with cashmere.

Sadly, this was not to be. The development agency in Wales we approached could not appreciate the vision or see the value of the proposal. No finance was forthcoming for any research and development, production or marketing. Quite simply, they didn't back the project. So instead, Scotland took up the baton and our beautiful guanaco fibre was woven into fabric that today carries the label 'Made in Scotland'. With the slogan '*More sashay than cashmere's cachet*', our marketing consisted of me walking into Harrods in my jeans and presenting the fabric roll under my arm to their head buyer. With a very discreet nod, the fabric was approved and was sold at £1,000 per metre in Harrods and at Gieves & Hawkes in Savile Row. Never mind – there's plenty of coal and sheep left in Wales.

But all this was to be in the future … for now, I was having just as much trouble convincing INTA in Patagonia of my proposals. My conclusion was that no one knew anything about this animal and they didn't care about the valuable fibre it carried on its back. They just kept repeating that it was a dangerous wild animal that couldn't be tamed.

I believed that, throughout history, many wild animals had been tamed – surely it couldn't be that difficult? So, after another tedious meeting with 'Mr Cow Head', I decided to hit the desert to look for my brother Fredy, whom I hadn't seen for many years. He was the only person I could think of who would at least *listen* to my idea.

I hadn't a clue where to start. I didn't even know if he was still alive and, if he was, where I could find him. To me Patagonia looked bigger than Russia today. Communications were wickedly poor and people still respect the silence, so they don't talk. My brother was a nomad, and he used to tame horses on his way to nowhere for a living, staying for a maximum of four or five months at each ranch. When I finally found him around Christmas 1988, I could see that around eight years had passed since the last time we saw each other. He was looking incredibly old in his early Forties. He was holding a big knife and his hands were covered in blood. He had just killed an animal for his supper.

I asked if it was possible to tame the wild guanaco and his response was 'Why not?' Then I invited him to join me in the project of taming and farming them for their fine wool. His response was 'Why not?' After a few days of monumental silence, and with the back of my jaws hurting from chewing so much guanaco and ostrich meat, I decided to leave. It was early in the morning and, except for two children of about eight years old, there was nobody else on the ranch. They gave me a piece of bread for breakfast but I couldn't eat it because it was rock hard, so they threw it into a bucket of water and then they put it in the oven. That breakfast was a luxury and I was amazed by those kids. They were Mónica Ruth and Elio René, my niece and nephew. They were living alone with their father in the most isolated part of the Patagonian Andes. But at that young age they could cook, wash their clothes and iron them, they could kill a lamb, and on horseback they were impeccable riders. They were little adults. Before leaving I agreed with my brother that we would meet again in a few weeks' time to start the adventure of trying to catch some *chulengos*[21] in an area of the desert inhabited by millions of the creatures.

We caught all of those *chulengos* with the *boleadoras*, on horseback. The *boleadora* is still the most efficient weapon to catch the guanaco alive. It consists of three pieces of metre-long rawhide tied in the middle, resembling a star. At each point there is a ball of stone, each weighing two hundred grams or more, and by throwing it at great speed it blends,

21 *chulengos* – baby guanacos

twists and tangles itself around the neck of the animal. The more the animal jumps around in order to get rid of the unwelcome *boleadoras*, the worse it becomes for him. There are two kinds of *boleadoras*: the 800-gram type is to catch wild horses by throwing them around the horses' legs, and the much lighter one is for catching ostriches and guanacos by throwing it around their necks.

The guanaco is a very successful survivor in the desert. The gauchos kill some animals from time to time to eat and, sadly, sometimes for a bit of sport. To catch an adult guanaco you have to be a very clever hunter, relying only on your horse and your *boleadoras*. They can't half fly up and down the hillsides of the desert, disorientating and watching the lonely frustrated hunter. Both horse and rider are constantly in danger of performing a somersault at any time. This happens because the desert is inhabited by billions of ants and these infernal insects make their nests in the ground. Therefore, if your horse steps into one of these nests, you can guarantee that it'll end up with a broken leg and you'll probably have a broken neck. A nice day out!

And then we have the beautiful penguins along the deserted shoreline of the Atlantic posing a threat to the gauchos. Millions and millions of penguins come every year to breed even more millions. People believe that penguins live in the sea, and they are right in thinking that, but once a year the penguins settle down in isolated places on the mainland, and on nearby islands. They come to breed in a very noisy way. They dig a burrow where they lay two eggs and then they don't have much to do until they hatch. So they spend those days making melancholic noises. These are the Magellan type of penguin, very friendly little creatures which walk awkwardly in a very peculiar and laughable way, stumbling over every desert stone they come across. They let humans get very close to them and are not at all afraid, but if you touch them they will chop your fingers off, as their beaks are so strong. Sea life is abundant in Patagonia, especially throughout the Peninsula Valdes, a sanctuary for wildlife. When the breeding season has finished, the penguins all jump into the Atlantic Ocean and vanish for another year, leaving behind a desert full of shit and holes – and that definitely means more broken necks for the poor gauchos.

Unfortunately, no alternative way has been found of catching the guanaco alive in the desert in respectable quantities. Rifles and bullets kill, so that's no good to anyone. I have been told of many other methods of dealing with the guanaco but they all fail, as these animals when fully grown have the facility of performing a suicidal show, and they do it at any opportunity. The government has tried many times to round them up like sheep and drive them into a trap made out of wires in the shape of a funnel. It doesn't work because when the guanaco finds out that he has been cheated, he turns back and, at full speed, will go through anything imaginable – people, horses and gates. The guanaco's brain is a little like mine, it's black or white, and that's it. So they'll pass through, or they'll die on the spot. My advice to any amateur is: don't stand in their way. Modern tranquillizer darts are too expensive and slow and it requires too many people to carry the sleeping beauty. So it was back to the Indians, gauchos and *boleadoras* and to the pain in the neck that all of this was sure to create.

We were four riders that first day of hunting, carefully choosing the best, most sure-footed horses but not particularly the fastest. We carried three to four sets of *boleadoras* per rider and began to spread out to cover more land. It was an uncomfortable cold morning, with a constant wind that chilled our bones. As the sun began to warm up our faces, one of the Indians caught the first *chulengo*. As I was preparing this little baby guanaco for transportation, my brother came along with two more and then more and more, until I counted seventeen *chulengos* and decided that this was enough to start the madness with.

Carrying them on horseback was not easy, and teaching them afterwards to drink milk from the bottle was a chaotic nightmare. The Indian workers were looking at me through lidded eyes and my brother wasn't looking at all. I am sure they all thought I was totally insane and probably they were right. They'd never done that kind of thing before, catching the guanacos alive and, on top of that, feeding them milk! Indeed, it was a messy and heart breaking business. Some of them died in our arms and we felt as vulnerable as they were. The change in their diet, the stress of travelling, first on horseback and then in the back of my pickup for hundreds of miles, the *boleadoras* around their long thin necks affected some of them and they fell into a kind of depression from which there is no turning back. There were no vets in the area, and even if there had been, it would have been pointless to call them as the vets don't have any idea about the animals of the desert, especially the guanaco. The Indians and the gauchos are too rough, too unkind and a bit afraid of the guanaco, which is understandable as they've never had to breed them for anything before.

But these initial problems were short-lived and breeding the guanaco became a strange reality. For the first time in Patagonia – indeed, in the whole of the Americas – I soon had a ranch with some two hundred tame *chulengos*. The Department of Wildlife had issued me with a licence, No.001, to breed guanacos. My brother Fredy and I learned from zero the way to handle and behave with these clean and elegant animals. The guanaco is an intelligent, stubborn and suicidal creature. Somehow he is also the ancestor of the *llama*, which was successfully tamed and bred by the Inca and Aymará people in what is now Bolivia and Peru. But the camel is also the ancestor of the guanaco, so a very confusing family, because there never were camels or llamas in Patagonia.

Now that we had our first livestock safely on the ranch, new problems presented themselves. Life in the Andes is very different from anywhere else, both emotionally rich and very frustrating at times. It's easy to turn a tiny insignificant problem into an indisputable nightmare, perhaps because you can't catch your horse one morning, or because the telephone doesn't work. And that day of course, it just happened to me. I went from the ranch to the village to make an innocent telephone call to my lawyers, because something was going on with the 'inheritors' of the ranch. But one of the posts which carry the telephone wires had fallen down in a storm and we had to put it back up before I could use the phone. I found a few Indian friends and we managed, in the middle of a windy storm, to tie back the wire and lift the long post quite straight. Eventually I was on the phone,

THE BROAD AND NARROW WAY.

Matthew VII., 13, 14.

'The Picture' – *The Broad and Narrow Way* (1883), **Anonymous**

My school in Bryn Crwn, Gaiman, which Juan Domingo Perón forgot to repair.
© RENÉ GRIFFITHS

The wagon that we used to move to the hills during the floods.
It took up to three months for my father to travel in this wagon
from Gaiman to Trevelin in the Andes during the 1920s.
© YVONNE CHEAL

Two of my grandfathers and assorted relatives with the Ford car that no one could drive.

© UNKNOWN

A typical Sunday lunch
that always lasted much longer than the services in the chapel.
© YVONNE CHEAL

In the role of Sitting Bull for S4C's film *Rough Riders*.
© MEDIA WALES LIMITED

In the role of 'The Gaucho' on location in Andalucía.
© GAUCHO FILMS CYF.

Surveying the ranch that once belonged to Butch Cassidy.
© FREDY GRIFFITHS

First day on the new ranch.
© RENÉ GRIFFITHS

Taming the 'dangerous and wild' guanaco.
© FREDY GRIFFITHS

Spot the difference!
© RENÉ GRIFFITHS

The proud and stubborn Juanita.

© René Griffiths

100% pure Patagonian guanaco fabric.

© Keith Morris

Fredy preparing his horse for a trip across the desert.
© HAYDN DENMAN

Fredy surveying the desert from a high rocky outcrop.
© HAYDN DENMAN

The remains of Butch Cassidy's house in Cholila.
© RENÉ GRIFFITHS

René and gauchos driving livestock to the *veranada*, or summer pastures.
© JASPER WINN

With Gruff Rhys discussing filming of *Separado!*
© DILWYN GOCH

With Ainsley Harriott following filming of *Ainsley's Big Cookout* on the ranch.
© PAUL MCNICHOL

trying to make some sense through the horrific noise that was plaguing the line.

Apparently, some of the 'inheritors' had employed lawyers to sell the ranch I was buying, and some 'inheritors' had not. Some 'inheritors' didn't want to sell the ranch and others were desperate for money. This is where the lawyers earn their bread and cheese – by stirring the mess for months on end and creating a chaotic turmoil of it all. The more prolonged the sale, the fatter the fees will be. I was getting tired of seeing in my mind's eye the deceitful faces of those lawyers every day so, as I had secured the property transfer from the majority of the 'inheritors', I was legally able to take possession of the ranch before heading back to Wales to organize the importation of the guanaco fibre.

— 23 —

IMPORTING THE GUANACO FIBRE

LITTLE green Wales was pretty in the spring of 1990, and was still dreaming of becoming a free nation. I went to my old local pub to have many beers and little food. The same grey faces with faraway dreams were hanging around, like always, undisturbed by the beautiful spring. A small group of students were still talking about the Falklands War in Welsh. They were sure that some Welsh soldiers had killed some Welsh Patagonians in the Malvinas War. They were against Galtieri and against Mrs Thatcher. A laughing girl said, 'We should kidnap them, stuff them with marijuana and send them both nude to the Antarctic.'

I made many television programmes that year, played
a few concerts and made another film. I was trying to get
some money together in order to invest in the ranch and to
pay for these lawyers who were crawling inside my Welsh
telephone line. Yvonne fought on the front line by my side
when barriers began to show their rows of rotten teeth, not
knowing that impenetrable obstacles at the bottom of a rare
abyss were waiting for us, swimming in a sea of wasps and
jealousy – otherwise known as 'importing the guanaco fibre'.

The word 'guanaco' aroused many suspicions. Many
flights to South America and many international phone calls
were made, and the importation of bales of guanaco fibre into
Cardiff Airport didn't sound quite right to the authorities. I
noticed that my telephone was tapped, and outside my house
in Llandaff men were sitting inside their cars, looking at
newspapers and watching at me passing by. I noticed that too
but, apart from being a bit concerned, I was not fully aware
of the silliness of the situation. So by the time the first bale
of guanaco fibre arrived at a warehouse in Cardiff Airport,
the Customs & Excise gang had arrived as well. They were
looking at my bale of fibre which, after the eight thousand
mile journey, resembled a huge meatball.

I checked my Argentine meatball and knew that nobody
had opened it so far, so I was sure it didn't contain any
contraband. The Customs & Excise gang began to cover
their hands with transparent, fresh gloves and their feet with
new Wellingtons. By now I was more suspicious than they
were. They were a very serious bunch and I began to feel
nervous. Did I check the bale well? Could anybody have put
something illegal into my insignificant bale of wool? I looked

at Yvonne; she was calm but with a serious fierce anxiety about the situation. A spectacular flash of stupidities crossed through my mind as the inspectors put their hands into the intestines of my adorable and dramatic meatball. I was sweating and imagined that my poor bale was full of cocaine and marijuana and I was guilty. I was going to spend the rest of my life in jail! Oh my God! I was really sweating by now. Then a thin, young Customs & Excise trainee approached a fat, old one and said, 'Sir, I've got something here.'

I didn't faint, because I was paralysed with fear. I wanted to run away. The thin man had a smile on part of his face and he was showing the rest of the gang some small round white objects. I was not sweating any more, I was in a trance and I was going to be the first stupid Patagonian to smuggle small round white things into the British Isles. I was done, busted, cornered and I was going to be bitten to death in a wet cellar of a monstrous prison where I was not going to be allowed to speak Welsh.

I knew I was going mad. But then an angel came with a miracle and the fat Customs & Excise man, after smelling the small round white things, said to the trainee with disgust, 'These are mothballs! Come on boys, we're onto a no-no here.' The gang disappeared through a big door, leaving Yvonne and me shattered and leaning against the poor defiled bale. 'Hhhhhuffff!!' We had completely forgotten the dozens of mothballs that I had carefully placed inside the bale in order to protect the fibres, as the experts at Dawson International woollen mill in Bradford had advised me to do. We rented a van after successfully clearing the customs trauma and drove our woolly whim to Bradford, deep in thought.

That sample of merchandise was of excellent quality, the best apparently that the company had ever handled. They were willing to buy as much as we could produce. That cheered us both up for the day and we smiled most of the way back to Cardiff, singing Welsh songs.

— 24 —

INTO THE HEART OF THE DESERT

IN order to fulfil the order we had received from Dawson International, I spent countless days alone in the desert of Patagonia, searching for guanacos and guanaco fleeces, driving many thousands of miles and regularly changing tyres that kept exploding on the sharp stones of the pampas. Up to a certain point, I was enjoying it all, the colours of the desert, the silence and even the conversations with the desert people who were completely unworldly. Yvonne joined me on some of these trips during the last days of a severe winter.

After a few thousand miles across snowy desert in the winter of 1994 we arrived at the desolated village of José de San Martín. As this extra-terrestrial village doesn't have a single hotel, we had to sleep in the back of the pick-up, while the temperature was around ten below zero. About five in the morning I couldn't stand it any more. We were paralysed and slowly dying of cold. I jumped out from the back of the pick-up and knocked at a door that said RESTAURANTE in big letters. I knew the owner, but at five in the morning he was still snoring with all his clothes on. So I dragged him out of his cuddly burrow. I don't remember his name but I do remember his trousers, hanging down with a big stomach hanging over the top. He didn't wash because the water was frozen in the buckets and he began to light the fire. The 0.25-star 'restaurante' filled to the ceiling with smoke.

We couldn't breathe normally and poor Yvonne was shivering with cold and coughing with the smoke, and she didn't want to talk. The fat man was not cold and he was not worried about the smoke at all. He said with a big smile, 'Don't you worry, my friends, I will make you a big cup of coffee and *maté*, and breakfast. Do you like eggs?' He was showing off his huge stomach, moving around the place that was supposed to be a kitchen but was, in fact, a bar. He gave me a strong alcoholic drink, which he said would help me with the cold weather, and Yvonne pulled a funny face in disagreement. So I had a few glasses and it was magic. It really worked wonderfully well. I was feeling energetic and happy once again.

The owner realized that I was enjoying the liquid breakfast, so he put the bottle on the table with a bang, like the cowboys do in films. Yvonne was anxious to go to a faraway town for a shower, but I wasn't. We began to disagree about just about everything. I was enjoying my Patagonia, but she wasn't. She went to look at the cooker and the eggs that were sizzling in the frying pan and she said, 'I'm not having breakfast.' The stove and the frying pan were so dirty that she had completely lost her appetite. I, however, was enjoying my breakfast in below zero temperatures when the owner of the restaurant said to her, 'How can a pretty girl like you put up with someone like him?' Meaning me! And she replied, 'I'm thinking of leaving him right now.' The fat man looked around and said, 'Ah, but you don't get rid of thistles that easily, eh?' We laughed loudly and I was really enjoying his eloquence. A guitar was hanging from a nail on the wall so I played and sang and drank more of that stuff called *caña quemada*, which means 'burned sugar cane'. It is a cheap and delicious drink, thick and sweet, which vividly induces the most abundant hangovers I ever had. As I was getting too happy, we soon left the place.

It was snowing when we left the 'restaurante'. I was driving carefully, trying to concentrate on the road that kept disappearing. After driving for many miles through a kind of *altiplano*[22] in a frozen breeze, I looked back and, thank God, the village was disappearing fast. It was just a tiny dot in the desert, a forgotten frozen mirage with an important name.

When travelling through the desert, you can be motivated by a mysterious feeling that entices you to look intensely at both sides of the road in the hope of seeing anything at all that is alive. Perhaps after hundreds of miles you might think you saw a hawk standing rigid like a statue on top of a fence post, but are not entirely sure of that either. A dusty whirlwind can distract from the emptiness, with tumbleweed rolling frenetically in the wind, giving the sensation that the barren land contains some kind of life in another dimension. Rarely would anyone compose a love poem or a romantic piece of music dedicated to this empty and monotonous stretch of flat stony land. You imagine that only a masochist would choose a place like this to live, a place so hard on the eyes. And then again, it contains something that is beyond our understanding in this complex modern world, and I don't know why the desert becomes even more confusing at night.

22   *altiplano* – high plains or plateau

I remember my father telling me that when he was travelling on his horse one night in the desert, he decided to stop for a rest and to have something to eat. He lit a fire, ate, relaxed and after a good rest he saddled up his horse and continued on his journey. After a while, he noticed that his old companion was disobeying his command; he was trying to go to the left and my father was turning him to the right. Hours went by like that, with both of them trying to move in different directions through the bushes, until my father saw a tiny fire in front of him. He thought that someone was camping for the night, but he was wrong – it was his own fire, left hours ago, and the breeze had kept it alight. My father realized then that he was totally lost and that his horse was right. My father had pushed the horse to make a perfect circuit, leading nowhere and losing precious time. The feeling of being an idiot, lost in the desert at night was enough to make him cry, so he crossed the reins over the saddle and let the horse decide his own path. The horse turned abruptly left, and with a smooth trot both of them were safely home in no time at all. Strangely enough I experienced the same thing whilst lost in the foothills of the Andes, and it was my horse that saved me then by turning abruptly, plunging into the river and carrying me upstream until we arrived at a gate that I recognized.

The desert can be cruel, disorientating and in a strange way beautiful, but although it is not in any way the Garden of Eden for me, I observed a peculiar view on the subject while travelling in France with a group of friends from Paris. We were passing through an area of fertile land with its magnificent undulating fields of wheat, maize and sunflowers.

Modern tractors were powerfully pulling expensive ploughs and trailers close to beautiful farmhouses and chateaux, but none of my friends cared a fig. Later on, when we entered a dry and obviously less prosperous part of France in the Massif Central, everybody spoke at once: '*Regard ... que belle ... c'est jolie ici.*' To me, the area was similar to the desert of Patagonia: barren, empty and sad, and for a long time I couldn't understand why my friends were astonished by a sterile area that could hardly feed a goat.

My Patagonian mentality couldn't understand it. I was born in the desert, and I believed that anything fruitful is good. So when I saw an extremely poor-looking old man herding his thin goats through thorny bushes in the Massif Central, it reminded me of the place I was born in South America where you can become crazy with solitude and poverty. The desolation we were driving through was not '*jolie*' for me. We drank wine in the car as we drove. I was quiet and pensive and my friends couldn't understand what was wrong with me. Of course, my friends were suffused with the wondrous aromas of tobacco and coffee on the streets of Paris, by clean avenues and magnificent architecture, and by adorable stylish women walking like elegant gazelles. They were satiated by restaurants and arrays of extravagant food and wine, by friendly social aperitifs of Pernod before the four-hour lunches on Sundays, and by seeing beautiful topless girls on the rivieras.

In the 1970s Bruce Chatwin, the English author and travel writer, was rambling around the desert of Patagonia too, although he doesn't mention San Martín at all in his book In Patagonia. Either he missed it altogether or the village was so insignificant that he didn't find any words small enough to describe it in his book. I was surprised and impressed by the analysis that Chatwin made of the word 'Patagonia', as I agree with his conclusion. He believed that 'Patagonia' is not a Spanish word, but a Greek one. The Patagon was a giant in Greek mythology and because the Tehuelche Indians were very tall people, Magellan on his voyage around the world called the country the Land of Giants, in Greek. I agree with that. Chatwin believed that 'Patagonia' doesn't mean 'big foot' at all, and I agree with that too. If the Spanish people called it Patagonia because the Indians were wearing some kind of skins around their feet, leaving big footprints around the place, then the whole world should have been called Patagonia, as all our ancestors around the world were wrapping their cold feet in animal skins. The correct Spanish word for 'big foot' is *pie grande* and in slang we say *patudo*. I never heard the Spanish people call those unfortunate souls who were born with extremely big feet 'patagon', and anyway, 'pata' in Spanish means a female duck.

I enjoyed and agreed with most of Chatwin's writings, but unfortunately he got my uncle's name wrong. His name was Alun Griffiths, not Alun Powell! Nor do I agree with Chatwin's observations on the gauchos' diet – eating meat and drinking *maté* and dying young of ulcers. I really don't know what he's talking about here. What can be wrong with eating an organic armadillo, or a *pudú*[23], or *huemul*[24], puma, or wild horse? If the gauchos lived in Britain, as Chatwin did, and were eating a beef burger every day with a tiny leaf

-----

23   *pudú* – the smallest deer in the world
24   *huemul* – another type of small deer

of lettuce, tomato sauce and the risk of Mad Cow Disease
inside, then I could believe that at the end of the day they
might have an ulcer. But in a place that has officially been
designated by environmentalists 'the least polluted place on
the planet'? I don't think so.

Perhaps Chatwin would disagree with the Atkins Diet
as well. Our diet on the ranch is exactly the same as Atkins',
and consists mostly of lamb for breakfast, lunch and dinner.
Research has been carried out in Argentina to find out where
in the country the healthiest people can be found, and what
a surprise, it was in Patagonia, where cholesterol levels are
extremely low. Before white people arrived in Patagonia,
the Indians lived purely on meat. Their diet consisted of
guanacos, ostriches, armadillos, pumas, skunks, foxes and
birds. Lettuce and asparagus were not on their menu and,
even today, they think that vegetables are only for rabbits.
With no words in their language for salads and vegetables,
the Indians thought that the Welsh must be very poor, as
they were eating 'grass'.

— 25 —

UNCLE LEWIS AND HITLER

ONE story that Chatwin didn't hear while with my family was
the story of Uncle Lewis and Hitler. This came back to me as
I was driving away from the village of José de San Martín.
The continuous flakes of snow falling slowly began to freeze
on the windscreen of the pick-up, and I had no idea which
road to take. Soon enough I found out there was only one

road out of town so I took it without blinking too much and hoped for the best.

I was driving with extreme care but at least I was moving somewhere when, as if I didn't have enough to think about, memories of my childhood came to bother me. I thought of those two roads in the picture on the wall of my family home. What if there is only one road – do I take it? As it was, I took this one with some regret as it kept disappearing in the snow, and perhaps I was heading straight to hell, instead of Esquel. In an eerie silence I drove slowly on top of the frozen snow for many miles. It looked like Antarctica as no roads could be seen until a sign appeared – Tecka 80 km.

I thought of my uncle, Lewis Griffiths, who had lived in this area all his life; he owned many houses in the village of Gobernador Costa, including the police station. He also owned and drove lorries, was a shopkeeper, an hotelier, and had even been the first lord mayor when the village was not even a hamlet. All that, with the temperature at times falling to minus 30° Centigrade, and gusts of dusty winds that appeared to be against all God's creation. Lewis spent half of the year drinking milk and the other half of the year drinking whisky. Had I lived here as long as he did, I would have probably ruled out the milk.

Uncle Lewis was a man of few words, unless in his spirits, of course. Then he could talk and laugh throughout an entire night with a rascally look on his face. One of the stories that fascinated me was the construction of an 'airfield' and the beer-making factories. 'An airfield here? Who for?' I asked. José de San Martín is not exactly a tourist destination.

Towards the end of 1800 and the beginning of 1900, hundreds of German pioneers settled throughout Patagonia, many of them in the vicinity of José de San Martín. The Germans were good ranchers, very brave and hardy people indeed to survive in that desolated flat land, which at least at times could easily be described as hell on earth. But the German people were well organized and prosperous in their own right. A general store called Casa Lahusen was probably one of the first in the desert to accumulate enough macaroni, wines, saucepans and saddles to satisfy the whole of Argentina. The company also bought wool, hides and whatever those ranchers could produce, including the by-products of wild animals, such as fox skins and ostrich feathers and so on.

Casa Lahusen was a serious well-established import-export company and I believe its headquarters were in Germany. The company had all types of lorries for the transportation of goods, warehouses to store them, and offices in all the major towns of Patagonia. Because Uncle Lewis owned some lorries and pick-up trucks he would from time to time, in order to break the monotony of the village, transport over thousands of miles a truckload of goods for Casa Lahusen. I joined him once when he was driving a lorry full of boxes of Nestlé chocolate on a freezing night to the town of Comodoro Rivadavia on the Atlantic shore.

We had an unlimited number of hours to fill, and he drove in a very slow, ponderous way, while I was making *maté*, sandwiches, peeling salami and passing the wine bottle. Lewis was a peculiar man; he could spend hours without saying anything and then, without any warning, like a roar of a jet fighter, he would tell me a story and that tale could last for hours, until the lorry broke down or until we stopped to stretch our legs. Being the owner of the only hotel in the village – the central gossip depot – Uncle Lewis got to hear all kinds of rumours, stories and hypotheses, some with a few facts thrown in. Whilst I don't remember his exact words now, this is the gist of one of those endless sagas.

The airfield in José de San Martín was apparently built under the instruction of Adolf Hitler while the Second World War was at its height and Hitler was stealing billions from the countries he was conquering in Europe, making Germany an extremely rich nation. As Hitler was planning – along with Japan – an attack on the United States of America, a huge percentage of those billions was sent to Argentina, and the José de San Martín area was chosen as one of the centres for German air force operations. Juan Domingo Perón was climbing the political ladder very fast in Argentina; he had become a General in the Army, a Vice President and finally, in 1946, President of the Argentine Republic. And for some obscure reason, he was a great admirer of Mussolini and Hitler.

In order to conceal the facts of what was really going on at the semi-built airfield in the Province of Chubut, the government of Argentina sent a small group of the Border Police Force to settle in San Martín. These Border Police are called the 'Gendarmería Nacional', with a reputation of being well educated and very tough, and the force was created for the sole purpose of guarding the nation's frontiers. This was done, for example, by intercepting drug traffickers and smugglers, and providing information to the Army immediately in the event of any developing friction with neighbouring countries. The problem is that in San Martín there are no borders with any other country, so the poor Gendarmería didn't have a clue why they were there. Anyhow, a basic runway was finally opened and the gauchos and the guanacos could watch some heavy, slow aeroplanes landing, once every two or three months in summer. In winter there were no landings because everything was covered with snow. Uncle Lewis thought the construction of that runway was the idea of some idiotic politicians, and that it would be better to repair the roads and put asphalt on them so we could arrive at Comodoro faster and without bursting so many tyres. 'Pass me the wine.'

Comodoro Rivadavia is the biggest town in Patagonia, an ugly and windswept coastal area where most of the country's petroleum is extracted. Hitler's plan was clear and clever – he would have a vast amount of petroleum at a reasonable distance from the programmed airfield, and from there the aircraft could fly a short distance over the Andes to the Pacific Ocean where aircraft carriers would be stationed. Also, the Nazis had chosen the town of Bariloche in the north-west of Patagonia as a base for the Fuhrer élite to control this entire and monumental operation. This area is situated in the heart of the lake district of Patagonia, a vast region of unparalleled beauty and an ideal hideout for outlaws. A replica of one of Hitler's houses in Bavaria was built in a secluded area of the Andes which could be reached only by boat across Lake Nahuel Huapi, or by helicopter. The house could not be seen from any road, but it would be from here in Bariloche that the delusional leader planned to achieve his dream of the Fourth Reich controlling the entire world.

The town of Bariloche was constructed mostly by Germans and in fact, by the time the Second World War ended, Adolf Hitler and his companions allegedly escaped the Russian invasion of Berlin and took refuge in Bariloche, where they controlled many important businesses. By that time Juan Domingo Perón had become President of the Argentine Republic, when the country was one of the richest on the planet. Europe was in ruins, but it was paying Argentina good money for grain and meat and the Central Bank and government houses were stacked to the roof with gold bullion. On some of his road trips to the north, Uncle Lewis stopped off in Bariloche, and regularly met up with a woman who had apparently worked as a housekeeper in Hitler's remote house. Recent research has uncovered others in the region who remember working for Hitler, or for his network of safe houses across Argentina.

Adding to the incredible irony of all this, the British engineer, Alan Arnold Griffith, had designed an aeroplane with jet engines, and his theory was put into practice by German engineers in Argentina. Kurt Tank, a German scientist and designer, manufactured the jet in the Province of Cordoba in central Argentina in the late 1940s. The jet plane was called 'Pulqui' which means 'arrow' in Araucano Indian. Perhaps it wasn't the best aeroplane in the world, but it flew at great speed and many countries showed great interest in buying the Argentine Pulqui with its revolutionary 'sweptback' wings. Other nations envied the advancement by Argentina in jet propulsion, but still, Argentina in a supersonic way, managed to fall into bankruptcy. All the gold in the country mysteriously disappeared, and a freshly made army general took over the country through a *coup d'état*. Perón was forced to flee for his life, but he was captured and thrown out of the country like an old unwanted rug. Kurt Tank left Argentina and ended up working in India before returning to Germany in the 1960s. Perón ended up safely in a mansion provided by Francisco Franco in Spain – another fascist criminal, responsible for lighting the first match which ignited the Second World War.

In some place – I had no idea where – Uncle Lewis and I stopped to repair some tyres. The tyres on three big wheels had exploded on the rough rocky tracks, the night was still young, and we had run out of spares. Changing these heavy tyres was an adventure in itself. One person must hold a paraffin lamp and try to keep the flames alive while the wind is trying to extinguish them, while another person is loosening the nuts of the wheel and swearing with sweat and cold. The frozen spanners and iron bars would stick like super-glue to the hands and we used hessian sacks as gloves to prevent losing our skin. A filthy tyre repair man had to dismantle the heavy duty wheels with crowbars and hammers in his dusty ramshackle shed. From time to time the tyre man would have a swig from a bottle of very high alcoholic stuff. I tried it and it made me retch.

The man repaired two of the tyres with reasonable ease; pieces of hard rubber were stuck on with glue and the tyres were fitted back onto the lorry. The third tyre was a write-off, so the man with such obvious experience of tyres stuffed sheep's wool inside where the inner tube should have been, and with a smile he assured us, 'It doesn't look very pretty but it might take you out of the shit.'

Uncle Lewis was cheerful and quite drunk when we climbed back into the lorry and drove back onto the interminable desert road, and although my uncle was a bit eccentric and temperamental, I appreciated his formidable father-like companionship and I believed he could drive his lorry blind. He switched off the headlights on the lorry because they were interfering with the glowing shine of the full moon on the horizon. This happens a lot in Patagonia, as the moonlight on a clear night is much stronger than the headlights. Surreal shadows appeared as if by magic in front of us with hypnotic silhouettes, and I had never before experienced such an astonishing view of the pampas at night. It is easy to believe you are on another planet when this phenomenon occurs, and it is quite a unique experience. It would be impossible to even attempt to describe how special and other-worldly those moments were in the desert that night. Uncle Lewis had driven those roads hundreds of times, hundreds of nights and hundreds of moons, and although for me this trip seemed an almost impossible undertaking, for my uncle it was just another night out.

Uncle Lewis appeared to be in a world of emptiness as he drove in silence, and I was not entirely sure if he realized I was a passenger by his side. So I asked him, 'What about the beer making plant in José de San Martín?'

'Aah!!!' He looked at me as if I was a ghost and continued driving his lorry in silence. I said nothing more. After half an hour or so, he began, 'I don't know ... well, I do know, yes, but I don't know why they wanted to make beer there, because nobody drinks beer around there. The gauchos drink gin, grappa, or wine, nothing else.'

'What about the Germans?' I asked.

'Aah … bueno … si … the Germans drink a lot of beer, and sometimes nothing else. The strange thing is,' he added, 'there were plans to construct many beer-making plants in Bariloche, in Bolsón, in Cholila, in Gualjaina and there in San Martín as well, but I don't know why.'

'Maybe they were expecting many German colonists to settle down around there?'

'Yes … I don't know … perhaps,' he mused.

Something was beginning to make sense, but it was like trying to find the fifth leg on a cat. Because of the Nazis and the catastrophic Second World War, many people were reluctant to talk about things German, with the exception of Mercedes Benz or Deutz tractors. The fact that dozens of German submarines had been found all over the coastal shores of Argentina, and most of them in Patagonia, implies that something important and well planned was going on in this forgotten land. It is suggested now that Hitler was in one of those German U-boats, and as Perón was pro-Nazi the subject has been kept under wraps. The shores of Argentine maritime waters were unpatrolled and safe for the Nazis to disembark. Nazi sailors were scattered throughout the Patagonian ranches and when I was a kid I met lots of them, but my father told me to be careful with those Germans because he believed they were all totally mad.

Not many people in Patagonia then knew where Germany was and they definitely had no clue about anything to do with any war. It must have been difficult for the Patagonian-Welsh farming community to understand those tall people with penetrating blue eyes who had difficulty in pronouncing the letter 'W' and explaining that they had just popped out of a submarine in Puerto Madryn. Most of those Germans were scientists and engineers so they would have been light years ahead of the Patagonians in everything, with the exception, perhaps, of singing in the Eisteddfod.

Hitler's dream didn't materialize in Patagonia after all. Rumours abound in Argentina that he fell into a well-earned depression, trembling with Parkinson's disease, being generally sick and lonely in his nightmares as most of his friends abandoned him. They said he died probably in Bariloche sometime in the 1960s. Other sources claim that Hitler as an old man spent the last days of his life in southern Chile, where there is a strong German community in a place that even today is extremely secretive.

Argentina fell into a catastrophic turmoil that would last for many years. Corrupt governments fed the corrupt oligarch élite, and in order to maintain a state of fear in the lower class of the population, they would succeed every few years in arranging a bloody *coup d'état*, and changing presidents became a routine disappointment. Perón returned from Spain to Argentina in 1973 as an old man, he took the presidency for a third time, but soon died. His newest and third wife, María Estela Martínez, took over but the military junta threw her in jail. A new Army General was put in charge of conducting the out-of-tune orchestra. This ultra right-wing new general was called Videla, a vicious evil man who, for the Argentines, was a million times worse than Hitler, Mussolini and Franco put together. About 30,000 people disappeared during his regime in the late 1970s. The majority of these unfortunate people were musicians, psychologists, journalists, poets and writers. In fact, anyone with Marxist ideals was likely to be tortured, drugged and put onto planes with a 'death' tag. The armed forces' propaganda machine tried to explain to the disorientated population of Argentina that many of those people were communists, therefore they had left the country and gone to Europe and the United States – when it is becoming ever more clear they were thrown out of aeroplanes and drowned in the middle of the Atlantic Ocean.

— 26 —

FREDY

SINCE I left Patagonia in 1972 to study in Wales, I was not caught up in this turmoil. Neither was my brother Fredy, who continued to play guitar on ranches in the desert, far removed from any military activity. He spent his time horse-breaking for a living until I went in search of him in 1980 after most of the madness was over. The next time I saw him was 1988 when I wanted him to join me in the guanaco adventure, and from then on we spent a lot of time travelling through the desert together.

Travelling through the south-west of the Province of Chubut on one of these trips, following the River Senguer, we crossed through a small handful of villages in the desert, all of them squatting in the bushes among the wind and dust, and crying out for something to happen. We were visiting a breeding station to buy good horses for my ranch, and stopped for a break in one of the few bars along the route. The leathery skin and the foggy eyes of the residents in the bar told me that the weather had not changed much in the last million years. Fredy and I ordered coffee to warm us up, and that reassured the villagers that we were not going to create a revolution that day. The gauchos turned their backs to us and carried on engulfing themselves in their emptiness.

I knew that this was the area where the Swiss veterinary surgeon, Tschiffley, bought the horses that were to carry him to the United States in 1925. The two *criollo* horses were Mancha and Gato, and what a hell of a journey they made. It really proved that the *criollo* is the toughest breed of horse in the world. They have to be in order to survive in this harsh environment. But what surprised me was that these horses were in such good condition by eating just hard grass and bushes, and they were not too small either – I would say around 14-15 hands. That's a lot taller than the Shetland ponies, or the ones in Iceland, where the weather is more or less similar to this area of Patagonia.

Tschiffley rode from Buenos Aires to Washington in two and a half years, getting good publicity for the *criollo* horse along the way. He did a wonderful job because, since that ride, the *criollo* horse is finally recognized as a breed, and the toughest of them all. I showed Tschiffley's book to Fredy, and he just said, 'Bahh, anybody could have done that, with all that money and help from Europe.' He was referring to when, many years before this conversation, my brother also began one of his many rides in Patagonia from around here, but in a very different way to that of Tschiffley. My brother didn't want any publicity because he was escaping from the police.

Apparently, he had had an affair with the wife of one of the gendarmes (border police), and these guys were after him. They never caught him, though!

On that occasion, my brother had fifteen young unbroken *criollo* horses with him, an old mare as the madame of the team, a pack horse to carry some belongings, and a butchered steer for his long lonely suppers in the desert with Clavel, his Border Collie dog. He knew it was too dangerous to stay around that area, as the police had long-range rifles and they could get him at any time. So he challenged them by going right into the middle of the province, where the terrain is too harsh for any police to survive. And he proved to be right. Worst of all, the woman was in love with him, and that is too dangerous for any man in the desert. He needed to disappear.

Fredy was breaking in the young horses whilst on the move, so he always had fresh ones in case of emergency. Travelling east, towards the Atlantic, he was hunting animals for survival and finding (very scarce) food and water for the horses. He was making shoes for Clavel, as his poor paws were bleeding from the stones of the desert. At one point, he told me, the horses couldn't go any further, as his way was blocked by a range of high sierras, a massive rugged outcrop of rocks which dominated an otherwise interminably flat desert which alternately boils and freezes like a never-ending argument. It was too steep for the horses and was similar in magnitude to Ayers Rock in Australia, only many miles wider. He dismounted and went to investigate the rocks. But when he was on the top, contemplating his bad luck and surveying the step-formed plains in the distance, all the horses began to move and climb the sharp rocks towards him. The old mare was in front, and my brother didn't try to stop her. 'It was unbelievable,' he said, 'because not even goats would cross those rocks.' It seemed as if the horses were not touching the rocks at all, a bit like floating. They all arrived in perfect condition at the top and then they stood calmly by his side as if nothing had happened.

My brother is the most atheistic person that I ever met but on that occasion he told me that something, or someone, was there with him and with his horses. Call it God, *duende*, spirit, or something like that, but there was definitely something powerful there guiding this adventurous nomadic group. Apparently, the same thing happened to Shackleton on his amazing voyage to the Antarctic in 1915, when his ship *Endurance* was trapped in an ice floe. For more than a year he and his crew camped on ice floes, crossed the sea in an open lifeboat, and finally crossed the mountains of South Georgia on foot to reach a whaling station. He felt that at times during this enforced expedition there was somebody or something else walking alongside him, even though he couldn't see anyone. Apparently, each member of his team had the same feeling and finally the entire crew was rescued. Years later in 1922, when he had fully recovered and appeared to be in perfect health, Shackleton went back to South Georgia, the place he loved in the South Atlantic, and died suddenly of a heart attack. Isn't that strange?

The gendarmes never found my brother, and after a few months without seeing another human soul, he arrived at his destination on the Atlantic Coast with all the horses in impeccable condition, and looking twenty years older. 'It was a hell of a trip,' he told me between tears, and I believe him.

— 27 —

The Three-Day Train Trip

I also had a hell of a trip of a different kind on one of my
return journeys from Wales. It was the beginning of another
winter time in the southern hemisphere when I took a 747
plane from Heathrow to Buenos Aires. The long trip was as
uninteresting as always, with tasteless food to eat on board,
and a beautiful-looking film that irritated all the passengers
as we could see it well enough but couldn't hear it as the
sound system refused to work. Some people were well
annoyed and complained loudly. Others were happily drunk
with all the wine and whisky. I was trying to entertain myself
by writing down all the surnames that I could remember
from my village of Cholila, in Patagonia. The tiny village
surprised me as I realized that the inhabitants today were the
descendants of Welsh, Germans, Spanish, Indians, Italians,
Irish, Lebanese, Bulgarians, Turks, Russians, mixed with a
few bastard descendants of the Butch Cassidy gang and those
of Sheriff Perry from the United States.

I felt I had arrived home when everybody clapped as
we touched down safely at Ezeiza airport in Buenos Aires. I
thought that in about three hours' time I would be arriving in
my village in Patagonia as it was only 2,000 kilometres further
to go on an internal flight. I was wrong. There were no flights
and, after examining all the possibilities, I had no choice
but to take the only available train to the south. Instead of a
three-hour internal flight, I arrived vaguely near my village
three days later by train. During those interminable three
days I had a bit of time to think and a bit of time to write

some stories and a few songs. The trip was as monotonous as the pampas we were passing through, with not much food to eat and with the only drinking water in the toilets tasting of paraffin. The flat pampas was dotted with black Aberdeen Angus cows, and very little else to see. I immersed myself in my imagination and story-writing, as this was the only place I could find any entertainment.

The tragic story of **John Glyn Jones**, told to me by himself when I was about fourteen years old, came to rescue my thoughts:

JOHN GLYN JONES

JOHN GLYN JONES was a friend of my father, a Welshman with a farm close to ours in Gaiman. One year, John Glyn earned a good price for his wheat, and decided to call in at a hotel in the village of Gaiman for a drink before going home, and to give his horses a rest. Two days later his three Shire horses were still tied to a tree in front of the hotel. The police came and told him to go away, and he went. A few miles out of Gaiman, he fell asleep while driving his four-wheeled wagon with his three horses. With John Glyn sleeping, the horses were free to wander in the desert and, smelling the water, they made their way through a canyon where they lost their grip on the rocks and fell twenty metres to their deaths down a railway cutting. The horses died, and John Glyn was knocked unconscious during the accident. When he regained consciousness he saw that a wheel of his wagon had crushed one of his legs, trapping him under the weight of the dead horses.

Somebody found him half dead, and brought him to the little hospital in Gaiman. They amputated one leg, and they left him to die in peace. But the Welshman from Caergwrle, near Wrexham, was not giving up just yet and managed to ring the bell by his bed, and ask for something to eat; he was a bit hungry after that tragic week. A few days later the little hospital caught fire in the middle of the night, and again he rang the bell repeatedly, but this time no one came. In the morning the smell of burning bodies was unbearable, but the voice of John Glyn was heard saying, 'There is a fire in my room, take me out.' No one understood how he survived, but he did, and he did for many years – years of hell, but always with a big smile, holding bottles of wine and visiting us regularly to sing Welsh songs. When he was about eighty years old, a dentist dragged all his teeth out, and soon after he died in our house. He was a very little man by then.

Very, very, *very* slowly the train left behind the humid pampas of the province of Buenos Aires and we were beginning to slide into the mouth of the Patagonian tongue. The grey and brown scrubland of this deserted paradise didn't want to smile very much at me but the red sky in the dusk on the horizon was, if nothing else, the most spectacular sight I had ever seen. It didn't last very long but it seemed as if the sky had joined the desert, to fuse together in a multitude of infernal red fires. Then it was gone, leaving a few horizontal lines of dark clouds hanging there, and with it, the cold night began to crawl through the legs of my trousers like a ghost that has spent several months in a freezer.

It is surprising that a country or land has to be of a certain colour in order to satisfy the whim of the moment. Sometimes I see Patagonia as brown, grey and sad in its loneliness, crawling for thousands of miles of desolate wasteland. On other occasions I love the way it is, with the wild enchanting sounds of the wind and birds, which in that glorious and savage environment are as melodious and wonderful as anything can be. Every time I come back to Britain I experience its phenomenally green land. It makes me feel soft and secure in its cradle but after a while it becomes monotonous and sad, as if the land is tired of perfecting the angles of its fields for thousands of years. The green seems to be not so adventurous or deep. At that point the nostalgia takes over and then I imagine the colours that cover the land of Patagonia – yellow, green, blue or violet hills crashing through the white kaolin, surrounded by arid brown, black and red wilderness. The train stretched his long body and headed furiously towards the mountains of the Andes, but I wouldn't see them tonight, nor tomorrow.

I was trying to keep myself warm by running up and down the train and doing some exercises, press-ups and so on, like I used to do when younger when I was boxing with my friends on my father's farm, and later on in the Navy. But now it didn't work in the same way. This time I was getting tired of jumping and exercising without much joy and I was still very cold. I put on all the clothes I could find in my bags and with the help of a torch I outlined some more stories, which in the morning were difficult to make any sense of, as my hands were getting so cold that I could hardly feel the pen. My fingers were white with the lack of blood circulation. The train was like a panther in that cold black night, feeling very carefully every millimetre of those long steel parallel lines.

LAGARTO

HE was the best; nobody could beat Lagarto Iâl when he was in the ring with the right gloves. He often challenged boxers much heavier than himself, and because there were not many of them about, he just challenged anybody. He was truly an entertainer and he boxed for a bit of a laugh. Sometimes he would just stay in the middle of the ring dancing, with his hands hanging down, while his opponents were desperately trying to knock him out. But they never succeeded and, worse for the opponent, he used to spit with rage at the punches that were coming at him, making his opponents furious.

An Indian died on the outskirts of the village, so that night Lagarto went with a friend to pay his last respects. There was nobody else in the house of the dead friend and after a while both of them were tiring of each other's company. So Lagarto sent his friend to the village shop to buy some wine. While he was gone, Lagarto removed the corpse from the coffin, propped him on a chair holding a newspaper, and climbed inside the box. When his partner came back with the wine, Lagarto stood up in the coffin with his arms spread open, shouting. His friend threw the wine to hell and ran back to the village to inform the police that the dead man was alive. It took a long time for the police to understand the message – the poor man was white with fear and his tongue paralysed with panic. The police realized, however, that something was wrong, and decided to investigate the drama. The police, his friend, and many others came as well. When they opened the door of the dead man's house, they saw Lagarto sitting in a chair reading the newspaper and saying, 'What the hell kept you so long?' The police and the neighbours weren't happy at all, going back at three o'clock in the morning, and the poor partner was never the same again. He was a bit 'loco' for the rest of his life.

'Lagarto' means 'lizard' in Spanish and his surname was, like many of the Welsh people, Jones. All the Joneses were of a very respectable extraction, but Lagarto was not too well respected socially because he laughed a lot, drank a lot, boxed a lot, and was the black sheep of the family, even though I doubt if there has been a single person in his life who didn't respect Lagarto Jones in the boxing ring. And when he was too old for boxing, he got a job at the local hospital helping people. He was quite an alcoholic by then, but he was very good at his job, especially delivering babies; he was the best at that as well. He remained a great character, full of tricks and totally unpredictable until the end of his life.

FOR some inexplicable reason, when it seems there are still a million miles to go, you keep looking at your watch every five minutes, thinking something is wrong with it. This train was definitely not in a hurry to arrive anywhere. Neither was I but this slow trot was getting really silly now. I was checking my watch, I was checking the immensity of the desert, I was checking if I could see a guanaco, a gaucho, or anything at all that moves a bit. But there was nothing.

And the day after that there was nothing either. This part of Patagonia in the province of Río Negro must be the most fantasmal in the whole world; at least it was for me at that moment. I was imagining all kinds of things that could happen when someone is totally fed up with boredom. It's a mild hallucination that inspires reality to be part of a dream. The brown skin of the desert continued stretching with the weight of the massive anaconda's rocking body, and I asked myself 'Why do people do certain things? Why don't people do certain other things?' My thoughts were passing through a wonder world of fantasies packed with theories. Charles Darwin, of course, was around here in my head with his theory of the origin of the species. Who can really say whether he was right or wrong?

It has been said, and there is no doubt about it, that Charles Darwin had interesting theories, but it has also been said that his theory of evolution was first put on paper (although not published) by a Welshman called Alfred Russel Wallace. Darwin just pipped him at the post after spending five years sailing around the world on board The Beagle under the command of Captain Fitzroy.

I remember reading some of Mr Darwin's observations about South America, when he encountered some undomesticated indigenous people in Tierra del Fuego. I believe those people were the Yahgans or, as some people like to call them, the Yamana Indians. Darwin clearly disliked those people from the Land of Fire and he made some abominable remarks with childish stupidity when he saw Indian girls without clothes playing in the snow. Challenging God, he said it was difficult to believe those people belonged to the human race. It seems from his writings Darwin didn't know that the Yahgans and the other tribes in Tierra del Fuego had families, children, religion, festivals and a language that still fascinates the world today, as it doesn't relate to any other language and it contains more words than English (if English had no loan words). That means, if we brushed out the influence of Greek, Latin, French, and others like Brythonic, Quechua or Hindi, English would be left as a very under-developed comparator.

On the other hand, it is difficult to comprehend how on the island of Tierra del Fuego those indigenous hunters had developed a magnificent language, when they didn't have houses, proper clothes, pens and paper or a computer to keep all their thoughts and verbal inventions safe on a hard drive. For example, the Yahgan canoe was described by many different words, depending on what kind of canoe it was and for what it would be used that day or next week or next year. I can't find anything like that in *my* English – 'maybe there is none!' For instance, the word 'canoe' was adopted into the English language from the Spanish word *canoa*, and the Spanish took the word *kenu* from an Indian language in the Caribbean.

I am not sure now if it was Robert Fitz-Roy or Captain Cook who asked an Indian in Tierra del Fuego something in 'English' and the smiling Indian replied – 'Ala-ca-luf', which apparently means 'I don't understand you'. The Europeans asked again and again and the Indian shouted back ALACALUF. So the tribe was named the 'Alacaluf people', or 'the people who don't understand you'! The real name of that tribe was Kaweskar, now extinct due to the progress of the Europeans.

I don't know why I was thinking so much about Darwin on that train trip; probably because in his books he described Patagonia in the worst possible way, or because I was not too happy at that moment. At least I thought his debatable theories would be a great entertainment for the next 1,000 km. I desperately needed him in order to criticize someone, but I felt like opening the window and throwing all his books out. I am glad that Mr Darwin was not sitting down next to me on that train, otherwise we would have murdered each other, or I would have committed suicide like Captain Fitz-Roy.

A mosquito was sucking blood from my arm and Darwin's theory of evolution was poisoning me. This bloody mosquito has been doing exactly the same for millions of years, and I don't understand why Darwinian theory can't change it into a bird of paradise or something similar. The monkey is still screaming and running around naked and the cockerels, after millions of years of evolution, are still singing the same song, one song!

By now my little Patagonian train was puffing away and showing off that he was a good smoker and I thought that at times his lungs were giving up. He was so slow that I thought he was going to stop, and he did. Now I was an extra millimetre worse off, as the train wasn't moving at all. It just stopped dead in the middle of the desert. That was … I don't know what it was … just beyond belief. I was looking into the imposing sky above me with its amazing constellations and I offered the night a kind of prayer, to see if an extra terrestrial would come and tow this ancient evolved locomotive to its destination. But nobody came.

I didn't know what to do with myself, so I thought of making a film in Patagonia. I ate the last available chicken on the train and felt very colonial as the waiter put an impeccable white tablecloth on the table, with napkins and a bottle of white wine with an extraordinary taste. Coming from Wales I was as white as all those things put together and the white pages became the film idea for *John 'Patagonian' Jones*, based on a true story.

JOHN 'PATAGONIAN' JONES
A FILM IDEA: BASED ON SOME HORRIFIC BUT TRUE STORIES

WALES: John is fishing in a beautiful river in north Wales in the early 1900s. He notices a gamekeeper watching him, so stealthily he puts all his fish into his pocket, knowing he is being watched. But the pocket is a false one and the fish disappear through the unstitched bottom of it back into the water, under cover of his long coat. He is taken to court, but is not charged. This kind of thing happens several times – sometimes he is charged a small fine for trespassing on the estates of powerful landlords, but nothing much. Welsh is the most common language in the area, but in court he is forced to speak English.

One day John and his son meet an old Welshman on their way to the private estate rivers and he is warned by the old Welshman of the danger of new keepers on the estate. John thanks the old man, reassuring him that he will never be caught red-handed. Son and father jump the big wall of the estate and begin to fish in their own

unconventional way. While his son is cleaning and
gutting, and also pulling the skins off some rabbits, John
is passing on his skills as a professional poacher to his son
in his own wild and foxy way. Two gamekeepers appear on
the riverbank with guns; John throws his son into the river
and tells him to get away, but one of the keepers shoots
him dead in the water. As the body of the child floats dead,
John reacts and attacks the gamekeepers, who knock him
to the ground. John is dragged away and again he appears
in court, but this time the judge is fed up of seeing his face,
and deports him. Showing him the world map on a globe,
he points – there … Patagonia … and goodbye. John never
sees his family again. He looks grim and sad; he knows
that his life has been broken for ever.

PATAGONIA: Sunday afternoon and the chapel in Gaiman is
packed with people singing hymns in Welsh. Not far away
there is an untidy farm with a bar inside – this place is
also full of people but their faces reveal the mixed ethnic
groups of the area – Welsh, Indians, etc. The barmaid is a
fat Welsh Patagonian lady who commands, with authority,
a handful of laid-back, part-time prostitutes, part-time
housekeepers …

The owner is Mr Chingolo, a full-blooded Welshman
of huge dimensions, a lovely man, a character with a
broad and tricky smile. He is attending his private zoo
and talking in Welsh to his strange creatures. He is a great
believer in God, so he devotes most Sundays to caring for
his animals with love and tenderness. It's not a public zoo,
it's for himself.

The same Sunday, in the desert, a mad Indian is cutting out horses' tongues and eating them raw. Two men approach – one is a huge old Indian known as Old Fuentes, the other is Welsh. The Welshman takes out his knife and lifts the little mad Indian from the ground with it. The poor bastard dies in the air and he's left there for the vultures. The same Sunday, a boat arrives at the shores of Patagonia and John is left alone on a desolated beach.

THAT SUNDAY NIGHT IN CHINGOLO'S BAR: The Welshman who killed the mad Indian is drunk and he's showing the locals how he did the killing. He is waving his knife in the air in an exaggerated macho way. The police arrive at his home later and arrest him. As they take him away, his wife and four or five children are crying. The old Indian is quiet by the fireplace but, observing the circumstances, he stands up and declares himself responsible for the killing. The Welshman rejoins his family but the crying gets worse. The respectable figure of Old Fuentes is now languishing in prison. Everybody knows that Old Fuentes is innocent, and everybody knows how much they are going to miss him, but there is not a single Christian who will stand up for poor Old Fuentes.

The same Sunday, night is falling, seeping into the poor wretched soul of John. The immensity of the desert does not welcome him. As he walks, hungry and thirsty, he imagines he is being followed, but every time he turns to confront his enemies, there is nobody there. Strange lights appear to follow him, he's sweating with fear, and he begins to behave very oddly. He catches a sleeping hare, snaps the head off its body and drinks its blood and devours the warm flesh. Blood is running down his unshaven face, and again he senses that he is being watched while he is eating, but again no one is there. He curls up in the bushes and he cries in his vast world of sadness.

He feels better as the beautiful dawn wakes him … the whispering wind and the huge clear sky give him the power to stand up and start a new day, and to walk the remaining miles to the village of Gaiman where, for the first time in many weeks, people welcome him with tea and cakes. These respectable people in the village of Gaiman remind him of Wales, where he has left part of his soul. He is a suspicious man by now; he has been betrayed in Wales and he is afraid of being betrayed again as the priest and police are asking too many questions. He is not the same man as he was in Wales; he is escaping from reality. Life has betrayed him and he is determined to change his destiny. He is not a son of God any more, he refuses to enter any chapel or take part in any religious festivities. For him, the best place on earth is Chingolo's bar, a natural refuge for lost souls. There he can do whatever he wants, and the Indian prostitutes provide all the sex he can afford. Sex becomes a natural show of his manic behaviour.

As John is an intelligent and charismatic character, doors are open for him. He uses society for his own benefit, chatting away with older women and playing games with kids. Nobody knows his past, nobody notices his indifference towards life, nobody can see his traumatised, evil thoughts.

Possibly he hates his Welsh heritage more than anything else. That is why he leads four gold hunters,

Welshmen, into the trap. It is he who organizes the one-way journey into the desert. It is he who tells the Indians that these four Welshmen were the rapists of their daughters. John stands back that day and enjoys the wonderful performance by the Indians. There is plenty of blood to be seen, the wild Indians tearing the flesh off the bodies of the poor unfortunate Welshmen. John laughs at the situation, and upon his arrival in Gaiman he reports that the group was attacked by Indians and that he is the only survivor.

He learns how to lie in order to be a hero. People think he is a good as Old Fuentes in the community, and although John never met the old man he is sure he could imitate that enigmatic image, and if possible be a better player. Old Fuentes was an Indian, so what could he possibly have to offer? Friends told John that Old Fuentes was able to see things that no other human being could see. Old Fuentes could see fire coming out of rocks, Old Fuentes could see the spirits in the lakes in the Andes and talk to them, Old Fuentes knows the man who has been galloping on a white horse across the pampas for centuries. John visualizes his first day in Patagonia and the lights that were following him – could there be any reason for those lights? Could Old Fuentes tell him what all those things were? Maybe, but first he must find that Fuentes Indian. He goes to Chingolo's place to look for an answer and to get a prostitute. The rough and sensitive farmers are there, and they clap when he enters the bar. But he is not happy – he asks loudly, 'Is there anybody here who knows anything about that Old Fuentes Indian?'

The ugly prostitutes and the pretty ones are in silence, looking at each other. The old farmers and the Indians are looking at their table, and Chingolo is looking at John. Chingolo walks towards John, looks him firmly in the eyes and slaps him in the face. And then he says, 'I am not surprised. The desert has gone to your head already. Don't ask any more questions about Old Fuentes and have a drink like everybody else.' An Italian farmer comes to the bar at that tense moment and accuses the Indians of being lazy bastards. One Indian moves and plunges his knife into the big stomach of the Italian. As he lies on the floor dying, the Indian puts his knife back in its sheath and asks John if he wants to know about Old Fuentes.

John moves on, but the image of Old Fuentes is bothering him, as are the stories of the strange lights and the fearless faces of the Indians. He decides to believe in his own theory and not in the rubbish of others. He will not be intimidated by all those stupid stories any more, so the rape of young girls continues, with the lies and falsities of a professional crook.

In the desert, John comes across a small group of men with wild suspicious looking faces. These men hunt Indians for a living, paid by rich landlords in order to exterminate the Indian population, and as the Indians are stealing sheep and horses from the European settlers and from time to time killing some white people as well, he decides to join these ruthless Christians and take part in an ethnic cleansing job. Money is good, and the Indians are easy prey. He doesn't care a damn any more about life, so he begins to chop the heads off the Indians and collect all the ears in his saddlebag. At times, and just for his own amusement, he cuts the ears off with his knife and leaves the Indians to carry on with their lives. But soon he starts to have some horrific nightmares – there are Indians eating him alive, and an old Indian that he has never met is showing him a photograph of himself and his son in north Wales. He begins to drink day and night and the nightmares and the alcohol transform him into a paranoid monster.

One day in Chingolo's bar, while John is in his delirium tremens condition, Old Fuentes walks in. Chingolo treats him with respect, followed by everybody else in the bar. John is in a corner observing, and he also knows that face, but he can't remember where he has met this old Indian. The peaceful and gentle Old Fuentes is telling stories to his old friends, standing at the bar with his back to John. Suddenly John remembers his face – this Indian has a photograph of his son … he must be the killer of his son. John walks towards Old Fuentes, takes a gun and shoots Old Fuentes in the back – but doesn't kill him outright. Old Fuentes gets hold of John's neck with one hand and squeezes until it breaks. Old Fuentes walks out and nobody sees him ever again.

John is buried in a traditional Welsh way, with songs and the minister saying kind things about him. Chingolo and all his prostitutes are there too, singing with the wind of the desert. Chingolo is back with some friends at the bar, they are all in silence. Chingolo senses something is not normal about the night – the air is different. He takes a candle and walks towards his animals and he sees a light

hovering just above them. Chingolo smiles and raises his
hand; he knows that Old Fuentes has come back to say
goodbye to his animals, and the light slowly fades away.

EVENTUALLY, of course, the train started up again. There's a
saying in Switzerland that if the platform clock says 2 p.m.
and the 2 p.m. train hasn't arrived, then either it's not a Swiss
train or it's not a Swiss clock. The destination for my train
was the German-Swiss settlers' town of Bariloche, high in the
Andes mountains, but even they haven't managed to prevent
the train being up to a week late, if it feels like it.

About 200 km before arriving at Bariloche, I needed to
change trains. From the middle of the desolated village of
Jacobacci, I began the final and the most tedious part of that
unexpected train journey, by transferring to the local steam
train, The Old Patagonian Express – Paul Theroux's name
for the slowest train in the world. Trapped in the rocking
wooden benches of my ancient wagon with a small cast iron
stove, I allowed myself to be deafened by a monstrous Belgian
steam engine. The Greenpeace boys wouldn't have been very
happy with it, as the intestines of that raging machine were
vomiting up all the lumps of smoke that its imaginative brain
could deliver, covering my Patagonian desert with a beautiful
coloured broken blanket of thick and sticky black stuff. I was
not very familiar with the area of the desert that the little train
was passing through, apart from knowing that it was once
owned by an English company, the Southern Argentine Land
Company. Now it belongs to a different type of 'gringo', the
Italian Benettons. One of their *estancias* is called *El Maitén*,
which in the Araucano Indian language means 'lonely tree',

the other *estancia* was called *Leleké* but I don't know what that means.

I have travelled by trains for years across many different countries and almost always I have enjoyed the freedom of travelling in a way which only the train can provide – with speed, comfort, unusual views of the countryside, and meeting other travellers with whom you can establish a conversation that can last for a day or two. You can have a party in the canteen of the train, or a wonderful meal while the train is moving fast. You can exercise, walk and even run between wagons, and of course you can read and sleep very comfortably. I was thinking of all those things while my noisy little Patagonian train wasn't at all comfortable. I was cold and I couldn't sleep, and it was better to forget about any party!

Crossing through the heart of a 300,000-acre *estancia*, and knowing that my adorable train was not in a hurry, I tried to put down on paper the story of a mysterious Bonnie and Clyde-type of girl who lived and died in this windy and rough terrain full of sheep and horses, condors and eagles, guanacos and gauchos, armadillos and numbness, and millions of years of wild solitude. Her name was Elena Greenhill and she was born in Bath, York or Ireland (depending on which version you wish to believe). In Patagonia she was known as 'La Inglesa'.

This confusing simplification of nationality is typical in Patagonia; you would never know for certain the nationality of a person, irrespective of who told you – whether a gaucho, a lawyer, an Indian or a judge. For example: a person, slightly touched by Arab blood or culture, is a 'Turco' (Turk), and many eastern European citizens are all Russians. My friend 'the Russian' in Cholila, is in fact from Poland. And everybody from the British Isles is 'Ingles'. So this English/ Irish outlaw girl could have been Welsh! Then, the stories about her would be more believable, even if they are a bit of a myth today.

THE ENGLISH GIRL

THIS 'Inglesa' girl arrived at the ranches of Patagonia towards the end of 1890 from somewhere in the British Isles with her father and mother. Therefore, being around at that time, she must have known Butch Cassidy, the Sundance Kid and Etta Place, as Butch's gang were living only forty miles away from her. Butch used to buy livestock from the English ranch and dine with her father, who was manager of the big Estancia Leleké. It was probably Butch or Etta who taught her how to use guns so accurately and how to steal herds of cows to be sold in Chile.

She married three times: she killed the first husband and the second also died in mysterious circumstances. The third husband was the closest to her wild adventures, as he thrived on robbing, killing and contraband. For years the police tried to track them both down in the desert and in the mountains, but it was always the same; she killed them and the bodies would be picked clean by the vultures. She would take from the dead police guns, bullets, horses and whatever information they were carrying with them. Once, she captured two policemen and instead of killing them she kept them as slaves in her house to wash the plates and the floors. Outlaws were everywhere in those days in Patagonia and, in my view, apart from the tactics, nothing has changed. The immensity of Patagonia and the difficulties of the terrain made it very hard for the police to get even close to these outlaws, but as often happens, one day the police caught up with 'La Inglesa'. They filled her head with bullets and buried her under the sand in the desert.

TODAY the wind has dried up her blood and blown away most of the stories my father used to tell me, and for some reason all these stories about outlaws have never been told properly and are still a kind of taboo today. I often wonder why my school teacher never told me these stories. She must have known them, as she knew everything else, especially about the Eiffel Tower in Paris.

As I am writing these memories now, and remembering the sour moments of cold and desperation, I realize how lucky I was that day as the lazy train slowly but firmly arrived at my destination. Had I taken the next train from Buenos Aires to Bariloche I would have grown old in one of its carriages, as the train broke down in the middle of nowhere and it didn't move for eighteen years. That was 1995, and only in 2013 was the line reopened and the service restarted.

— 28 —

Establecimiento Los Guanacos

THE steam train deposited me at Estancia Leleké, and I walked and hitched the remaining 40 km to my ranch, exhausted and racked with pain. The noise of that maddening train was still rattling somewhere above my head and the wooden benches of the wagon were branded on my buttocks. The ranch seemed quite abandoned as I opened the second gate. A few months had gone by since the last time I was there and the gauchos I left in charge were not the best people in the world for cleaning and tidying up anything, except (and just about) their own horses.

I put on some of the dirty working clothes which were available everywhere and began the huge task of cleaning up. I put the spoons in the correct place with the knives but I couldn't find any forks. It took me a while to realize that only very rarely would a gaucho use a fork, and a few days later I found some very dirty ones in a plastic bag in the tool shed. They hadn't needed them. I lit a good fire and I put a piece of suckling lamb on to grill while sipping plenty of *maté*. It tasted delicious after so long without it, and I carried on cleaning and putting myself on the right track in this forgotten corner of the world.

Later that evening, and without yet having seen any of my gaucho employees, I started to arrange the traps to control the field mice that queue in silence to visit us with the first frost of autumn. They take advantage of our generosity by sharing the living room with us although we can't see them. This is the only living area with a kind of roof and walls and a huge round chimney that we have in the entire ranch so far, but I'm sure the mice think it's a four- or five-star hotel. These field mice have the most irritating diet; sometimes it consists of eating the expensive sealed plastic containers with pretty colours that we bought in the supermarket 'La Anónima'. Parts of my camera and binoculars are also in their diet and rolls of film and pencils that I bought in London were also now inside the intestines of these lodgers.

In the adjoining tool shed the smell of skunks was unbearable. These fearless animals have the most efficient method of defending themselves, by peeing over the ground around them, and peeing on anything that moves in their territory. In fact, what we call pee is not pee exactly, it's a dreadful yellow liquid that they carry in a gland between the back legs and, by squeezing the muscles of their legs, they can project this revolting fluid a few yards with incredible accuracy. I was aware of this as I was trying to dig one out of the hole that he had burrowed in silence, very close to my bed. The smell was becoming unbearable and I couldn't breathe in that little shed. I had to go out, fill my lungs with fresh air and rush inside for another fight with that beautifully marked creature and his well calculated pee. Nothing seemed to work. The stubborn smelly creature didn't want to come out of his hole. I was fast losing my temper by now, I was sweating and swearing and I knew the gauchos would arrive at any time. They would find me in that state and, of course, they would laugh at me. So I burned him out – or I thought I did. The devil came out of his hole half singed and sprayed all over my beautiful French shirt. I kicked him out of the shed until he disappeared reluctantly into the bush.

Finally that evening two gauchos appeared at the ranch and we settled down to drink *maté*. 'Cuándo volviste?' (when did you arrive?), asked one. 'Recién nomás' (just a short while ago), I replied. The gaucho said nothing for a good few minutes, just drank his *maté* in silence. Then he said, 'Y cuándo te vas, che?' (and when you going back, then?) I was sure the gauchos could smell the skunk on me and they wanted me to go quickly back to wherever I'd come from!

I love animals, and I have been protecting and breeding all kinds of animals and birds for as long as I can remember. In fact, my small library on the ranch contains more books about animals than any other subject, and Gerald Durrell's experiences with animals make me laugh a lot. But I don't like skunks being too close to my bed or wandering around the place when I invite some Indians for tea. The other animal I don't like is the Patagonian puma. I am convinced that this animal is the son of Satan, or is possibly even Satan himself. Even the dogs are afraid of his yellow guilty eyes with his cold-blooded attitude of playful murder. No other animal, in my part of the world, likes this evil cat.

People who live in towns are totally ignorant about this type of animal, because it is not the same as having a cuddly little cat sleeping peacefully on a cushion by the fireplace in the living room while you are watching TV. It is an unscrupulous and selfish puma hurting, killing and ripping apart your best horses while you are having a rest at night. I lost one of my best foals early one morning. He was as promising and beautiful as the spring that year, and since then my hatred towards the mountain lion has grown wilder than the lion itself.

One puma, seemingly just for fun, will kill fifty or seventy sheep in a single night. One day I arose particularly early. The morning was majestic and healthful and, because of that, I was feeling powerful and in love with all the surrounding beauty of the ranch. The lake was a perfect oval mirror, reflecting the Andes in its crystal waters. I lit a fire and was preparing the *maté*, when Pinky my sheepdog came inside the hut and looked at me with a slightly sad face. In a split second I saw the picture. I didn't care about the *maté*, the fire and the water that was boiling furiously. Pinky and I ran towards the lake where the Merino sheep were supposed to be grazing peacefully. But the picture I saw at that moment was horrendous. There were dead sheep everywhere; some were still alive but only just. Others were moving and dragging their long intestines on the grass whilst the vultures were picking at them. The vultures had picked out and eaten the eyes of all the dead sheep and also some of those that were still alive. Pinky was chasing the vultures in rage, barking furiously from one carcass to another, and another, and another, until the poor dog was so tired that he came back to my side with his long tongue hanging out, full of froth, and looking extremely angry. The bastard puma had killed most of his sheep.

My temper was exploding in sweat. I took my knife from its sheath and cut the throats of the sheep that were still breathing in agony. Leaving the vultures to finish the job, Pinky and I walked around the ranch in search of puma footprints. We found them and I went to fetch the gun. My .44 Winchester was smiling at me, and he was also thirsty for blood. We couldn't find the puma that day but eventually he came back to my ranch. Then it was his turn. I split his brain in two with a single shot that went in through his nose. The National Parks are totally at fault by not letting in selective hunters and, as these areas are protected, they are the perfect breeding grounds for the mountain lion. The National Parks have expelled most of the gauchos and Indians that used to live in this area and that's a great pity as these mountain people are the experts at snaring the mountain lion as it crosses the rivers. I believe that all the farmers of the Patagonian Andes should get together and pay a good amount of money to the hunters in order to get rid of this Satan *non grata*. And if that doesn't work, we could probably sell the meat of the Patagonian puma to the restaurants. It is much better than beef and, of course, organic.

When the English were in Patagonia, farming the desert, we were better off. The Southern Argentine Land Company which ran from approximately 1887 to 1986 used to control the pumas, foxes, *caranchos*[25] and vultures. They paid good money to anybody who came to their offices with the tail of a puma or fox, or the head of the *carancho* or *jote* (vulture). Unfortunately, there are fewer people living on the scrubland today than a few decades ago. The painfully low price of wool on the world market has created a devastating scenario, leaving these huge *estancias* almost de-populated. Those who remain are considerably more isolated and poor than they have ever been. In consequence, there are not enough working people to repair fences and to take care of the livestock and the remaining few starving Merino sheep are trembling as they see the red foxes multiplying in their thousands. Without the rancheros to stop them, the future of the *estancias* is grim.

The infestation of the red fox is growing into a serious epidemic in Patagonia and I have been told that this red fox was introduced from Europe, as so many other animals have been, including sheep, cows, horses and humans. But

25   *carancho* – an indigenous scavenger bird

the red fox has grown much bigger, whereas the humans and sheep haven't. The truth is that the Patagonian red fox is an indigenous fox which, as well as being reddish in colour, is also grey and nearly as big as a wolf. A full-grown red fox can kill a ram. Such a thing is unknown in Britain and I think it's unfortunate for the rest of wildlife that this animal exists at all. Given that he doesn't have a natural predator, this killing machine demolishes everything in his path. Rhea eggs and rhea chicks are on his menu and for dessert he will probably choose baby armadillos. The fox will kill one or more lambs or sheep per day if he can find them and he will eat only the fat part of the breast, leaving the rest of the carcass to rot. In one *estancia* alone there were no lambs left by the end of the year.

— 29 —

'El Loco'

WHILE the *peons*[26] had a long weekend off from the routine work on the ranch, I utilized the opportunity of that idle existence to do nothing too extravagant worth mentioning. The *peons* had saddled up fast while dawn was breaking even faster on a crisp summer's day, and I was left alone in charge of the ranch. Being alone on the ranch doesn't mean I was in silence. The noisy birds in the Andes haven't yet evolved into singers; they scream as if they are in a constant state of desperation. But the haunting screaming of those birds in the trees and on the ground was in fact more entertaining and melodious than the horrendous noise a football commentator was making, shouting from the portable radio

---

26 *peons* – hired farmhands

on the table. So I switched off the radio and listened to the sound of the fire softly crackling in his homely corner of the wooden cabin, and as I was relaxing, as gloriously as a Roman Emperor, I stretched my legs and contemplated the hypnotic beauty of the ranch from the comfort of my arm chair. But, damn it, the wine was metres away and I had to get up to fetch it.

So many things had happened since I bought the ranch that, looking back at it now, buying it seemed like a dream that you never, ever, ever, ever want to wake up from. It is a kind of out-of-body experience, or perhaps a close encounter with a fourth or fifth dimension. Of course, if I mentioned anything like that to the gauchos, they would probably kill me, as they would think I was crazy, so in case they were correct I lassoed my thoughts and with great difficulty kept them to myself.

Very rarely is the word 'eccentric' used in Patagonia. Instead most people would use 'off your head', a 'silly slob', or an 'idiot', and of course all these synonyms are simplified in Spanish as 'loco'. Most of the time this word is used in a friendly way, to describe an unconventional person, or a person not totally 'square', and as soon as I arrived in Cholila I was given that nickname.

The main reason why the locals called me 'El Loco' was because I was experimenting with breeding the guanaco, instead of traditional farming of cows and sheep. The gauchos were disorientated and they couldn't understand why I was doing it. Nobody had bred any guanacos before me, so for them I was definitely 'off my head'. On the other hand, they respected and trusted me because one day a gaucho and I insulted a policeman and we were both thrown in jail for the night. On another occasion I was back in jail for pointing a gun at an ignorant drunken sergeant, and although I had a .22 rifle and 200 bullets in the pick-up, I don't recall threatening any policeman with it. Anyhow, my argument was not good enough and he decided to punish me by throwing me in the little dirty dungeon where someone had urinated all over the floor. I didn't sleep well that night and I'm sure if I had had a gun with me, I would probably have shot the bastard after all.

That brush with the law confirmed to the gauchos that I was one of them. Also, each time one of my gauchos ended in jail I immediately went to the police station, paid a fine, and took them out. On one occasion, it took me two years to take one of the gauchos out of jail. His detention was long because he had allegedly killed another gaucho with his knife, and couldn't afford bail before being acquitted. After taking so many out of jail I began to wonder if the police had decided to improve their income stream by taking money from this gringo 'loco'.

Also, over the years my Argentine accent had changed a lot, and because of that they called me 'El gringo'. (I don't know what the accent changed to, because it's not English or Welsh either.) So I was 'el loco' and I was 'el gringo' as well. They alternated the two nicknames depending on the circumstances and sometimes they joined them up, so for most of the time my name now is 'el gringo loco'.

Those days alone in the ranch were the best of the whole year for me. Of course I was not alone at all; there were cats, dogs, chickens, turkeys, cows, sheep, horses and the guanacos wandering around the ranch day and night.

Also, among the farmed animals there is an infinite amount of wildlife inconspicuously taking part in ranch life at night – a night at times so dark you just had to imagine what was going on. A fox could be slashing the necks of the tame lambs, and a puma could be chewing on one of your best horses. The stoats, minks and weasels might be having a feast by sucking the blood of the chickens, rabbits and hares, while the local people could be poaching anything they could find. The invisible thieves were too numerous and crafty for me to track them down.

One morning after a windy storm, I went for a stroll to suss out the damage to the trees and fences. To my surprise, a track left by a single cart wheel was fresh and clear on the ground. I followed it for a while through rocky slopes, bushy terrain and through an impenetrable forest of wild roses with their vicious thorns, before giving up. A gaucho living close by had seen the same track a few miles away and he couldn't understand how a cart could have moved around with only one wheel, and without a horse or oxen. Finally we found out that during the night a thief from the village had taken from my ranch an old wagon wheel weighing over 100 kilos, and had rolled it alone through an area that a fox would find difficult to penetrate. I will never know how this thief found the strength for that amazing piece of thievery, as I couldn't lift that wheel even for a second. I never reported the theft to the police, and in fact, in admiration of the strength of the man, I found a matching wheel and gave it to him so he could build an oxen cart to fetch wood for the winter. That day I pushed myself to be nice to him, even though something in my heart was telling me to break his neck.

Now that I was wheel-less I had more time for leisure, which is something that I always enjoy. Doing nothing, for me, means work for other people, as I practise the guitar, compose songs, drink wine and write pages and pages of stories. But probably my favourite hobby is thinking. I remember spending most of one sunny afternoon thinking how we, the Argentines, came to use the word '*boludo*' so much. The word '*boludo*' literary means 'big balls', but we don't use it in that sense. Everybody, regardless of age or sex is a *boludo*. I heard a mother say to her daughter of less than a year old that she was a *boluda* because she was looking pretty in her cradle. Also a lawyer who is not a gangster is a *boludo*. A person who is not dishonest enough to cheat everyone else is a *boludo*. It is common to hear people in the streets saying, 'good morning, *boludo*', 'happy birthday, *boludo*', 'let's go for a beer, *boludo*', or 'I am a *boludo* because I've forgotten my bus pass'. One day my brother told me that I was a 'gringo loco boludo'!

— 30 —

JUANITA

JUANITA was a female guanaco and she was the first of the two hundred or so that we had caught in the desert of the Patagonian plains. Juanita was different from the others and I never found out exactly why. She was the same colour as the others, the same size, she could kick, bite, push and spit like any other guanaco, and yet she was still different. She certainly had more personality than the others, and she was definitely more stubborn and immensely adorable. Of course, being like the first child, she was a bit spoiled with the best food, plenty of fresh straw for her to dream comfortably and, worst of all, we had the time to study her, to caress her, to imitate the soft sound that baby guanacos emit. We went for walks together, and she used to run like the devil around us. Guanacos are faster than any Porsche or Ferrari from the off and, although you can't teach them anything, they can go from 0 to 60 before you can blink, no matter what the conditions or terrain. I don't think the Ferrari would do so well in the rocky areas of Patagonia.

When I decided to breed guanacos for their fine wool, I knew that I would be alone as no one had done it before. Everybody in the village was very curious about it. Looking back now, I must have been a great entertainment for them. Everyone was calling me *El loco de los guanacos*. My brother said that I was bringing the clowns before the circus and an old woman said that I was going to change the villagers' diet. She was damned right, though, as I was losing many guanacos and I thought they had escaped. But, of course, they had ended up in the stomachs of the local people. Anyhow, I am proud to say that I learned much about the guanacos. These animals are very intelligent, stubborn, territorial, tremendously suspicious and very, very wild. And if they like you, you will adore them.

I wasn't put off by those kinds of serious challenges and today I still enjoy their companionship very much. The powerful landowners of Patagonia had portrayed the guanacos as ugly and destructive animals, killing them with long-range rifles and making this creature even more suspicious about the human race. My job was to prove to those ignorant and preposterous landowners that they were pissing out of the pot.

I laugh a lot with my guanacos. I find them extremely affectionate, caring for their family, clean, elegant and proud fruits of the desert. It is a great shame that the majority of the ranchers think in a different way. In their ignorance, they believe that the guanaco eats the same amount as seven sheep. I proved them to be wrong, and even though some old guanacos can carry scab, it is not the same type as in sheep. Therefore it cannot be contagious to their flocks of desert sheep. Trying to explain this to those arrogant landlords, who have spent most of their lives in the cities, is a huge task. I witnessed the most horrific and sad massacre of guanacos by the police, who had been paid by a landowner to clean up the ranch of wild guanacos. The police and the army used anti-tank bazookas to blow them up, leaving thousands of carcasses of the beautiful guanaco rotting in that dry land. Juanita was one of the lucky ones, she was with me. Fat, healthy and very elegant, but sometimes incredibly stubborn. One day I decided to teach her a lesson. I put a special head collar around her head and made her walk by my side up and down the farm. But she was in a very strange mood that day. She wanted to go in front of me and sometimes she didn't want to move at all.

After wasting most of the morning with her to no avail, I remembered that I had a meeting in the village. So I tied her to a tree until I returned and went on horseback, calling into different shops along the way. Juanita broke the rope and decided to look for me. She jumped all the fences and gates, calling in all the shops where I had previously been, creating a manic chaos, biting and throwing packets of spaghetti and biscuits around the place, then leaving at full gallop. Eventually, somebody got hold of her in the village and she was arrested. And to my knowledge, she is the only member of the camelid family that has ever spent the night in a Patagonian jail.

— 31 —

RANCH LIFE

AFTER returning with the fugitive, some gauchos started to arrive at the farm and more meat was thrown on the grill. More *maté* was passing from hand to hand and from mouth to mouth. Then a neighbouring gaucho arrived with our new horses, including a frisky golden colt. This colt, with the name Sol (meaning 'sun'), was the first of four that had to be tamed this year by the neighbouring breaker, but as he arrived he took the training saddle off and threw it on the grass. It was obvious that he and the horse had decided to stay the night with us. This man was not an Indian but his name was Mr Curru-huinca Curruleo. He said that tomorrow would be the final test for the horse as he had to go to the village of Epuyén and back – about ten hours each way – and this horse hasn't seen a car yet, he said, and the lorries … aye, aye, aye.

The stories flowed during a mixed grill of liver, heart, lungs, kidneys, glands, testicles, two kinds of chitterlings and the colon turned inside out, simplified as *achuras* or sweetbreads. The stories were unaccountable but the subject was the same: mice. Mr Curru-huinca hadn't been able to sleep in peace for many weeks because the mice were galloping in the ceiling of his tiny hut. And because the ceiling has too many holes the mice were galloping straight through the holes and landing in his bed at night. Then he would give chase to the mice in the dark with his gaucho whip but he hadn't caught one so far. The mice would climb back, using the table, and then into a secret passage in the wall. After that they would be back on the ceiling and the galloping dance would start all over again. Sometimes he would fire his .22 calibre rifle but in the dark it was useless and he never got one mouse with this method either. Also it was very expensive in bullets.

He couldn't keep a cat because the wild cats that lived around his hut would kill it. 'What about putting some poison around the place?' I said. 'Poison?' he said, 'poison? Today the poison is so weak that the mice are getting fat on it. Before, the English ranchers had a very good poison,' he said, 'and it came in a triangular tin with the name of Manchester on it. But now the English have gone somewhere and we cannot get the tins.'

After a solid two hours of talking field mice, he began to look seriously pensive and the long silence told me that the mice were having a great time inside his brain. And he still couldn't catch them. Our farmhand told him to fill a bucket half-full of water, then put a bottle standing in the bucket with a stick inside the bottle. The stick must have a lump of horse fat on top. From the rim of the bucket the mouse jumps onto the horse fat, the stick wobbles, and the mouse falls into the bucket of water and drowns. The stick returns to its upright position. He could catch hundreds of mice in one night with that simple system. Mr Curru-huinca was analysing the system very carefully and rolling his eyes, then he smiled and said, 'Aha!' I knew he hadn't understood a word.

The problem with field mice comes every twenty years or so. Apparently it's because the *colihue* cane – a type of bamboo, but not hollow – flourishes every twenty years and brings with it, for some reason, an invasion of field mice from the jungle of the *colihue* cane in the high Andes. There is no point in trying to kill them or get rid of them – it's like an invasion of locusts. Millions upon millions arrive overnight for a few weeks or months, then they disappear. But a few always remain as the best source of food for cats and owls, and to annoy the hell out of Mr Curru-huinca.

The next problem took only half an hour to solve. Mr Curru-huinca wanted to buy a calf to make a good barbeque but mathematics was not exactly his field. Now, a calf of around eight months old should weigh about 80 kilos clean and, at two pesos per kilo, how many pesos could it be? I said 160 pesos but he was not sure if I was telling him the truth. He knew I had a calculator in one of my boxes; he had seen it before and was extremely impressed with it because that calculator was an honest and intelligent machine that people use in the shops. It never lied like people do. And now that he was very close to it he wanted to use it all by himself. So I switched it on and he began to calculate with his cracked middle finger. After the equal sign he said, 'Oh shit, that calf is much too expensive, I knew they were trying to cheat me, I knew it! The calculator never lies, you see? It says 1,600 pesos, and that is too much for that Hereford-with-Brahman mix. People around here are bad, they try to cheat me because I come from the pampas of Paso del Sapo and Paso de los

Indios. Nobody lies around there, but here in the Cordillera
… *a la mierda!*'

I told him that he had probably put one zero too many
somewhere, and he said '*A la puta! Siiiii … si!*' He looked at
the calculator again and, without correcting it, he started to
smile. Two days later Mr Curru-huinca got up very early and
saddled up the young colt. He said he was in a hurry to go
back to his hut. It was pay day, and he was afraid of missing
his *patron*, who was coming in his new pick-up, a '3 x 4'.

— 32 —

GAME FISHING

IN order to generate some income for the ranch while the
guanacos were very slowly growing their fleeces, I decided to
set up a company that would concentrate on game fishing. As
the region surrounding my ranch is full of fish in rivers and
lakes, it should have been quite easy to make some money
out of this idea.

I had lots of connections in Britain so the obvious thing
was to begin with some Welsh and English anglers. I found
a good British ghillie and an all-purpose local guide, and
some ranchers promised to rent us their farmhouses to
accommodate the anglers at night. In a very short period
of time, after visiting a few game fairs in the UK, we found
an interesting numbers of anglers willing to travel to the far
southern hemisphere, and I began to learn all about this, in
my view, incomprehensible sport.

The first group arrived from England and in no time at
all they caught enough fish for breakfast, lunch and dinner.

But these maniacal English people threw the fish back into the river! My first thought was 'Surely they're drunk?' as they were drinking whisky all day long. My poor Indian guide was speechless, seeing all these beautiful fish disappearing back into the crystal-clear waters of the Andes. He asked me *'Están locos, o qué?'* – Are they mad, or what?

In fact, it was difficult to understand the situation. It was illogical, preposterous, incoherent: we had walked many miles through thorny bushes, climbed hills and sunk to our knees in mud, with thistles pinching and sticking in our socks and trousers, and waded through swamps of long reeds before finally arriving at a perfect spot teeming with big fish. But these *gringos* were behaving in such a strange manner – talking all day about fish, taking photographs of the fish, and then throwing them back into the river. Who on earth could understand that? And then, after throwing the fish back, they expected me to provide gin and tonic (with ice) on the bank of the lake or river. Where was I supposed to get gin and tonic from? – which you couldn't buy for a hundred miles around anyway – and the nearest ice was on the glacier at an altitude of 3,000 metres.

My guide didn't want to work with those 'maniacs' any more. I lost him, and my excitement about organizing game fishing trips didn't last long either.

— 33 —

THE SEASONS

THE different seasons in Patagonia are well demarcated. My ranch is at the edge of parallel 42° and, at a height of 650 metres above sea level, winter comes with rage. There is snow, frost, gusts of wind and lots of torrential rain throughout the months of June, July and August. By September the spring begins to show itself, with clear, green shining leaves on the willows and with longer and warmer days but with cold nights as the mountains are still covered with plenty of snow. By November the long spring is well under way. Days can be really hot and from there on we expect only the dry hot season. Midsummer is January and February, with temperatures reaching 40°C. This is the siesta season, as sometimes it is too hot to do anything but sleep.

The autumn begins in March and a phenomenal multi-coloured landscape materializes before your eyes. This is my favourite season, with its yellow poplars in the valleys and red *ñire* and *lenga*[27] trees on the mountainsides. Flocks of Andean parrots and parakeets fly from the mountains to pick the sweet apples, chattering in the still warmth of the afternoon. Herds of wild boar with their growing piglets descend from the forests to get fat on wild apples. The seasonal circle has been completed once again.

People in the ranches prepare themselves for another winter. Wood has to be collected, dried and stored, the pantries and *store*rooms will be filled to the top with dried fish and salted wild boar. Sausages and hams will be hung from the rafters, as well as dried wild mushrooms. The morel mushroom is known locally as the 'cypress' mushroom because it grows only where spores from the cypress tree have landed. It has the consistency and taste of dried venison. It is such a delicacy that most of the

27   *ñire* and *lenga* – indigenous Andean deciduous trees

morels collected are exported to France, the country that is so famous for its own morels! After truffles, the morel is the most expensive mushroom in the world and the vast majority comes from Patagonia. Wide expanses of virgin forest in the Andes are unscrupulously and deliberately burned because the locals know that the following year this will produce a bumper crop of 'cypress' mushrooms for export. In the meantime the fireplace will be busy devouring tons of logs and the gauchos will stretch their legs in relaxation for another four long months of Patagonian winter.

Ranch life becomes very quiet in winter. Most birds have migrated to warmer lands and those that remain don't seem to be quite so musical. They are the reluctant members of the international orchestra that performs so vividly in spring with its incessant cacophony of sound. People withdraw into indoor activities, such as sleeping, eating, drinking and trying very hard to do nothing at all. The only places that enjoy a great deal of life are the ski resorts in the Andes. The biggest and the best ski resort is the town of Bariloche, with thousands of people practising their sport. Some of those thousands are Brazilians who fly direct from São Pablo and Rio de Janeiro to Bariloche. The contrast between these permanently suntanned people and the white snow is quite amazing, and to many of them this is the only time they will have a chance to wear pullovers, woollen hats and socks, or to sit in front of a roaring fire at lunch time, and to see and touch any snow in their lifetime.

In the picturesque village of San Martín de los Andes there is another wonderful ski resort with great accommodation and service. The inhabitants of this village are descended mostly from Swiss and German immigrants. Esquel falls into a third category. It is the cheapest ski resort in the area, and if you don't mind waiting for long hours in the freezing air for the lift or for a cup of coffee in the canteen, the rest should be okay, with plenty of snow and not too many people. The resort is 15 km from the town/semi-village of Esquel and is called 'La Hoya', which means the cooking pot. A very cold cooking pot! Normally the skiing season in Patagonia is from July to September. It enjoys the reputation of free spirited sport, especially at El Bolsón, which has the wonderful feeling of being a family-friendly village. El Bolsón also enjoys the reputation of producing the best marijuana in the Andes – which comes highly recommended – and is *the* centre of organic agriculture in the Andes. In the autumn all the valleys are covered with fruits – cherries, gooseberries, strawberries, blackberries, raspberries, boysenberries, rose hips, black and redcurrants – an infinity of indigenous berry families, with Andean apples adorning the mountains and fields.

These berries remind me of an incident that happened to Lucas Bridges. Bridges was a remarkable man, born in Tierra del Fuego of English missionary parents. As the son of the missionary he spent most of his life as a rancher among the Ona and Yamana Indians of the 'Fireland' at the southernmost tip of Patagonia, as it was then called by the English. They were the first non-Indians to settle there. Living amongst the Indians, Bridges learnt from them the pros and cons of the land. His survival instincts were well developed and therefore he knew what, or what not to eat from the land, including the local berries. On one of his trips to London he visited the Chelsea Flower Show and seeing, on one of the stands, a rare vine full of berries he asked the attendant what it was. The attendant didn't know much about those berries, just that they came from Tierra del Fuego and that they were highly poisonous. Recognizing an indigenous species from his birthplace, Mr Bridges gathered up a handful of berries that had fallen to the ground, and swallowed the 'deadly' berries. He then walked away laughing, leaving the poor man on the stand white with fear and shivering in horror. Bridges' book is called *The Uttermost Part of the World*, a refined jewel which details a unique experience that no human being will ever repeat. The life in southern Patagonia that he describes in his book has gone forever.

A curious farming tradition occurs in the Andes. After the livestock (mainly Hereford cattle) has spent the winter in the low land of the valleys, in the spring all the gauchos round up the livestock and drive them into the hills of the Cordillera. This is called the *veranada*, or 'the summer place'. It's a kind of summer holiday for the cows as the only thing they do is get fat. This happens in November and the drovers take two or three days on horseback to reach the high pastures. A vast number of cattle with their calves, bulls, dogs, horses and sheep are driven in dusty clouds with the gauchos bringing up the rear. The loose horses will lead the way, followed by cows with calves and, lastly, the lazy sheep with dozens of dogs watching them and barking with excitement. The last in this long train are the gauchos, black with dust and sun, dragging in slow motion their *cargueros*[28]. The load of the *carguero* contains all the food and *maté* for

....

28   *cargueros* – pack horses

the trip, which should last for at least four months. The wine never lasts that long so from time to time the gauchos send a young courier towards civilization for more. Meat they don't worry about – they have plenty.

During those months there is very little for the gauchos to do in the mountains. The animals graze peacefully, so there's not much work. On one occasion I spent a summer with the gauchos taking care of the animals in the *veranada* and, yes, it was an extremely dull time. The days seemed never-ending and because no one did very much during the day we were not tired enough to sleep at night. We played cards and that was quite boring as well. Sometime we entertained ourselves during the day hunting pumas, foxes and wild boars. The area is infested with them and it is good sport on horseback through the mountains – though a bit dangerous at times. As the puma loves horsemeat, we always lose some horses as well as sheep. Every gaucho carries one or two pistols or a revolver. Some prefer the old .44 Winchester rifle as, in good hands, it is a very accurate gun, and the pumas will drop dead with a single bullet. But although we carried guns and knives all the time, the real hunters are the dogs. Without the dogs we wouldn't be able to catch any pumas easily, as this area is bushy and covered with trees, and it is quite difficult to hunt with guns.

The start of the winter time can be quite tough in the *cordilleras*[29] of Patagonia, and the month of June, with its long cold nights of frozen dew and the clear sky opened its belly to billions of stars which are like thoughts that never seem to end. But the following day it was pouring down with

---

29   *cordilleras* – Andean mountain range

rain, and the paraffin lamp was telling me that the fuel had run too low. The spare container was empty and the shape of the clouds resembled Charolais bulls' bums. They weren't aiding anything at all. The rainy season had begun.

It had been raining for the past three days, day and night without a single interval, and running to the far away toilet was quite a drama. There was no way of moving from the ranch for who knew how long. It was the beginning of winter in the Andes of Patagonia. I have tried my best to love Patagonia on those cold rainy long days but I'm not sure if I have succeeded, as nearly all the songs and writing I did then contained hundreds of grouchy words and not many happy ones. There was not much I could do, except eat and sleep, write and dream a bit, or get soaked while fetching pieces of wood for the fire – the only fuel supply available on the ranch that, even when wet, still burns well, especially the *espino negro* bush and *laura* branches. All the willows, poplars and pines are so soft that this persistent rain gets through them and they won't burn at all. I was reminded of discotheques in these moments because of the horrific noise they emit from inside their black boxes resembling unburied coffins, the trapped ghosts screaming indecipherable lyrics. But now, in the silence of the mid-Andean mountains, it was the noise of the heavy rain on the corrugated iron roof that was driving me mad.

It was past four o'clock in the morning and it was pitch black outside. Inside it was more or less the same except for the ghostly shadows produced by the flickering fire. There was no radio or television, no electricity or people, not even any paraffin left in the lamp. In fact, I didn't know if there

even were people still living in the world. I could have been
the only one left alive after some natural disaster or nuclear
holocaust. The only thing that deeply embraced my thoughts
was that it was still raining. It was an unlocked natural jail
that God had very thoughtfully provided for me, a school
without a teacher and an answer without a question.

I woke up in the middle of a confused nightmare. The
clever rain had found a hole in the roof and it was pouring
down onto my bed of sheepskins. It was a sticky business, the
drama of finding dry clothes on a muddy floor in darkness.
My mood was growing wilder as I fell over trying to put my
socks on. This was really a circus with only one clown and
20 billion drums of raindrops in each ear telling me that the
discotheque in the Andes was here to stay. I laughed widely
as I tried to get some more sleep in a very untidy wet bed.

It rained solidly for three weeks and the dogs and the
rest of the animals were looking very depressed. As a rule the
gauchos don't care very much. They entertained themselves
repairing the saddles, whips, bridles and lassoes by the fire,
telling 'true' stories that were not always true, and drinking
maté until their pee turned green. Most of the gauchos are
quite clever artisans, they can transform a good rawhide,
preferably of a good healthy Hereford breed, into various
working artefacts including head collars, reins, nightingales,
whips, lassoes, boleadoras and very tidy and intricate parts of
their saddles. The thread to tie, weave, plait and adorn these
ropes is made out of horse-hide, taken from the sides between
the belly and the ribs. Sometimes, when available, they use
the neck of the male guanaco for sewing. It is very strong
and can last for a lifetime or more. An Inca Indian told me

that the word 'gaucho' derives from the Quechua language, where their word 'guacho' means 'orphan'. And it's probably true as we still use 'guacho' today for orphaned animals or a lonely hill or a lonely tree, for example. In Chile they call the gauchos 'guasos' and in the United States 'cowboys' and in Wales nothing at all. Although the gauchos have been immortalized and romanticized so much by José Hernandez in his brilliant book of poetry called Martín Fierro, they are still the low class aristocrats of the desert.

But sadly these proud aristocrats of the desert are very ignorant when they step into the towns. At times they are the butt of jokes as they wear different types of clothing and they walk in long strides, but looking a bit like Charlie Chaplin. In fact, the comfortably wide baggy trousers they wear came from the Arabs to Argentina with the French army. Their language came from Spain and the word 'gringo' from an English or Irish folk song ('*Green grow the rushes, oh*') sung on the plantations in Mexico. The irony is that all of the gauchos are 'gringos' in one way or another but today the meaning of the word 'gringo' is 'foreigner'.

The rhythm of the gauchos' songs came from Africa, as at one point there were more black African people in Argentina than white people. Today it is difficult to find even one. They all died in the war against Paraguay and in fights between the Indians of the pampas. But the African rhythms remain very much alive today, as do many of their words, such as 'malambo', 'zamba', 'candome', 'milonga', 'mandinga', 'caramba' and 'la bamba', etc. I haven't met one gaucho yet who knows these facts but they can perform beautifully their songs with those rhythms, which vibrate in deep sadness. It makes me wonder if, in their subconscious, they know all about the tragic history of Argentina, a history in which thousands of black African slaves died in order to draw the boundaries of northern Argentina and preserve the white population.

— 34 —

Visitors

Back in Cholila, the famous celebrity chef Ainsley Harriott arrived at my ranch to make a programme on barbequing around the world for BBC2's *Ainsley's Big Cookout*. It was really odd to see all the macho gauchos with their big knives and guns behaving so shyly and apprehensively. Of course, they had never seen a black man before, and certainly not one riding a horse, laughing wide and loud with Ainsley's contagious and charismatic personality. And then cooking as well! The gauchos admired him when he took a knife and in seconds carved the bones clean out of the back leg of a lamb and put it on top of the grill on the open fire by the lake. The gauchos had never eaten 'Agneau á la Moutarde' before – what a treat that was for them! It wasn't the first time that the gauchos had seen filming on my ranch but Ainsley is still, to my knowledge, the only black man to have visited Cholila and the locals still ask me about him even now.

Barbequing is the traditional gaucho method of cooking meat, so Ainsley's open grill was no surprise, although in Argentina the word used is *asado* which means 'to roast' – usually on a spike over an open fire. The word 'barbeque' came with the Norman French to England as 'barbe-à-cul' which literally means 'from the chin to the arse' (barbe

= beard, chin; cul = arse), and described their system of
roasting a full pig on a spit, with the iron bar being inserted
through the length of the animal. As the French language
faded in Britain the word became 'barbeque', and now the
French have adopted the English spelling and pronunciation,
which doesn't mean anything in either English or French.
Spain has adapted the word from the English into 'barbacoa',
which also means nothing at all. The Australians use 'barbie',
and the Americans use BBQ, just to add to the confusion. At
least when someone mentions an *asado*, you know what to
expect – a succulent, roasted animal, whether a lamb or an
entire side of beef. I remember cooking a full steer once. It
took over six hours of hot, sweaty labour before we could eat.
At fiesta time in the local villages, the gauchos will start to
prepare the fires for cooking a day in advance, to ensure that
the eighty full steers and six hundred lambs are cooked and
ready to eat over the four days of fiesta.

The nomadic gaucho of the central desert of Patagonia
is a hardy type, reminiscent of the nomadic tribes of North
Africa. They are excellent carnivores and the healthy diet
of pure organic meat from the guanacos, sheep, horses,
armadillos and ostriches with their eggs can keep them alive
for a hundred years or so. But the solitude and the freezing
winds in the desert take their toll. It makes them look older
and dangerous. The gaucho's knife, the facon, is always
hanging from the belt across his back and, unfortunately, it is
ready to be used at any time, often with tragic consequences.
I've witnessed a few fights between gauchos. They move like
panthers to the kill, without feelings or regret. Generally,
those often mortal fights happen in bars after heavy drinking

sessions overloaded with machismo. It's understandable really, as the country itself has a hard, sad and cruel history, from the vicious *conquistadors*[30] of Spain to the vicious military of Argentina who destroyed democracy, or whatever crossed their path, at any opportunity and at any cost. The gaucho began to shape his characteristics when the royal family of Spain conquered the continent in the name of God, with a big Bible and with an even bigger sword. Some of the gauchos are the descendants of those *conquistadors* with Moorish blood, like the Yemeni-Andalucían thoroughbred-cross polo horses. Argentina exports thousands of these horses all around the planet but not many gauchos.

Apart from the fights that occur from consuming too much poor quality alcohol there is also trouble with the gauchos at shearing time. And this time it's without alcohol. The huge *estancias* can take up to three months to shear 70,000 sheep and they employ hundreds of people to do it. Indians, gauchos, and anyone willing, even inept amateurs from Europe and Buenos Aires, join the greasy job in the desert. The work is tough, the living is tough, and the lumps of meat are tough to chew. Some of these hard guys don't have any teeth left, so they have to swallow the lumps of meat whole, and that is tough too. But they make good money if they survive. Thanks to the tamarisk tree they have some shelter from the wind and under which they can lay their beds. These consist of a few fresh sheepskins with a canvas on top. It isn't an ideal place for a honeymoon and it is perhaps because of this that the gauchos can lose their temper as soon

30   *conquistadors* – soldiers and adventurers in the service of the
      Portuguese and Spanish Empires

as they wake up and provoke an argument with the cook, the manager or anyone who crosses their path on the way to the toilet. Some of them are like cats with nine lives; they don't die easily. They are very stubborn about entering their final journey for some reason.

On one occasion I took Señor Mansilla to the hospital with his intestines distributed all around the back of my dirty pick-up. He'd had a fight with a young lad and I thought he would die before reaching the hospital which was twenty miles away. But he didn't and ten days later he walked back to my ranch. 'The food is very good in the hospital,' he said. Another gaucho had four .38 calibre bullets in his chest but, apart from being a bit shaken, amazingly he survived. Another one was not so lucky. We buried him and that didn't take us very long. The boxes for the dead are made locally with good wood but the carpenters are not generally of a high standard. One of our neighbours, however, is a good carpenter, a great character, but he drinks far too much wine. Once he made some miscalculations in measuring a dead man and couldn't fit him in the freshly made box, so they chopped his legs off with an axe and then it was alright.

Most people think that the gauchos are the descendants of the Spanish *conquistadors* mixed with Indian blood. Well, in one way they are, but there are also Russian gauchos, Welsh and Polish gauchos and Czechoslovakian, Arabian and English. In fact, all kinds of races and nationalities are mixed into the browny soup of the desert. Some are serious and dangerous like a frozen night, some are more eccentric than any Englishman ever could be, some are incredibly comical. Romualdo, one of the farm workers, was a bit silly and a bit funny, yet also from time to time he had a lot of common sense. One hot afternoon Romualdo and I decided to go for a swim in the nearby river, together with some other gauchos, and about a dozen kids joined us as well. I lent Romualdo a pair of shorts which he carried very happily in his hands. When we arrived at the riverbank, Romualdo took off all his clothes and jumped into the middle of the river, while the rest of the group were laughing as he was the only one who was naked. Romualdo never understood why we were laughing at him while he was in the water and why we carried on laughing when he got out of the river and then put his shorts on.

He whistled nearly all the way back to the house, happy and light inside his body that had seen 75 years of poverty. He had never shaved because hair wouldn't grow on his face. He whistled, laughed loudly and told us many stories. He told me that when he was twenty-two he put on the first pair of boots of his life. He didn't like them at first, because his feet were hard like the skin of a wild boar and wide like a spade. He suffered a lot with those boots because he couldn't take them off. So to celebrate the new shoes and that pain, he bought a bottle of a strong caña. He got drunk and the police chased him on horseback but Romualdo, although drunk, knew his ground very well. He led the police and the galloping horses, which were getting closer, to a grass-covered swamp. The horses with the fat police on top went up to their necks in the mud but Romualdo glided through the swamp with the ability of a lizard. More laughter poured from his mouth, showing his perfect white teeth.

On another occasion, Romualdo arrived at the ranch in the early hours of the morning. He'd got lost somewhere after a party and was still drunk and laughing. He told me that he had seen three big fires coming out of the ground on his way back through my ranch, 'And that means,' he said, 'there's gold buried there.' It's difficult to believe Romualdo. You never know when he's telling the truth, as he's always smiling. But one afternoon on the ranch, with everything completely still because it was so hot and not a cloud to be seen in a perfect blue sky, I observed that it would be nice to have a drop of rain. The place was looking desperately dry and as Romualdo looked around he said, 'I can make it rain if you want.' I looked at him as he began to dance and jump around the woodpile, thinking that he was quite mad or drunk – when suddenly, after only a few minutes, the skies opened and rain came pouring down in huge drops. It was such a torrential downpour that all of us, dogs and chickens included, had to run for cover. The raindrops were as sharp as arrows. It continued to rain like that for two hours. As it had been so hot before this inexplicable rain, the humidity that was generated began to evaporate, causing the herbs and grasses to release an incredible aroma of freshness. Could it be possible that Romualdo, or any other Indian, could make rain after all? My brother certainly couldn't believe what had just happened in front of his eyes.

Early one morning, as dawn was breaking on the ranch, Romualdo arrived very excited. I had just woken up but he had been on his ugly little horse for about four hours already. He began to prepare the *maté* and I went to wash my face. As he was noisily sucking his tea, he told me that while he was crossing the shallows of the River Blanco, he saw a huge fish in a deeper part of the river. And that was that. Obviously I was curious and asked him what kind of fish it was – knowing that the answer was supposed to be something like 'rainbow trout', 'brown trout', 'brook trout', 'fontinalis' or 'perca trout'. He had the *maté* in one hand and was brushing and flattening his wild hair very seriously with the other. Suddenly he said that the fish was a *pescao-pescao*, which means it was a 'fish-fish'. After that clear answer from Romualdo I felt quite ridiculous for asking him the question because for all the Indians fish is something that they can eat. They don't have those fancy names. Just *pescao*.

On one of those enchanted silent nights when I had the most pleasure of being alive, I was sitting by the fire on my ranch and observing the old Romualdo Indian gaucho, and he, in a dream-like state, was observing the fire. From time to time he would stand up and look through a hole in the wooden wall at the pitch black of the night and then go back to his stool by the fire, locking his eyes into the flames.

He knew his friends would arrive at the ranch on horseback one of these days or nights, and that night he was sensing something in the air or in the fire, or perhaps in the behaviour of the dogs that were fast asleep by his boots. Who knows? Suddenly, he stood up and said, 'Ahí, vienen!' (they are coming). I couldn't hear anything, and the dogs didn't bark, but somehow he knew his friends were close to the ranch. I forced myself to understand the telepathic communication that the Indian was using so successfully.

I heard the hoo-hoo of a *nwco* (big owl) and the ri-ki-ki-ki-ki-ki of the kil-kil, a miniature owl that imitates birds' songs, gets their attention, and feasts on them. At long intervals, a fox would scream. The night had no other sounds that reached my ears, but for the Indian there was a different dimension to life, which for a white half-gringo like me was impossible to understand. And sure enough, a group of five horsemen arrived, immaculately dressed and with their faces shining with freshness. It was already late, so after shaking hands with the smiling new arrivals, I went to bed. They welcomed themselves with a noisy drinking session and a roast lamb on the grill. They kept me awake all night.

In the morning I sat and talked with Romualdo's cousin, Pichinian. He was an old Indian, probably in his 80s who had lived and worked as a fence maker all his life. He didn't have a house, as he was living and moving 'with' the fence as it grew and advanced through those huge *estancias*, building a new campsite every few weeks under a bush and always close to his fencing work. This work in the stony scrubland of the interior of Patagonia has to be one of the hardest jobs for any man but he was as fit as a tennis player. The galvanized wire dried and cracked his hands until they resembled ostrich's feet. The cold wind in winter and the scorching sun of summer dried his face until it looked like a long-dead guanaco. His diet consisted of meat and *maté* tea. The fencer is a hard man and very proud of his job, he prefers to work alone in the silence of the desert. The fence is his life, a harmonious past and future in a perfectly straight line.

Every six months or so, he would get paid some money and one day, with money in his pocket, he decided to pay a visit to a doctor in town because he had been concerned for the past fifty years about a growth on his neck. He had never been to town before and he had never seen a doctor before either, but the lump on his neck was growing larger and was bothering him. He wore his best shirt and headed to town on foot. The doctor examined the 'lump', and finding it was a malignant tumour on a very delicate part of the neck where it was not easy to operate, and also considering the Indian's age, he decided not to proceed with an operation. Pichinian walked back to his camp among the bushes of the ranch thoroughly depressed. After sipping his *maté* tea, and sharpening his knife methodically, he cut the malignant tumour off his neck with a single slash and threw it on the fire. He put some *salmuera* sauce into the wound, ate some meat and went to sleep. The following day he was back on his fence, happily whistling, and never again went to see a doctor.

— 35 —

TECHNOLOGY AND COSMOLOGY

THINGS are changing fast in my adorable wilderness of Patagonia. Technology has arrived faster than lava runs downhill, trapping the illiterate Indians with their mouths open. And now they are galloping fast into town to fetch an e-mail or fax which is waiting for them at the police station or *telefónica* (public telephone booths). It's a fascinating sight; rows of horses tethered to the trees outside the *telefónica* with saddles, guns and knives while inside, the staff of the *telefónica* are patiently trying to explain the intricacies of computer technology to the Indians and gauchos. Anyway, it's a great excuse for them to stay in town where they can find a bar and people to talk to, even if they have no idea what an e-mail really is. They are in no hurry to get back to their farm or ranch and usually some of them end up in jail. These events happen regularly and 'collecting e-mail' is a new entertainment and a believable lie to their wives.

Even the police station is now fully and dangerously computerized and the police officers look quite clean and efficient. It was so different only a few years ago when I had just bought the ranch. I went to the police to report a robbery. The policeman in charge shouted 'Come in!' and I said, '*Buenos días.*' He, without looking up, said, '*Qué pasa?*' (what's happening?). He was writing something on a piece of paper and appeared to be very busy because he didn't have time to look at me. After I explained that someone was stealing lambs from my ranch he responded, still without looking up, 'If you find those guys, shoot them.' I thought he was joking, so as a joke I said laughingly, 'Right, but if I kill those guys, what do I do with their bodies?' Still without looking up, he said with complete indifference, 'Throw them in the lake.' I gave him my thanks and drove my pick-up back to the farm, thinking that something wasn't right. This policeman must be pretty ignorant because, if I had to kill these thieves and throw them into the lake weighted down with a big stone, the water is so cold down there that their bodies would not disintegrate. And after a while they would pop up like balloons. Somebody would find them floating about and I would get the blame because the lake is within the perimeters of my ranch. Well, we haven't killed anybody yet but the lambs are still disappearing and some gauchos think that it would be better to burn the bodies of these thieves instead of throwing them into the lake. I'm still thinking about the whole dilemma.

The Tehuelche Indians think that the lakes in the Andes are full of bad spirits and won't go near them, which is something that has always intrigued me. I don't know if it's because they have been throwing bodies into the lakes as well or if there is something else there. The area is packed with strange stories, nearly always to do with unexplained lights at night, lights which follow you around, lights that grow from the abdomen of the lakes and silently shoot into the sky at great speed. Horses, oxen and carts have been dragged into the lakes and drowned for no apparent reason (even in far away Lake Titicaca in Bolivia the stories are the same). Innocent farmers have been transported on their horses many miles away from their wives without any explanation and, although some of them might not regret this paranormal divorce, this time-warp experience is still a peculiar thing to happen.

Every lake, lagoon and big pond has its own personal story about flying objects with peculiar lights, either hovering above the water, entering or exiting it. The speed of these flying objects varies all the time. Sometimes they travel so slowly that you can walk alongside them. At other times they move as fast as lightning and disappear in front of your eyes in seconds, always without any sound. In about 1992, one of these flying objects landed on my ranch, on a very high, flat part of a remote hill. My brother Fredy went to investigate, but by the time he arrived on horseback, only a scorch mark exactly 3.5 metres in diameter remained on the ground. After ten years, the mark can still be seen as the grass has never grown back where the circle marked the ground. Today, the grass is still a bit in shock and is struggling to grow.

These things are so common around Cholila that people take very little notice and they have definitely never been reported in topical magazines. Therefore, we don't even have a name for these strange things, except a peculiar local appendage – people call them 'those f**king round things'. Sometimes these 'f**king round things' just hang quietly in the air just a few metres from the ground. At other times they move very slowly in the sky and sometimes they go so fast that there is no time to believe or imagine anything or to wonder why they don't make a noise like an aeroplane or a helicopter. Sometimes they pop out of the water in a form similar to a crocodile, other times like a huge swan, but the locals say they are not swans.

One late summer evening two cousins of mine from the coast decided to travel across the 700 km of desert and visit Yvonne and myself on the ranch. For a treat we all went to a nearby fishing lodge. This lodge is the only typical Welsh tea house in Cholila, a hundred metres from the cabin that belonged to Butch Cassidy. The owners, Sr Miguel Calderón and his wife, Toli, provided an extravagant meal consisting of everything we could think of and a few extra things on top – my favourite was baked cream cake, a delicious dessert made with rich full cream straight from the cows on their farm. My cousins ate so much that they decided to go for a relaxing walk before going to bed but, as it was around one o'clock in the morning, I took the pick-up and went back with Yvonne to the ranch. As I opened one of the gates on the hills, a massive light appeared out of the sky a few metres away and hovered over the hill. It looked as if a number of lights were being switched off one by one. Then it vanished without a sound across the lake.

In the morning we joined my cousins for breakfast and I asked if they had seen anything strange while they were walking last night. Susana told us that they'd seen a bright light on one of the hills and the light appeared to be wobbling around a bit and changing slightly in colour. Her husband is a methodical, knowledgeable, well-read man, a very down-to-earth type, so he had told his wife not worry because those lights were coming from an *estancia* on the hill. But Susana was not convinced, because she couldn't remember seeing any *estancias* on that hill before. The mystery of that ghostly establishment in the hills became very eerie, however, when both of them saw the '*estancia*', or whatever it was, slowly rising with its lights into the sky. They trotted home as fast as they could back to the lodge, dived into bed and buried their heads under their pillows.

We said farewell to my cousins and later in the afternoon I went to fetch some of the workers who lived on the outskirts of the village. While I was waiting for them I had the opportunity to ask some of the children if they had noticed any strange lights about in the sky. 'No,' they replied, 'no lights, only those f**king things were around here yesterday, travelling very slowly on the hill slope.' I looked towards the hills and scanned them in the hope of seeing something so that I could convince myself that I had seen something extra terrestrial. But no, not even any non-extra terrestrial things were moving on those desolate hills and the kids weren't interested. They had more important things to do, they were furiously kicking a football made of old socks.

— 36 —

COLD NIGHTS IN THE ANDES WITH PIROLA

I was on my way back to Cholila again from the desert one night in my pick-up, when I noticed the water temperature gauge on the dashboard begin to rise dangerously, until the engine got too hot and the water started to boil. As I was driving downhill, I switched off the engine, put the gears into neutral and slowly arrived at the village of Epuyén. There I found a mechanic sitting on his door-step drinking beer at one o'clock in the morning, while a pack of dogs were barking madly at my arrival. Without any movement, the mechanic delivered a sharp whistle and all the dogs went quiet. '*Qué pasa?*' – What's happening? – he said.

His name was Pirola and he was a man of many skills, including being a top mechanic, storyteller, fighter with knives and drinker of huge quantities of wine and beer. He exchanged the radiator of my pick-up, in the dark, for one that had been lying around in his back yard, and the engine began to work perfectly once again. As it was late, he invited me to stay the night in his house and to drink wine. He was as wild as the wind and racing with motorbikes and horses were his great hobbies. Very alert even when he was drunk, his knife was always in the sheath on his left hip, ready for any kind of macho 'entertainment'. He had been in countless fights, but thanks to his ability and the speed with which he could use his knife, he had always been victorious even when someone put a gun to his head.

He had a 1940s four-wheel-drive lorry that he used to transport timber and, if he could, he would always try to drive his lorry at night, as it is easy to dazzle animals by the road side. If a cow happened to be wandering on the road while he was at the wheel, he would hit it at full speed with his lorry and in a matter of seconds he would load up with the carcass of the dead beast and drive home for a barbeque with lots of wine. His house was dirty and chaotic, but was a paradise for an anarchist like him and his drunken friends. The pungent smell of horse meat was everywhere in the house, even in the shower room that nobody ever used, and chunks of the wandering fat cows hung with flies from the rafters.

As we became good friends, I accompanied him on many adventures and on one occasion we were trapped in a snow storm in the middle of the Andes for a week. We were supposed to stay in that area for a maximum of two days. The only thing we had to do was cut and load the truck with bamboo-type cane and hurry back to the village. We built a campsite with some stones for the fire place and a hut with branches. It was a shameful 'building', with cold winds rushing in through gaps in the walls. Food and drink were getting scarce after three days, especially the wine, and besides salt and *maté*, there was not much else edible to be seen.

Pirola's strong hunting dog was surveying the situation idly. This dog was a dangerous beast and I was frightened of him, especially when he was turning his head from time to time and listening to the rumblings of his own empty stomach. That rumbling was a dangerous sign and we had to find a solution to this mess – and fast. We were sleeping fully-clothed when just past midnight the dog moved from his comfortable position and, with furious barking, sped out of the shack and disappeared into the forest. Pirola and

I woke disorientated and confused as we thought someone had arrived at our base camp, but that was quite impossible; outside there was over a metre of snow and no one would dare to attempt to visit us at night. From time to time we could hear the bark of the dog, but we could make no sense out of it. Why was the dog barking in the middle of the night in the snow?

We rushed outside, sleepy but still fully-clothed, and although we couldn't see each other in the dark, Pirola said, '*Vamos*' – let's see what's happening. We stumbled through trees, bushes and boulders to reach a nearby hill, with no sign of the dog, only snow and the nocturnal shapes of the cypress trees against the sky. As we stopped to get our breath back, a noise of swishing snow paralysed us and what seemed to be a huge wild boar flew past us. The dog had clamped itself to the backside of the wild boar and the creature was running for his life! The boar was dragging the dog like a sledge, upside down and against the trees. That type of hunting dog can lock its jaws, and when it does so it would rather die than release its catch, so it was a normal game for an experienced strong hunting dog to be dragged furiously with his teeth clamped to the wild boar's testicles.

When we thought about our empty stomachs, we followed the chase with difficulty, falling face down in the snow several times. The footprints left by the wild boar and the dog were clear in the snow, so we ran madly and sweat began to stick to our smelly clothes, while Pirola encouraged his dog by shouting '*Vamos … vamos perro … agárrelo … agárrelo, mierda!*' Finally the boar stopped, exhausted, and showing his massive tusks, sat panting on top of the dog, refusing to budge. Pirola took his sharp knife and slit the boar's throat, and in an instant he was dead.

We warmed up our hands inside the boar's belly for a while, gathered our breath and threw the inside bits of the stomach to the dog. We carried the carcass back to the hut, lit a fire, put a big chunk of fatty ribs onto the barbeque iron bar and the dog went to sleep in front of it.

The whole business could not have taken more than an hour, but it was an exhilarating experience that, after all these years, remains vivid in my memory as if it happened just yesterday and never since have I tasted a barbeque of a wild boar as delicious as that one. The dog with his belly full of food continued to snore loudly by the fire. Pirola and I also sat by the warm fire telling each other stories as we couldn't go back to sleep after that unexpected rush of excitement. Some of Pirola's stories were fascinating and real although some, I believe, were of his own invention. At any rate, in that snowy and isolated environment, any stories, any song, any unusual behaviour which in normal circumstances would be classified as utter madness, was well received.

We put more wet wood onto the fire, drank more wine, and ate more wild boar. As the dawn was breaking Pirola continued to tell me stories. He was getting more and more excited with each tale and his natural gift to exaggerate amused me, as I thought the stories could possibly be true, and perhaps they were. Nearly all of Pirola's stories were surreal, but I had heard similar stories separated by thousands of miles across Patagonia, so they may have contained a few grains of truth as well.

In one, Pirola was travelling very slowly in his Second World War truck, packed with timber from the mountains. On a flat part of the road he spotted a strange animal running in front of him. His first instinct was to kill it by running it over with the heavy truck, but when he was very close to it, the beast with its long tail pushed the lorry into the bushes, and it was stuck there for a day. Pirola grabbed his shotgun and fired a few shots at the huge dinosaur-type lizard, but the creature got away, jumping the fences and bushes like a kangaroo, and vanished. A family of Gypsies told me a similar story 500 miles away from Pirola's incident, but this time the entire family saw the strange animal jumping fences while they were travelling in a pick-up.

In another place a gaucho saw a creature resembling a huge hairy man with a lizard's head wandering around the corrals, but while the gaucho was fetching his gun, the creature disappeared, leaving no footprints. Of course, not everyone believes in those stories; to most people they are the ramblings of drunken idiots or mad Indians and we shouldn't listen to them. Nevertheless, I am attracted by the unknown and I find it fascinating that people can say something like, '*Yo no creo en brujas, pero que las hay, las hay!*' – I don't believe in witches, but they definitely exist!

— 37 —

THE CRAWLING STONE

AFTER returning from that trip I was still fascinated by the flying objects suspended in the air, so I called all my gauchos together on the ranch and we organized a barbeque party which lasted for three days, with plenty of wine, guitars and stories to break the monotony of the everyday drag. The gauchos can be very entertaining indeed, full of curiosity and superstition. Some can lie with a noisy and contagious charismatic laughter, while others remain inscrutable, like those big statues on Easter Island. Whenever I touched on the subject of mysteries, they all talked at the same time and I couldn't make any sense of it. The bottles of wine were emptying rapidly – they are very good at that – but I had plenty on 24-hour standby. Some of them were curling up for a nap, and then they would continue drinking and eating meat in a very interesting macho way, half drunk all the time. One of the freshly fallen artists was mumbling something between his teeth and from beneath his huge untidy moustache. I thought he was dreaming so I didn't take much notice of him but when he mentioned my name with respect, as in 'Don René', I began to listen more carefully to his semi-coherent words. He was asking me a very serious question, apparently – 'Do you know about the stone that moves?'

I heard all the other gauchos muttering, '*Ahh, si, si, si,*' and I didn't have a clue what any of them were talking about. My first reaction was that he was hallucinating. A moving stone? A joke, surely? But why had the others agreed with him?

'The stone is not very big,' he said, 'if you can find one, it will fit in your hand. And there are two *estancias* where you might find such stones: on the south-east of Estancia Leleké, and in the north part of Estancia Quichaura, close to Tecka. You must follow its trail, which is similar to that left by a snake on the sand. It could take years to find it, and maybe you never will, because they look exactly like normal stones and the place is full of stones. They don't have a head or legs or mouth or an arse. They don't make any sound and they don't fly. I don't know what they eat or where they sleep.'

He had seen 'the stone' only once and that was in a bar in a small village in the desert. An Indian who was very drunk had it in his pocket and showed it to him. But the Indian went off with the stone and he has not been seen again. 'The stone exists, because everybody knows that it exists,' the gaucho said.

This story was, and still is, totally beyond the reach of my imagination. I was convinced that this gaucho was not telling me lies but it sounded too fantastic. The subject of flying objects ended in the mystery of a crawling object, an incomprehensible stone. Days later I prepared my pick-up and drove about 300 miles to Estancia Quichaura. I knew the manager, Sr Courteney, a typical gaucho of the desert. He was born close by but his grandfathers, he said, were from Ireland, although he didn't know where that was.

I brought up the subject of this mysterious stone and asked if he knew something about it as the gauchos told me that the stone existed on his ranch. 'Of course I know about the stone,' he said. 'Well, everybody knows about the stone around here but nobody has seen it. I've found its trails but I got tired of following it after so many hours on horseback. The terrain is tough for the horses, a lot of sand and full of all kinds of stones anyway. The stone moves in a kind of circle on the sandy part of the pampas. The trails are clear but lead nowhere, maybe it jumps or flies. I don't know more than that – although I believe that it could be a prehistoric animal that sleeps most of the time, I don't know. There are so many stories around here, God knows if they are true or not. Some of them are true of course, but others are difficult to believe. Some people think so much of these strange things that they go totally insane and end up in hospital or commit suicide. The desert,' he continued, 'is a very dangerous place to live, too much silence, too much wind and all that vast immensity where the human race hasn't set foot yet. It could contain anything, even dinosaurs perhaps. There are plenty of stories about it. People keep disappearing with their horses – where do they go? They don't leave any clues to look for them, exactly like the stones. I've been all my life in the desert, and my fathers too, and I'm telling you that although it's a bloody strange place to be, I would never change it for the towns.'

I left the isolated and massive *estancia* with its clumps of silver alder trees around the main house. I wasn't sure what to do – carry on looking for that very precious stone? Or abandon the crazy idea? I drove on and my pick-up was heading back to my ranch against a 100-mile an hour wind. The strong six-cylinder Dodge was bravely tackling the pampas without complaining and the wind was whistling, out of tune, all the music of the desert; a wild symphony with a cold title, spreading dust and rage on the desolate roads. I was content with myself, driving my thoughts through this semi-nomadic, unconquered, unwelcoming and amazingly beautiful slice of the world. The Andes were getting closer now, I could smell the green forests in the mountains and the glaciers and pockets of snow lying quietly in the shelter of the blue rocks were telling me that home was only a few hours away. I caught two armadillos for supper on the way and killed nine hares with the pick-up. Well boiled with potatoes and wheat, the hares would make a good meal for the dogs.

The gauchos were having a barbeque of lamb. What a surprise! But when I showed them the armadillos covered with yellow fat, they all moved at once and in seconds the two hairy armadillos were lying flat on their open bellies, looking down into the fire from the top of the grill. I forgot about the stone that moves without legs or an arse, but I did remember Sr Courteney and his prehistoric animals – I was eating one.

— 38 —

ALL THE COUNTRIES OF SOUTH AMERICA

ON one of my trips back to Wales, I decided to travel through all of the countries in South America except for the Guyanas and Surinam. Leaving Argentina behind, I entered Uruguay and then Brazil, Paraguay, Bolivia, Chile, Peru, Ecuador, Colombia and Venezuela. The trip took a hell of a long time, nearly a year, much more than I had intended because I had decided to travel by land, and I didn't know that South America was as big as that. It looks so different on the map, like looking at the moon. It seems to be so small that you can hold it in your hand.

After a few days in Bolivia I was a bit concerned about the fetid smell in the streets. For days I couldn't work out the reason until one day in La Paz I was buying some sweet oranges, delicious tiny bananas and a few ounces of coca leaves for the altitude sickness and I saw something that opened my eyes about the smell. The woman selling the fruits and leaves bent down to fetch the bananas from the floor, and I saw that she was wearing no knickers – but she had about twenty skirts on and with a funny little hat on top of her head, she looked quite ridiculous. The truth is that most of these women from the Aymará and Inca tribes don't wear any underwear and when the skirts of these South American mountain girls get dirty, instead of washing the dirty skirt, they keep adding clean ones on top of the dirty ones. At least, they look clean but they smell rancid and, unrestricted by underwear, it is much easier to do their business anywhere and very fast. No one can see what they are doing because everything is hidden under a pile of skirts! They don't use toilet paper and they don't wash themselves either. So I peeled my oranges and bananas very carefully. I chewed lots of coca leaves and then I didn't give a damn about anything.

To me, all the countries in South America are spectacular, and their people are magnificent. Exploding with colour and music, they have the best rhythms in the world and in my opinion the best writers and poets. The best coffee beans and marijuana plants are from Colombia, the best sweet corn from Peru, the best meat from Argentina, the best coca leaves from Bolivia, and so on. The place is boiling with life, mysteries and craziness, all mixed up in that turmoil of poverty and wealth in a wonderful atmosphere, but surrounded by danger. As the media reports on a daily basis, it is a disgrace that the western world is interfering so much and at every opportunity in South American countries by destabilizing their economies, supporting *coups d'état* by the ruthless militaries and sending gangs of death squad criminals to kill innocent kids living on the streets.

The people of what is today known as Peru had the greatest empire in the Americas, and although their empire was destroyed with the arrival of the conquistadores, the descendants are still there scattered over a large area of the Andes. These people are the Quechuas, and those who commanded and advised them were the Incas, who seem to have been like some kind of chief-Gods. These controllers were a different shape from the Quechuas, and stories of these Gods being very tall and with fair hair abound in many areas of that Andean region. Also in the jungle in Paraguay the stories of tall blond Gods have striking similarities. Certainly if those Inca God-like people were equivalent to the Pharaohs in Egypt, I believe it's possible they originated from the same race.

There is evidence of Inca skulls being large and elongated in the same way as those of Tutankhamun and his father. Many people including myself believe that they were extra-terrestrials and, if that is true, then the mystery of the pyramids in Egypt, Mexico and the magnificent ancient constructions in Peru and Bolivia begin to make sense. The quiet local people of the *Altiplano* between Bolivia and Peru think the Inca Gods still live at the bottom of Lake Titicaca and they can see them coming and getting out of the lake. I stood all day long staring at that lake once and saw nothing.

The central government of the Incas was based in Cuzco, and from there they controlled 5,000 km of the Cordillera from Ecuador in the north, to Chile and Argentina in the South. It's difficult to believe the Quechuas travelled all those distances on foot – they didn't have the horse or the wheel, they had only their own legs to rely on! I imagined sending a message to Mr X for a meeting to be held early tomorrow morning. Off you go then, only 5,000 km, and don't be late!

The mysterious city of Machu Picchu, high in the mountains and not far from Cuzco, raises many questions and offers few answers. It was called 'the city of the Gods' but even National Geographic magazine is still debating the reasons why it was built. One of the theories it investigates is that Machu Picchu might have been a temple devoted to the Virgins of the Sun, a holy order of chosen women dedicated to the Inca sun god, Inti. These women (usually beautiful young girls) were all virgins and they were kept well fed and safe as they were property of the Gods. After struggling to the top of the citadel, I thought these Incas must have been fussy buggers. But when an archaeologist discovered Machupichu by chance in 1911, the city had been long abandoned and nobody knows when or why.

Machupichu was probably the most difficult city to build in the entire world; a phenomenal architectural work, high on the mountain slope, an inaccessible paradigm that some of us see as paradise. The Quechuas had to flatten the rocky mountain top with their hands and then carry millions of stones up the mountain from far away quarries, then cut and fix them in the most intricate forms. Suddenly it seems they abandoned the magnificent citadel as if it was no more than an overnight camp site.

The other place in South America that I enjoyed is the mysterious ruins of Tiahuanaco. This mind-blowing place is located in Bolivia, close to the shores of Lake Titicaca. Tiahuanaco probably precedes all civilizations in the Andes, so is pre-Quechua, pre-Aimara, pre-Inca gods and pre-whatever was there after Tiahuanaco was built. The lack of information we have about this unusual place is surprising, in comparison with Egyptian or Greek ruins. It lies there in ruins as if a terrible earthquake or an atomic bomb has shaken most of it to the ground. But strangely enough the biggest stones, like 'The door of the sun', are still standing, as if someone has just erected them. Some of the building stones are so big and have been cut so perfectly, that you really wonder if it was possible then for those little Quechuas or Aimara people to have accomplished such a magnificent achievement with limited ancient tools. I would love to see the best engineers and architects of today build a replica of Tiahuanaco using ancient tools.

I consulted some serious looking books in order to see if they would provide answers to satisfy my thoughts, but no. In fact I think I was worse off after reading those reference books. For example, the Tiahuanaco people had shaped out of stone something that looks like a tube, but this 'tube' is cut in half, immaculately polished and then put together again to create what looks like an enclosed channel. No one knows what it is. The archaeologists, with all their imagination, think they are water pipes, and that's it. Enclosed canals made out of stone? To my knowledge, water flows freely in gravitational terrain through all kinds of obstacles, rocks, soil, jungle, etc. The meticulous Romans and many other old civilizations cleverly constructed canals which we thoroughly admire today, made with common sense and shovels, so why didn't the people of Tiahuanaco have the same common sense in construction as the rest of the world? Or perhaps they were not stone-made pipes for the transportation of water at all. They could have been carrying something a bit more technological inside. Telephone cables? Computer connections? Or something that perhaps we have not discovered yet? I don't know if we will ever find out the truth about Tiahuanaco, but it certainly deserves a full investigation.

When I felt I had had enough of everything to do with Tiahuanaco, I went for a long walk on the arid soil and tried to find an answer to the magnificent legacy of the Gods. I had plenty of coca leaves in my rucksack but I needed food. On the shores of Lake Titicaca I found a dilapidated building with a sign saying 'restaurante'. The 'restaurante' had been built with reeds from the lake and mud from the streets. The ceiling was unusually low and I had to bend to get through the door. A candle shone lazily from the wall and a teenage girl walked sluggishly from table to table, dragging her dirty feet. In the twilight of the little place I saw the silhouettes of two Indians eating soup and talking in Aimara very fast. I lit a cigarette and ordered a beer from the sleepy girl, but before I had a chance to relax, a child-sized waiter put a big plate of food on my table and the smell that came from that broth was heavenly. Without doubt, that moment was the best part of that day in Bolivia, but there were no signs that the Inca Gods had been in that restaurant for a very long time.

In the mountains of Puno in Peru I ended up five kilometres high in the ranch of an effeminate German with a round face and a short fat body. He was driving his four-wheel drive truck while I was hitch-hiking and he wanted extra passengers to weigh down the vehicle. So I accepted his invitation which took me to the highest place I have ever been in the mountains. In one way the place was heavenly, in another it was very desolate, devoid of trees and with an uncomfortably cold breeze. I saw many llamas, alpacas, vicuñas and condors and some extremely quiet people ploughing the hillside with a hand-made type of potato planting fork in sub-zero temperatures. These Quechua people workers had rock-hard faces which I'm sure they needed in order to survive this bitter weather. My Lord, it was cold!

An Indian from the lowland jungle of Peru was staying with the German and they gave me a ceremonious welcome consisting of chewing three coca leaves each and reciting the usual greetings: 'Welcome to Peru my friend, welcome to the land of the Incas my friend, this (coca) will keep you healthy my friend, I hope the roads are clear for your travels, I hope God protects you my friend.' The strange ranch even had a small church with a bell on the tower in order to persuade all the Indian population to attend an oppressive service on Sundays. The Quechua workers didn't receive any wages for ploughing the land with that fork. Instead they received a patch of land for planting their own potatoes.

I was not happy there. I was thinking about those Catholic missionaries who came here, robbed the Indians, killed their children, raped their wives and built chapels in the name of a God from a faraway land who didn't chew coca leaves. They had a cross, a symbol that meant nothing to the Incas, and their images of a crucified Christ, which meant even less to the poor disorientated sons of the sun.

Apparently one Inca God was a woman. I was fascinated when I found out that the place or centre of the Incas in Cuzco is called Sacsayhuamán – similar to 'sexy woman'.

This goddess came from the centre of Lake Titicaca, gave birth to ninety children and then flew to the skies. Now, Sacsayhuamán is a very strange site, it's neither one thing nor the other. It's not a house, a castle, a temple or in fact anything more than just a massive lump of stones, cut and put together systematically and perfectly in the most difficult way possible. It would probably be impossible to match, even with all the technology, tools and equipment of today. And why would we build such a difficult thing for no reason at all, anyway? Why did the Incas do it? – or did they? I know that today they are still ploughing the mountains by hand with the only tool they've invented, a kind of fork. Did the Spanish gold hunters, criminals, *conquistadors* with their Bibles, take away the Inca brains as well as their gold? What on earth happened up there?

The people are mysterious and the place is full of mysteries. The vast deserted area from Nazca to Tiahuanaco is full of bizarre drawings of spiders and monkeys, all of them with unusually disproportionately long legs. I thought that those Inca artists were worse than Picasso, chewing too many coca leaves, for sure. They talk about airports in the desert when in fact they don't even have a mule to go about on. And where was the saviour Sacsayhuamán goddess when Francisco Pizarro came and smashed the heads of the Incas?

I took a last look at the sexy woman of Cuzco and headed north to Ecuador. But I couldn't put out of my head the stories of the 2,000-year old airport or the woman giving birth to ninety little Incas. How to choose their names? How to celebrate their birthdays? It's quite dramatic enough giving birth to one child; imagine ninety of the little offspring!

— 39 —

GRAHAM PROSSER

THE surreal stones of Cuzco were fading away in a mirage of heat and laziness and they were haunting me by now. I was walking north with my thoughts, wandering through the mountains, gliding through the valleys like a lonely condor. Memories were coming and going, leaving little behind. In one of those drifting moments, a great friend of mine, who sadly died, stood there on top of those big stones on his horse, proud of his adventurous life, carrying in his saddle bags the immortal head of an Inca that he had found not far from here. Graham Prosser was born in Llantwit Major in south Wales, and since an early age Graham had shown a great interest in adventures. He spoke many languages, drank a lot of beer, played the guitar and sang and did many other things that interested his disquiet brain. He headed for South America and based himself in Buenos Aires, learned Spanish and taught English for a living. When he'd earned enough extra money, he bought a horse and together with two English friends traversed 3,000 kilometres through the Andes in nine months, to arrive in Cuzco and then Lima.

Somewhere in Peru he found the skeleton of a human being lying in the sand. It had a most unusual head, the cranium elongated towards the back. He was very excited with his discovery, so he picked it up and carried it everywhere with him in his saddle bags. The Indians could see that he was carrying a forbidden treasure and they advised him not to do that, to leave the head where it belonged. But Graham was not a superstitious man. He was too busy taking care of his friends and his horses. He had to plan carefully the route through the mountains, jungles and deadly deserts and to find food for the horses and for his team. Survival was uppermost in his brain and he thought that nothing could stop him. But when they arrived in Lima they stopped because they had run out of money, so they sold the saddles and the horses and they took a train back to Buenos Aires. Desperate and penniless, he couldn't go back to his beloved Wales, so he went to the British Consulate, explained the situation and asked for a boat ticket. He was willing to pay for the ticket by painting the boat and things like that. The officials at the Consulate were about to throw him out on the street when an English sea captain popped his head around the door and said that he had a dead man on board and he would like to find a live one to take his place, because the captain wanted to bury the dead man in England, not at sea. Graham jumped into the captain's arms and offered himself up to do whatever the captain wanted. His carry bag didn't contain very much apart from the Inca head and again, during the journey, people were telling him not to carry the head because it would bring bad luck to the ship and everyone on board but again he didn't take much notice.

The boat caught fire as they arrived at Río de Janeiro harbour and some passengers and crew were burnt to death but Graham and his greatly-prized head survived. The trip to England took longer than scheduled because people were still mysteriously dying on board. The refrigerator was full of dead bodies and the captain was not very happy. But arrive they did and Graham stretched his legs and disappeared into the beauty of the English countryside, heading for Wales with the ghoulish head still inside his bag.

Graham left the Inca relic to rest in the attic of his parents' house in Llantwit Major and went to find a job. Shortly after an interview in London he was flown back to South America to start work with Longmans publishing company in Río de Janeiro. Within a short time he died in an unexplained car accident in northern Brazil. Afterwards, Graham's family decided that the Inca head would rest better at the Natural History Museum in London. Bad luck, superstitions, Inca heads, adventure and craziness, Graham Prosser had it all. He was such a natural ambassador for mankind that it's difficult to believe he has gone. I'm sure I am not the only one to miss him at this very moment.

— 40 —

Colombia and Back to Wales

I crossed the Equator from south to north while I was in Ecuador. The small pretty country was full of bananas and I didn't stay there very long. Colombia was waiting for me with its voracious anaconda's mouth. There is no other country in the world quite like Colombia. There you can find the best people on the planet – and the worst. They will invite you into their homes offering everything they have – even in the worst circumstances of poverty they will offer you their hearts or they will recite you a poem. The words *compañero* and *camarada*[31] are pronounced often enough to make you feel really at home. If they like you they will protect you, they

---

31   *compañero* – companion; *camarada* – comrade

will steal for you and they will kill for you. But if they don't like you they will not protect you, they will not steal for you and they will kill you, rape you or rob you as many times as they wish. I was very lucky, I was robbed only twice on the same day, once while I was sleeping on the bus, the second time by the Superintendent bastard in charge when I went to report the first robbery.

I stayed with friends I had previously met in Wales in the wealthiest area of Bogotá. The house had a guard at the gate on 24-hour duty (even at night), and two fierce-looking Alsatian guard dogs, very well trained, were awake and barking all night. God, I was so irritated that if I'd had a gun I might have shot them. If I had to go to the centre of Bogotá, I had to go with a bodyguard. I felt like a prisoner in that grand place and, for sure, the house was not a happy one.

After a few weeks the bodyguard let me go alone into the city and, of course, it was much better. It was dangerous, yes, but full of life and totally crazy. I liked that. I discovered a place called 'Barrio Kennedy' on the outskirts of Bogotá, a very poor area packed with unwealthy people. I met a ninja fighter there and I stayed with his family for about a month. They didn't drink coffee or tea, only cocoa, a chocolate drink made from the bean of the cacao tree. They showed me what the real Bogotá looked like and how its people really lived. I was astonished to find out how many people can live and sleep in a single room. They were practising yoga and kung fu, they had slim and sleek bodies and they laughed a lot. They had very good books on Chinese philosophy and when they were drunk with agua ardiente (a vodka-type drink, literally meaning 'burning water') they were creating and reciting freshly made poetry. Meanwhile the young lads would go to the supermarkets and steal everything they could carry.

Sometimes a big gang would hold up the supermarkets with machine guns and, after filling their lorries with merchandise, they would distribute it in the poorest areas of the city. The system worked well in Colombia and I was wondering why we couldn't do the same in Britain's poorest areas, places like the coal mining areas of the north or the south Wales valleys, for example. Probably some British Lords would disagree with this system, although it was popularized in England by Robin Hood and he was very good at it while he was jumping through the woods of Nottingham. The folktales in Britain say what a good chap Robin Hood was. Nice songs are sung about him and everybody is proud of the fact that he was English but, ironically, if we tried to behave like him we'd end up in an English jail.

Everybody in Colombia is involved in the marijuana business, whether they like it or not. Thanks to the massive consumption of marijuana in the United States and many other countries in the northern hemisphere, some Colombians are getting very rich. It grows more easily than coffee and they get a significantly higher price for it. This commodity is a highly profitable business, a 100% pure, organic and ecologically sound product that grows everywhere and creates a solid source of employment. It is much better for the farmers to produce marijuana or cocaine, as the other commodities like cotton, bananas, beef or potatoes are risky crops, constantly attacked by viruses, pests and falling prices. But the price of these stimulants is getting higher every year and, like many other countries, death and corruption in Colombia is part of everyday life. If marijuana was legalized Colombia would, for certain, be one of the superpowers of the world. That's probably why it's not legal in many countries yet!

Nearly every farm has an airstrip, so the valuable merchandise is transported from the mountains on donkeys and mules. The police turn a blind eye when they see a mountain of marijuana being transported on a donkey's back so I don't know why the police searched me twice in one day on a bus full of Japanese tourists, understandably afraid of the police with macho moustaches and machine guns. I was wondering if it might have been easier and more 'incognito' to travel on a donkey packed with marijuana. In the small village of Poponte on the border with Venezuela, I saw seven huge lorries packed with marijuana leaving for the port of Barranquilla, and passing through without question. Everybody in the village knew what these lorries were carrying and I talked to some of the drivers. They were totally relaxed about it. It was as common as transporting a bale of hay or straw but obviously a bit more expensive, they said, and they all laughed loudly.

One Colombian Welshman invited me to go to his ranch in the area of Honda in his car. His car was a Jaguar 'made in England'. He was a great man and we talked a lot about cattle during the trip to the ranch. He kept many thousands of them on one of the most extraordinarily fertile pieces of land I ever saw, with an astonishing surrounding beauty. Wales was still his motherland but it was history to him now. After Colombia, Miami was his second home. As we arrived at the main gates of the ranch, Mr Hughes told me something that I thought was quite remarkable. 'Most of the rich people of Colombia have a house in Miami – I have two,' he said, 'and their kids are educated there. Primary school consists of learning how to speak the English language with an American accent. College consists of how to become a successful money-maker, and university consists of how to live in Colombia without being kidnapped. But, of course, sometimes we fail some exams.' As a consequence his sister was kidnapped for ransom for six months by a non-governmental organization, an idealist group called M19. Interesting, eh?

I was enjoying every second of this mad country. Even now, after so many years, the memories cascade through my mind with an insatiable pleasure. Daylight starts in Honda at 6.00 am and it ends at 6.00 pm. There are no winter or summer months; in fact there are no seasons at all, but a concoction of hot, humid and intolerable rainfall makes life an irritable experience. Snakes, killer wasps, scorpions and thieves all add to the insupportable tropical heat, wrapped in a conundrum of wealth and misery.

I found a job at a ranch in the scorching valley basin that was surrounded by the green natural forested mountains of Honda. This land with its extraordinarily beautiful topography was owned by the wealthy ex-north-Walian gentleman, and neatly farmed with an abundance of horses, tractors, cows, cowboys, and bare-footed Indians. Huge rivers of fertile brown waters criss-crossed the land, carrying dead trees, dead cows and live piranhas, and it was not unusual to see a human body floating by in the company of a swarm of flies, while frantic toothed fish fought each other for a piece of juicy Christian.

My work consisted for a while of supervising on horseback a team of Indians and *mestizo*[32] labourers who swiftly climbed the hills, each with 30 kilos of watered chemicals to be sprayed over the sticky leaves of those bushes that the cows didn't find tasty enough to eat, and which had to be destroyed. The job for the labourers was very tough indeed, though they managed to do it with a smile. Intrigued by the wellbeing of the mostly Indian labourers, I began to investigate the reason why they were continually smiling. I thought they were probably smoking marijuana or chewing coca leaves. I was wrong. These Indians were not drug addicts at all, and what was happening was the effect of an innocent fruit juice called *guarapo* that had fermented during the hot day.

Every day, each working man on their way to work on the ranch carried a 5-litre plastic container in one hand, and in the other hand a machete. The 5-litre container is prepared early each morning with different kind of fruits, corn, *panela* (unrefined sugar cane blocks) and yeast, so that for the first half of the day it's a clear, cool, fresh, and non-alcoholic juice. For the second part of the day this drink is warm, thick, and dark. It ferments during the hot day with flies and wasps committing suicide, drowning in the bottles. It looks like fresh vomit. I asked the nearest Indian for a bowlful. He smiled and gave it to me. It tasted delicious, and the Indian poured me another bowl while the rest of the Indians were laughing loudly, as they knew it was the end of the container and therefore should be very strong in alcohol, and surely I would get drunk.

....

32   *mestizo* – of combined European and Native American descent

Slowly, the whole gang started to move towards their homes at the centre of the ranch, some on mules, and some walking and dragging the stubborn mules along the dusty track. Dusk fell suddenly and magically, bats in their suicidal madness flew over and around us, hunting their insect dinner in a wonder of acrobatic disarray. The *guarapo* made us happily tired, dreamy and mellow. Nobody argued or complained, and although we were dirty with sweat and dust, everyone had a picaresque smile on their faces. The smell of roast beef cooking entered our nostrils as we approached the ranch hamlet. Tall palm trees waved their massive leaves in a gentle breeze, displayed heavy bunches of dates and, from the corrals, fresh and warm cow dung steamed spicily towards us. We unsaddled our horses and mules, brushed and rinsed the sweat off, and let them loose in an open field till the next day. We washed our hands, sat around the table and waited for our plateful to arrive, warm, rich with meat, beans and dead flies.

The Colombian adventure was coming to an end. I was getting fed up with the marijuana business, the mafia, the thugs, the heat and the noise, the desperate faces of the poor and the mistrustful faces of the rich. I was angered by the corrupt police, army, religion, freedom fighters and all the establishments that really stink like the decomposed corpses we found in the jungle, killed by one of these ambitious organizations. I needed a nice cup of tea and a bath, so I flew back to Wales.

In Wales I could talk about romantic Druids reciting poetry on hilltops in the rain. I could eat huge amounts of wonderfully greasy fish and chips with salt and vinegar wrapped in dirty newspaper. I could get paralytically drunk on Saturday nights and, on jolly Sunday, go to the chapel, as high as a kite, to sing a few hymns and pray for God to cure my hangover. I could do all these things in Wales without too much of a problem. But first of all I desperately needed a long and extra large bath to wash away all the sweaty nightmares that I was carrying with me from South America.

Back in Cardiff, I met my old friend Alan Jenkins and, of course, he invited me to celebrate my arrival with Welsh beer. I accepted his invitation with enthusiasm but first, I said, I needed a bath. As we were very close to where another friend of mine, Catrin, was living we decided to go to her house for a bath. I rang the bell several times but nobody answered the door. Then I realized that one of the windows on the top floor wasn't totally closed, and I was sure that I could squeeze through it. We found a long piece of wood in the garden which we leaned against the wall at a good angle and, with Alan holding it, I began to climb like a monkey. And I was right – I managed to pass through the small window.

Once inside the house I opened the door to let Alan in, and I started to prepare for my long-awaited bath while Alan was making a nice cup of tea. I took my clothes off and had just put one foot in the bath to feel how hot it was, when the bloody doorbell rang. I wrapped myself in a towel that was much too small and ran downstairs to see who was bothering me now. I opened the door to see a young man standing there like an idiot, asking me what I was doing in the house. Of course I replied, 'I'm having a bath.' Then four policemen appeared from nowhere and I realized that the young man with the idiotic face was a policeman as well. Oh shit, I was the idiot now! Alan had stopped making tea and was no longer smiling. One of the policemen ordered me to put some clothes on. He followed me to the bathroom saying, 'Come on, let's go to the station.'

It was obvious what had happened. An elderly neighbour with nothing to do had seen me climbing the piece of wood and, thinking I was a burglar, had called the British 'law-and-order' to stop me having my bath. Sitting in the back of the police patrol car, my brain couldn't cope with more words than 'Bollocks, I'm still dirty and can't even have a peaceful bath in Wales.'

Whilst in the police station I noticed that Alan was white in the face. He was serious and quiet. Later, I found out that the reason for this was that he had some grass hidden in his boots. He hadn't had enough time to remove it when the police arrived by surprise at Catrin's house. Anyway, we were inside the police station talking to the Chief Superintendent in charge. This man, with his calm Welshness, seemed to have had a lot of experience in policing the Welsh people and with a bit of a smile on his face said, 'So, having a bath, hey?' And I said, 'Yes, sir, just a bath, nothing else … well, Alan was making tea, but we didn't have time to drink it … in fact, I didn't have time to have a bath, either.' And then he began to giggle. His face went quite red and then he laughed loudly, throwing his large body backwards on his chair. He was laughing so much that another policeman entered the room to see if everything was alright. The Chief Superintendent was laughing so much that he couldn't say anything at all, so the policeman left the room leaving his boss laughing his bollocks off, and Alan and me not knowing what to do.

The police station turned out to be a friendly one. The police knew we were just two innocent idiots but the problem remained unsolved. I had the telephone number for Catrin's office but I hadn't seen her for a few years and the policeman told us she was no longer working there. 'You're not doing too badly, boys,' said one of the policemen cynically and again we didn't know what to do. When, finally, the police traced her, I was a bit nervous and confused and still dirty. On top of that Catrin was bollocking me on the telephone. We didn't end up in jail after all, and she laughed a lot about that silly incident. I'm sure she's still laughing every time *she* has a bath. But I was very pissed off that day and ended up drunk in a pub in Cardiff without any hope of having a damned bath. The only thing I remember from that night was someone saying to me in the pub, 'Sut mae'r hwyl René? Pryd ydych chi wedi dod yn ôl?' (How's things, when did you get back?) And I said, 'Y bore 'ma' (this morning). And he said, 'Pryd ych chi'n mynd yn ôl, te?' (When you going back, then?) I thought to myself, 'Back? I've only just bloody arrived. And I still haven't had a wash or a cup of tea!'

— 41 —

R. BRYN WILLIAMS

I wasn't having a bad time at all in those days but I couldn't find many interesting people to talk to in Cardiff, so I headed off to mid Wales. After navigating the miniature village of Pontrhydfendigaeth, I arrived at Llanbadarn Fawr on the outskirts of Aberystwyth. A great poet was living there and I wanted him to help me with some songs that

I was writing in poor Welsh. Mr R. Bryn Williams greeted me loudly in Spanish because he knew how to do it. He was the Archdruid that year in Wales and had spent many years in Patagonia. He believed I was related to him somehow. He was getting old, but had not lost his peculiar sense of humour; a bard with luxurious fantasies, a *troubadour* with his horizons wide open, and an impeccable historian on the South American Welsh. He had written dozens of books and some of them were quite complicated for a 'gaucho' like me to understand, with their elaborate and poetical Welsh words.

I asked him if it was true that Charles, the Prince of Wales, had come to Aberystwyth to study Welsh. He took his time and then said, 'Yes, he was here.' I wasn't sure if it was wise to ask him any more questions. Sometimes he was a lay preacher as well. He used to go from chapel to chapel entertaining his friends and preaching away until he ran out of time and had to go home to make lunch because he was living alone now. He had just divorced for the first time and he was in love with his new girlfriend. All through that afternoon we talked, sang in Spanish and Welsh, drank tea with strange biscuits and played the guitar. We also managed to tidy up my new compositions in Welsh.

In the morning Mr Williams lit the fire, poured the inevitable cups of tea and prepared his pipe for an early smoke. I wished I had a camera with me at that time as he was looking like the father of poetry and philosophy, relaxing in his big chair, puffing away at his pipe. He was the picture of an ancient Greek philosopher, a Celtic druid from a book of fables, a hermit half buried in a garden of books. The smoke from the wet wood on the fire combined with that of his pipe created a magical atmosphere in that room full of books and spiders' webs.

On the third day of my visit I think that he must have got out of the wrong side of the bed because he didn't say 'good morning' to me in Spanish, he said it in Welsh. That was a bad sign. He hadn't had his morning wash and he was walking like a zombie with the only few hairs that he had left standing up on his head. The English punks would have paid a fortune for that hairstyle but Mr Williams hadn't seen himself in the mirror yet, and to make matters worse, an Englishman came to visit him to pick his brains about Patagonia. The Englishman was very polite and he excused himself for everything, even for not speaking Welsh. He said that he could understand most of the Welsh language but that he couldn't speak it. Mr Williams replied that he had a dog that could do exactly the same! Then he continued by saying 'Don't worry my friend, nobody's perfect!' The poor Englishman stood there in that untidy room, trying his best to adjust his brain to the situation but, unfortunately, he couldn't do very much that day against the unpredictable personality of Mr R. Bryn Williams. On another occasion while Mr Williams was travelling through Europe, representing Wales at a conference, someone approached him and asked 'What's all this fuss about being Welsh? You look exactly like the English.' To which he replied 'Yes, that's because I've just been sick on the plane.'

— 42 —

BUTCH CASSIDY

IN those three days staying at the bard's house, I probably learned more about Welsh literature, history and the annoying mutations of the Welsh language than during my entire time travelling around Wales. Bryn enjoyed talking to this Patagonian peasant because I was extremely ignorant in comparison to his massive knowledge. When he couldn't find a certain word in Welsh, he could say it to me in Spanish – or vice versa. He asked me to accompany him to the cinema because the film *Butch Cassidy and the Sundance Kid*, starring Paul Newman and Robert Redford, was showing. I enjoyed that film but he didn't. Bryn said that it was pure fantasy and that Butch and Sundance never went to Bolivia, and that they would surely have died crossing the Andes when they escaped from Cholila to Chile in 1907.

I asked if Butch had killed Llwyd ap Iwan in Patagonia and he said very firmly 'No.' Then he explained to me a bit more. At the beginning of the 1900s there were many outlaw gangs in Patagonia, a bit like now, but with the difference that Butch Cassidy is not there now. For sure, there were plenty of North American outlaws in the area of Bariloche but there were also Welsh, Spanish, Italian and English outlaws. There were also many mercenaries brought from Europe to kill the Indians but, in fact, they were free to kill anybody they didn't like. These ruthless people were always blaming the Butch Cassidy gang because the Wyoming guys were really the professionals and, although they spent only six years in Cholila, they managed to amass a huge amount of publicity.

Therefore, whatever went wrong in Patagonia at that time, Mr Cassidy had to cope with taking the blame. They were still blaming him many years after he'd gone.

So, Bryn Williams didn't know who killed Llwyd ap Iwan in Arroyo Pescado ('Nant y Pysgod' in Welsh, 'stream of the fish' in English) south of Cholila but he reckoned that it could have been the outlaws Wilson and Evans, who were probably British. These were the same guys who robbed the bank at Río Gallegos in the south before being killed, apparently in Río Pico, which is also south of Cholila. Their killers were border police who decapitated the bandits, put their heads in a barrel and covered them with alcohol. Apparently these heads made their way to the United States labelled with the names of Butch Cassidy and the Sundance Kid and the remains of the two bodies are buried on a farm close to Río Pico, under no names at all, with just two wooden crosses.

Michael D. Jones, the creator of the Welsh colony in Patagonia, was getting a bit old for the job of being the eternal leader of the colony, so he appointed his son, Llwyd ap Iwan, to take over. Shortly afterwards someone killed him. He was educated, he was a strong athlete, and with a good brain. I believe that under his leadership the colony could have been a very successful new Wales, totally independent of any other country or colonies. And it is true that some of the Welsh were getting very rich by the end of the 19th century. They were much better off there in Patagonia than in the coal mines of south Wales or the slate quarries of north Wales. They didn't suffer or experience any wars like the Europeans did and they had a global open market in which to sell their produce. They were as modern and prosperous as any other part of the world and, in some cases, much better. Farm machinery was coming by the shipload from Canada and the United States to this Welsh part of Patagonia. But after Llwyd ap Iwan was killed, everything fell apart. Why, though? What really happened? Was it just an accidental killing by some petty thief? Or was it programmed as an assassination?

Ap Iwan was probably the most important person at that time for the Welsh Patagonians and after his death there must have been hundreds of letters from Patagonia to Wales describing his tragic end. But where are they? I came across a nine-page letter, hand written by a Mr Roberts of Arroyo Pescado to his family in Aberystwyth, dated Wednesday 5th January 1910. In this long letter he described – as if he was under some kind of torture – that in December 1909 two 'Englishmen' came to rob the shop and they shot Llwyd ap Iwan three times, killing him instantly. Then they disappeared at full gallop into the vast desert on their horses. So if the murderers were English, as Mr Roberts indicates, and not North American, what happened to them and why did they blame Butch Cassidy? Was it a cover-up? It sounds to me like: 'Enemy destroyed, case closed – next!' The little shop in the desert closed down, Mr Roberts went back to Wales, Llwyd ap Iwan was buried a few yards away from the shop and the wild wind devoured the Welsh flag on top of the flagpost.

The stories of Butch Cassidy in Patagonia are fascinating. Some stories are true of course but some are not. One of the stories that I particularly like goes like this: Butch and Sundance were bored one day on their ranch in Cholila so, to entertain themselves, they decided to plan a few hold-ups in the area. One problem was that there were no banks in Cholila (there are still no banks in Cholila today!) The nearest bank at that time in 1905 was 800 km away to the east, on the Atlantic coast, in one of the Welsh hamlets.

They must have been totally inspired to decide to cross the desert from the Andes in the west, to the coast in the east, with nothing in between. They were aiming for a place called Tre-lew (which in Welsh means the place, or hamlet, of Lewis). In this Trelew, an outpost type of village, there was a bank which is still there. It is El Banco de la Nación Argentina, established with money from Lloyds Bank. Lloyds Bank had branches in Patagonia as the wool business was thriving there. The Welsh people kept their savings in this bank and Butch knew it. There was no other bank, the next one being 1,500 km away. That was too far for the horses. So Butch and Sundance booked into the only hotel in town, which today bears the name of 'El Touring Club'.

After the 800-kilometre trip through the desert the gang was thirsty and after emptying several bottles of whisky they decided to organize a party. Butch and Sundance invited everybody in town to the party at the grand saloon of the Hotel Martino (as it was called then), owned by Anita Howell Jones. Of course, the guests were all Welsh. And these Welsh guys could also speak English, as well as Spanish. Their wives danced with Butch and the Welshmen drank all the whisky that was available. The Welsh colonists delivered the greatest social event that Butch and Sundance had seen for many years, and they loved it! They danced, sang and drank whisky all night long. Then Butch fell in love with a blonde Welsh teenager.

Butch and Sundance had such a good time with the Welsh that they decided not to rob the bank after all. They stayed in the Chubut valley for several weeks, relaxing and socializing, practising with their guns by day, and partying at night. Soon the news of these great North Americans reached every home in the valley. Everyone wanted to meet them, every wife wanted to dance with them, and the Sundance Kid would show off his accuracy with his revolver by shooting the heels off the women's shoes while they were dancing. Then he would give them money to buy new ones.

Butch Cassidy returned to his ranch in Cholila not knowing that he had left the Welsh teenager pregnant. No one seems to know what happened to this girl, or the baby Cassidy. He wasn't known as Cassidy of course, so the baby Cassidy must have borne one of the Welsh surnames of the colony, names such as Evans, Williams, Griffiths, Jones, Roberts, Powell, Davies, Jenkins, Rhys, Lewis, Morgan, Hughes, Rogers, Pugh, Phillips, Lloyd, etc. We will never know for certain which Patagonians are carrying the Butch Cassidy genes to this day – it could be anyone, including me.

It was a shame that Butch and Sundance were hounded out of Patagonia as they were the masters of bank robbery and today they could have been useful teachers to those who don't have any other way to earn a decent living. When they arrived in Patagonia they had the equivalent of a few million US dollars, enough to have a great party in the desert and make all the guanacos dance around the fire. So they had no need to rob a little Welsh shop in Arroyo Pescado. I know that Butch and Sundance left Cholila in a hurry in the month of May when the autumn was well under way, with lots of snow and ice. Crossing the mighty Andes in those circumstances is lethal. So did they cross them or not? If not, then what happened to them? They had probably crossed the Andes several times before in order to familiarize themselves with the fastest escape route into Chile but when the mountains are covered with snow it's a different story. The mountains transform themselves into an infernal labyrinth of snow, rocks and bamboo-type canes where no one can survive for very long, especially carrying all that money and with pack horses and mules transporting belongings. Not long ago some Italians went to climb those mountains where Butch had supposedly crossed but the bad weather trapped and killed them. They are still there today, buried under millions of tons of snow in the glaciers. And these were professional mountaineers, well prepared for the circumstances.

The local story in Cholila is that one day two gaucho ranch workers were sent by Butch to Estancia Leleké on a routine visit to bring back horses, bulls and rams from the massive English sheep station about 40 miles away. After a few days the gauchos arrived back at Butch's homestead in Cholila with all the animals needed and, in the saddle bag, an English newspaper printed in Buenos Aires, given to the gauchos by Butch's friend in Leleké. There was a photograph of two outlaws in the front page, Butch and Sundance, with the caption: 'Wanted – dead or alive'. As those gauchos couldn't read in any language, they were not suspicious that their boss was in mortal danger. The newspaper with the photograph of their famous 'patron' left a bitter taste in Butch's mouth and it is not difficult to imagine what the outlaw heroes said when they saw themselves in a national newspaper ... 'Goddamn it, let's saddle up!'

The other local story is that Pinkerton's Detective Agency in the USA had sent various detectives to Argentina to track down Butch and Sundance. They all failed, but an astute Texan sheriff named John Comodoro Perry succeeded. The irony is, according to Perry's family who live in Cholila today, that Comodoro Perry and Butch were friends, and it was Perry who informed Butch that Pinkerton's was closing in, and that they should do something about it – like bugger off, fast. So, the story goes, Perry reported back to Pinkerton's that he would stay in the area, waiting to ambush Butch, and would bring him to justice in the USA. He had a long wait.

There are hundreds of versions and legends of those amazing 'bandits' in Patagonia and, like most tales, some don't make any sense at all. I believe that Perry invented most of it, for he and his friend Gibbon ended up keeping most of the stock, chickens and dogs that belonged to Butch, including a huge piece of land where Perry's descendants still live today. Perry was a tough man, an impeccable shot and he represented the USA law, so who would argue with him?

It is obviously a bit odd that a policeman sent by Pinkerton's Detective Agency, after travelling for thousands of miles to the south of Argentina, found the bandits' hiding place without the bandits, and decided to stay and become a rancher in the middle of an isolated place in the Andes. Why he didn't go back to Texas where he had a proper job? Butch was a well respected man, a great character and very sociable, so it would have been easy for him to pay few dollars to his neighbours and friends and tell them to distribute the story around that they had gone to Bolivia, even though not many people knew were Bolivia was.

The gang definitely headed towards Chile, but there is no sign of them anywhere after they abandoned Cholila. Most people swore they went to Bolivia, others said Paraguay and so on, but when the entire world thought Butch was heading north, I believe he was heading south. If they managed to cross the Andes, they could have arrived on horseback at Puerto Mont in Chile without much trouble, and from there taken a boat to the far south of Chile. They would have arrived clean and smartly dressed in the busy international port of Punta Arenas, where many English and German people lived. From there, they could have gone anywhere, their lives would be free and open for them and, according to the most adventurous story tellers, Butch, the Sundance Kid and Etta Place settled down in Australia, which was then a heaven for outlaws being sent from Great Britain. Of course we will never know, but with all their connections in Welsh-Patagonia, they could have ended up in Wales!

— 43 —

THE INDIANS

BUTCH never seemed to have any problem with the Indians, but going back to my childhood in what I thought was a beautiful sleepy valley, I remember many silly and sad incidents that amused us with the great entertainment they provided. We didn't have electricity, gas or television of course, but the social events were much more fun than they are now. There was no need for the law to interfere in the colony and as the police didn't have anything to do they joined us in some chaotic incidents, breaking the law in every possible way.

Houses didn't have locks on their doors because nobody was afraid of robbery in those days. There were parties everywhere with barrels of wine and tons of Welsh cakes. Most of the Welsh integrated naturally into other communities, especially with the Italians, and we were just like one big tribe under the sun. On Sundays the churches with their different religions separated us for a short time but as soon as someone opened a bottle of wine we were reunited in a loud party once again.

Only the Indians were a bit different and, although some of them could speak Welsh, they couldn't integrate into the community as the others did. So they were softly rejected by the brownish-white Welsh Patagonians. One of the weakest points of some Indians is that they enjoyed stealing things, even if they didn't need them, and consequently my mother was losing some precious cutlery that she had inherited from my late grandfather through her unlocked doors. My father had only one Indian farmhand and he always managed to look a mess. He never washed or combed his long coal-black hair, he never wore socks and he never took off his ridiculous hat. He tried to grow a moustache and a beard but the hair refused to grow on that part of his body, only a few hairs here and there adorned his ugly face. When my father sent him to do something, he stood straight as a soldier and said, 'Si señor, si señor,' but he did bugger all. I saw my father in a temper many times because he had to go after him and do the job himself and when my father found out about the petty theft of taking the cutlery that was it – that was the end of the farmhand.

Early one morning my father called him and told him to saddle up his horse. He sent the farmhand as a messenger to another ranch with a piece of paper in his pocket with the message written in Welsh. After galloping all day, the Indian arrived at my uncle Alun Griffiths' ranch. Alun read the message. Then he told the Indian that he needed to give that piece of paper to another of my uncles who was living in Ty'r Halen, so the messenger spent his second day galloping through the Chubut valley until he arrived, late in the evening, at what he thought was his final destination. But again this other uncle sent him on with a message. And another sent him on again. The last news we had of the unfortunate man was that he and his horse had arrived in a desolate village in the middle of the province, 300 miles from where he had started. The village is called Paso de los Indios (the Indians' Pass). The paper contained the following message: 'Please, keep sending this idiot onwards'. We never saw him again.

This Indian was not a Tehuelche, he was an Araucano. These two Indian races were constantly at war with each other. They don't resemble each other in any way. It is said that the Tehuelche were then the tallest people on the planet. Apart from that we don't know much more about them and we will never know anything else now because, as they were a nomadic tribe in the desert, the early landowners killed them all.

The Araucano Indian has similar features to the Chinese and, like the Chinese, there are plenty of them. The

Araucanos always lived in the Andes, sharing the borders between Argentina and Chile. They were incredibly good fighters and in fact they were the last Indians in South America to be conquered by the *conquistadors*. Ironically, today the white people are erecting statues in honour of these brave and savage people who, in their natural huge refuge of the Andean Mountains, had plenty of time to reproduce themselves. These Araucano Indians developed a beautiful language and a very repetitive dance.

In 1884 a tragic incident occurred between the Welsh and the Indians, the first and only one among the settlers. Three gold hunters and a guide saddled their horses and decided to follow the river Camwy (*Chubut* or *Chupat* in Tehuelche Indian) up-stream, in search of gold. The adventurous Welshmen were John Hughes, John Parry, Richard Davies and a guide named John Daniel Evans.

The Welsh version goes like this: The three Johns and one Richard were peacefully traversing the pampas, twisting and turning with the topography of the land where the river Camwy lies ('camwy' means 'winding' in Welsh). They found insignificant little pieces of gold buried in the sand on the river shores. As no white man had ever been there before, the desert was unchanged Indian land, inhabited by the Tehuelche nomads. Some 300 miles west from their starting point in Trelew they met a lone Indian on horseback. This Indian could speak some Spanish and he told the little Welsh group that it would be wise if they followed him towards the *tolderias* (Indian camp) to ask permission of the Indian casique (chief) to travel across Indian land. In the area of Lepa, which today is Benetton land in the foothills of the

Andes, the mistrustful Welsh thought that the lone Indian could be setting a trap for them. They turned back, light with gold and heavy with fear. The Indian continued on his lone journey towards the *tolderias* and the Welsh did a 'U' turn and headed towards the east and back to Trelew.

The Welsh had Remington rifles and revolvers but so far they had used them only to hunt wild animals for food. Early one morning, after some 200 miles from the turning point, John Daniel Evans, the guide, saddled a special horse 'El Malacara' (which in Spanish means 'Bad Face') and began to ride towards the valley. What was supposed to be another monotonous day in the desert turned out to be a catastrophic day. A thousand wild looking Indians descended on them with hurricane force. Arrows and lances rained on the poor defenceless Welsh who fell from their horses like sacks of potatoes, their bodies pierced by the four metre lances. The deadly war arrows were encrusted in their Welsh intestines. John Daniel Evans somehow avoided all the arrows and lances and, at full gallop, disappeared from the chaotic scene. His horse jumped a *barranca*[33] and somehow landed perfectly – somewhere. John hurried on the 'malacara' towards civilization some 200 miles away. After arriving on this magical horse and breaking the tragic news to the Welsh, the leaders of the colony organized a trip in order to investigate what kind of fate the remaining Welsh explorers had met at the hands of the Indians. The horrific site was inconceivable. Davies, Hughes and Parry had been torn into pieces, their testicles cut and stuffed into their mouths, and vultures had taken part of their bodies. After collecting the remains of

33   *barranca* – slope alongside a river

their bodies a hole was dug and the leftover body parts were buried in it. The hearts had been removed from each corpse and were never found. Traditional Welsh hymns were sung at that funeral for the first time in that part of the desert.

The Indian version of this tragedy is quite different. I have been told this story by an Indian in the Andes. This Indian has died now and, although no one knew his real age, some reckon he died aged 120. No one knows if the story that follows is correct, although it makes sense and could be true.

An Indian party of Araucanos (Indians from the mountains) was hunting in the foothills of the Andes and they caught two ostriches. A youngster was sent on horseback with the two ostriches to the *tolderias*[34] so the women could start cooking while the rest of the Indian party continued hunting. John Daniel Evans, the guide of the Welsh party was also hunting for breakfast, and the two met. John Evans shot the Indian boy dead and took the two ostriches and his horse, the famous 'malacara'. John left the boy in the bushes and rejoined the Welsh party, without knowing that a group of raging Indians was following him. The Indians gathered all their warriors in the *tolderias*, painted their faces with red lines and then danced their war dance. The Indians followed the Welsh party for 200 miles without being detected. In a high rocky area that is now called Los Altares (the altars) – and which is supposed to be an Indian sacred site – the Indians attacked, killing the Welshmen, tearing their bodies into pieces, and, as the ultimate punishment, castrating them and stuffing their mouths with their own testicles.

---

34   *tolderias* – Indian camp site

This was not a simple act of war but more a case of revenge, a retaliation of some kind. The fact that the Indians followed the Welsh party until they arrived at the sacred site before killing them suggests a particular meaning. My father told me that John Evans found that 'malacara' horse somewhere, because it didn't belong in the Welsh colony, and that it had been broken and tamed by Indians – hence its stamina and endurance. The 'malacara' could have jumped the *barranca*, but so could the Indians. When I went to visit the site of the miracle jump, I couldn't help thinking that I had done those jumps around the place on horseback hundreds of times and probably in some circumstances more dangerous than John Evans'. Indian people are not afraid of dying, so why didn't they even try to jump that *barranca*? I believe that if the Indians had wanted to, they could have killed John anywhere on his retreat towards the valley. The deadly young warriors could have followed him to his doorstep but they didn't. Was John Evans there when this massacre took place? Or was he far away, hunting or surveying the desert, finding a safe place for the Welsh to cross the river? Who knows? To me, the romanticism of the 'malacara' is far from romantic. Something terrible had to have happened in order for the Indians to behave in that vindictive way.

Whatever the true story is, there is no doubt that John Daniel Evans was a great man of the desert. He was born in Wales and arrived in Patagonia when he was only four years old. He was an impeccable horseman, he spoke English, Welsh and Spanish, as well as some Indian languages. He did much for the Welsh community and was the first to build a flour mill in the Welsh-Andean village of Trevelin; a tough man who has entered the history books.

Apart from this isolated incident, the Welsh Patagonians were apparently very friendly with the Indian population and vice-versa. In fact, on at least one occasion the casique (chief) asked the Welsh if they could teach one of his sons to speak their language, as the casique was so impressed by these friendly people. The Welsh accepted and the son of the chief became fluent in the Welsh language, singing in the chapels and participating in the Welsh festivals, the 'eisteddfodau'.

— 44 —

INTO THE ANDES

IN 1884 a man named Fontana arrived, dusty and exhausted, to the Chupat valley. This man of Italian descent was a Colonel in the Argentine armed forces, and he was appointed Governor of the Territory of Chupat by the Argentine government. In other words, he was sent to 'keep an eye on the Welshies'. John Daniel Evans was employed by Fontana as a guide, due to his extensive knowledge of the interior of the Province of Chupat.

Now, the original name of the river flowing through the centre of Patagonia where the Welsh first settled was called 'Chupat' by the indigenous Tehuelche Indians for as long as they can remember. The Welsh called it 'Camwy' and in both languages the name means 'winding'. In the old books of expeditions to the area, writers make reference to this river Chupat, but somewhere around 1900, I believe, the name was changed to 'Chubut'. It is unusual to change an innocent name for no reason at all, a name that has been in the guttural vocabulary of the Indians for possibly over 20,000 years. Invisible to us, they have special sites or meeting points for their hunters, sacred areas with prehistoric paintings, and a constant flow of clean drinkable water that runs for 800 km from the high glaciers in the Andes into the Atlantic Ocean.

So far I can think of only two reasons for changing its name: the first one I believe is to do with alcohol, as the word *chupar* in Argentine slang means 'to drink' or 'to suck'. Therefore a person who comes from that province of the river Chupat would be called an alcoholic or a sucker. Although perhaps the next example is more credible, as by the end of the 19th century Italians started to arrive in Argentina like ants, and lots of them ventured south to Patagonia. In a short period of time those Italians, who we called 'tanos', had settled down permanently in the Chupat valley, therefore they were called 'Chupa-tanos, which means 'Italian suckers'. I am convinced that some respectable priests, military and businessmen with an Italian surname didn't like to be called an Italian sucker, therefore the name had to be changed.

The peaceful Welsh settlers were living free of tyranny in this new land, so they were surprised and not very excited when Fontana – or anyone else for that matter – presented himself in an army uniform and began to give orders around the place. Fontana had been posted before to different locations in areas of conflict on the Argentine borders. He had years of experience in commanding soldiers and in dragging mules on the sierras of northern Argentina, but now he was here to keep this foreign settlement clean and tidy, and although his surname was as foreign as anything could be, these people were Welsh foreigners.

Being an army Colonel, his shoulders were loaded with the indoctrinated burden of discipline, so the hard man would ensure that under his command the little colony would respect him in the same manner as any of his subordinates. When he finally settled down comfortably in the valley, he noticed that the Welsh were a tame lot, and apart from the noise they made in the chapels on Sundays, the place was peaceful and he wondered why he was there at all.

Soon he began to enjoy the parties in the company of these funny and friendly Welsh people, and the teenage girls with their horse riding skills fascinated him. Mr Fontana didn't have anything to do apart from sending some useless reports back to his Buenos Aires headquarters from time to time, when a boat was available to carry the post. In a way he was living in a state of permanent idleness, until an order arrived from Buenos Aires from his superiors, stating that he must investigate the interior of the territory of Chubut. As he didn't have the luxury of a regiment with him, he gathered thirty of the fittest Welsh lads available and set off with almost 300 horses and many wagons packed with bedding, food, guns and bullets to the west of the territory. Those enthusiastic recruited farmers were not soldiers in any way; they were much better than that. They were young, strong and healthy; they knew how to use the *boleadoras* as well as their rifles and knives; and they were unequalled horse riders. And, more useful than anything else, they had a good knowledge of the desert. They knew how to smell danger and how to hunt wild animals and how to sing, too.

Years ago, Colonel Fontana had lost his left arm in a fight with Indians in north Argentina, and since then he had become terrified and paranoid about Indians; when he was on his horse trotting about the valley my family thought he looked like Napoleon. Fontana soon realized which one of the little Welsh army was the best lookout – he chose Mr Jenkins for his determination and efficiency was extraordinary, but mainly because Jenkins had extraordinary eyesight.

When they were well into the desert they saw huge clouds of dust far away on the horizon, and Colonel Fontana asked Jenkins, 'What is that?'

And Jenkins replied 'Indians.'

'Indians?' asked Fontana and Jenkins said, 'Yes sir, Indians.'

'Could you tell me more or less how many there are?' asked Colonel Fontana and Jenkins replied, 'One thousand and three.' Colonel Fontana was amazed by that answer. He knew that Jenkins had the most extraordinary eyesight in the world but this was a bit too much as poor Fontana couldn't see any Indians at all. So Colonel Fontana asked Jenkins, 'How on earth do you know there are one thousand and three Indians up there?' And Jenkins said 'Because there are three over there and there must be a thousand behind them!'

The Indians were not at war that day so they left Fontana and the little group of exhausted Welsh souls to pass through the desert without molesting them. After six hundred kilometres of desert terrain they arrived at the foothills of the mighty Andean mountains. As they were following the River Chubut, the little group arrived eventually in a place without a name. They dismounted for a long time as there was plenty of food for the horses and then they stayed a bit longer, because someone said, 'Hey, this is a beautiful valley, isn't it?' And that was it – the name Beautiful Valley, or Cwm Hyfryd in Welsh, or Valle Hermoso in Spanish, was branded forever on that truly spectacular area of the Cordillera de los Andes. The town that grew up to serve the valley is called Trevelin ('the place of the mill').

A few years ago it was immortalized on film when a Welsh production company made a film called *Cwm Hyfryd*. I played the part of a Welsh-Patagonian and we returned to the valley in 1993 to shoot the final scenes of the film. This film had an interesting start in life because it was written by someone who was conceived in Poona in India. He was born on a boat off the coast of Liverpool, was of Norman-Irish-Scottish descent and brought up in England. He married into my distant family in Llanuwchllyn and ended up writing a script in English about a Welsh-Patagonian (without ever having met a Patagonian), which was then translated into Welsh for filming by S4C. The film was a co-production with France, was produced by an Indian and directed by a Welsh-speaking Cornishman – a very multi-cultural heritage!

— 45 —

SEPARADO! FILM

BACK in Wales, a few years ago I found out by accident that I was in another interesting feature film, and had no idea that I had been involved in its production. As it seems that I was the inspiration for the film, I would normally think that I had been more inattentive than usual, but on this occasion

I need to share the blame with a distant relative (who I was also unaware of, so I was possibly doubly inattentive). This distant relative turned out to be quite famous, and I didn't know that either, so all in all the entire experience was quite a revelation.

From my side, the story began in the late Nineties when a friend of mine asked if I could help him with his floor-restoration business. He had received an enquiry from a client in Cardiff, and had no one to help him with that particular job, so one far-too-early morning we went to assess the work. We had just started measuring up, when a tall thin man with long hair and a long beard appeared, stared at me for a moment, and then offered us a cup of tea. While he was opening all the cupboards in his kitchen in search of sugar, he said to me, 'Um … ehh … I think we're related.'

I said, 'Oh, really?' Now, I get told quite frequently in Wales that I am someone's relative, and I have no idea usually what the connection is. This was no different.

'Um … ehh … yeah … uh … from Llanuwchllyn,' he said.

'Oh,' I said, 'I've got family in Llanuwchllyn.'

'Yeah … uhh … my name is Gruff,' he said, but didn't elaborate further.

Gruff wasn't really very talkative, but we were sitting at the table and having our tea without sugar, when he fetched two guitars and invited me to play. *So this guy is a musician, then?* I thought as I picked up one guitar and started to tune up. It wasn't a good start as I sing in Welsh or Spanish and Gruff sings in Welsh or English. So we agreed on Welsh as we knew some of the same songs, but we were playing in totally opposing styles; he is a left-handed guitarist and I am right-handed; he plays on steel strings and I play on nylon strings. We couldn't follow each other at all, and the whole thing was a bit of a disaster, messy and out of tempo but we forgot about the floorboards for a while. We gave up with the guitars after a bit more mess and I went back to the job. The floors were finished by the end of the day, and as we prepared to leave Gruff appeared from somewhere and said, 'Ehh … um … I would like to make a film about our grandfathers one day … ehh …yeah …'

I said something like, 'Yeah, sure.'

What I didn't realize at the time was that Gruff was the famous Gruff Rhys, lead singer of the rock group The Super Furry Animals, and that we were third cousins once removed. Although the music we were trying to play at his kitchen table was in different styles, it was also the rope that bound us, because the seeds of our music – which germinated in different hemispheres – had been sown many generations previously in Llanuwchllyn, and we were connected to music through our family genes.

Anyway, many years later I had a call from Gruff, asking if I would record an interview on film and sing a few songs with my guitar. I agreed, and once again found myself sitting at his kitchen table, but this time in front of a microphone. Gruff told me the story of the old family and our great-great-grandfathers in Llanuwchllyn, and how we were related, and said he'd like to interview me about our shared heritage.

He also said that the first time he saw me was on television in the Seventies, when he was only a young boy. He said I was singing a gaucho song in Welsh and wearing a red poncho, and he had asked his grandmother who I was. She told him that I was from Patagonia and was related to him. Gruff was so impressed by the way I was playing the guitar on that TV show, that he decided to buy a guitar and learn to play himself. As we were talking, and as his crew was preparing recording equipment for the interview, I suddenly began to realize that this was *the* Gruff Rhys, from *the* Super Furry Animals, and I couldn't believe that I had been restoring floorboards in a room of his house eight years earlier!

I was moved by those words from Gruff, as he said it was I who had influenced him to become a world famous artist, and I wondered how many more people were (or are) influenced by my Patagonian cultural inheritance, who I have not been able to meet or know about. I assumed he wanted to capture some of that shared inheritance on video and so had a very entertaining day with his recording crew, also filming outside in the park as it was a beautifully sunny day. But in all the excitement of discovery *I did the interview without asking what was it for* and after that brief togetherness in Gruff's house in 2008 we separated again. I went to South America, or wherever, while he continued to tour the globe with his band and we lost contact once more.

About eighteen months later, I had a call from a film producer, inviting me to see the rough-cut of a film called *Separado!* (separated) at an edit suite in Cardiff Bay. She said some of it had been shot in Patagonia and, as I wasn't doing anything on the date she suggested, I said yes. Well – what a shock! The film *Separado!* was about me! In the intervening years between my sorting out his floorboards and this screening, Gruff Rhys had been on a journey to South America to sort out the connection between me and himself.

His film was based on his personal journey in search of René Griffiths, a distant relation who had influenced his music career, and who was infamous for being extremely elusive. Without me knowing about it, Gruff had been in Patagonia with a film crew, filming my (and his) family and everything else that moved – except me. Gruff had included in his film archive footage from various television programmes I had made over the years, and I sat and watched myself singing in the 1970s, arriving onstage on horseback, ranching in Patagonia, and finally myself playing the song we had recorded eighteen months before in the park in Cardiff. So that's what that day had been about! Gruff hadn't said, and I hadn't asked, but it was for the concluding scenes of his film.

The opening scenes of his film are set in the early 1880's in Llanuwchllyn around two brothers from the Jones family who had a serious disagreement whilst in a tavern. In order to avoid a fight, the story goes that these two wild characters from the Aran Mountains arranged a race, each providing their own horses and riders. The race was from the tavern, to an agreed point, and back through narrow paths full of brambles and trees on the hills. The brother whose rider lost the race would have to surrender and pay for the drinks.

Dafydd Jones was my great-grandfather, and his brother was Gruff Rhys' great-great-grandfather. My great-grandfather was definitely not willing to lose, so in the *Separado!* version of the story he organized some young lads to distract his brother's rider during the race. As the riders came to a bend in the road at full gallop, the lads stretched a rope across the rough path and his brother's horse was brought down. The rider fell and either died or was seriously injured, but my great-grandfather's rider won the race. Another version of the story is that my great-grandfather switched the riders' horses, so that his horse was being ridden by his brother's rider. He knew that his own horse would turn sharply for home when approaching the bend in the road, allowing his own rider to continue straight on and win the race. In this version his brother's rider was thrown from the saddle at the bend but survived.

Either way, all I know is that my great-grandfather landed in the Welsh colony in Patagonia around 1882. The other Jones brother stayed in Bala and became Gruff Rhys' great-great-grandfather. That incident in Llanuwchllyn was the beginning of over 100 years of family separation. The horse race was forgotten in Llanuwchllyn and was never mentioned in Patagonia. So Gruff and I were brought up in different cradles and on different continents, separated by history, fate and generational silence. Now, in front of my eyes, I was watching this story unfold on the screen for the first time.

Even though Gruff had not made a film before, somehow it worked extremely well! I laughed throughout the film and enjoyed the psychedelic musical journey. Even the obvious mistrust shown by the more traditional Welsh Patagonian families towards Gruff was fascinating. I must confess that seeing most of my family on film was quite emotional, especially my uncle Bryn who was over ninety years old at the time and still smiling. When asked the secret of his longevity, with impeccable wit he replied, 'I never smoke in bed!' I have seen many films shot in Patagonia, but I congratulate Gruff for being the first to make a film about Patagonia that is not boring, and which is not overly romanticized. In fact it was entertaining and outrageously funny and the psychedelia must have been a shock for many Patagonians with their self-imposed silence and the monotony of so many years of isolation.

The next contact from Gruff was an invitation to attend the première of *Separado!* at the South Bank Centre in London, in August 2010. We also agreed to perform in public together for the first time, and I appeared on stage after the screening as a surprise guest to play with Gruff and Tony da Gattora (a Brazilian percussionist), followed by some solos from me. The London audience was magnificent; they really enjoyed the film and my surprise contribution to the night. I realized that night that people honestly adore Gruff Rhys. This courageous and charismatic musician with no experience in film making, a minimal budget and a simple idea, managed to make a movie that has been successful worldwide. Our great-great-grandfathers and their descendants were separated for over a century, but Gruff's *Separado!* brought us together again. The DVD of the film also contains the interview I recorded sitting at his kitchen table, in an additional feature called *Juntos!* (together).

In April 2012 I played a concert in Gruff's home-town of Bethesda in north Wales. He couldn't make it that night, as he was playing a concert with his band in Plaza Palermo open-air stadium in Buenos Aires. That's what I call a great Welsh-Patagonian cultural exchange; separated again but somehow linked together across the cosmos.

— 46 —

EPILOGUE

OF all the experiences, adventures and stories in this book, many remain with me in memory only. The enduring elements are those which are still part of my life today. My story, and that of my ancestors, has been one of constantly having to choose which path to follow (metaphorically and literally) from the moment my great-grandfathers decided to leave Wales and fulfill their dream of establishing a new life in Patagonia. 'The Picture' was an ever-present prompt which no longer traumatises me, but definitely accompanied me on my travels.

The truth is that, thanks to the decision of my great-grandfathers, I have a story to tell and by returning to live part of my life in Wales, that story has come full circle. The separate roads taken by those who originally went to Patagonia, and those who stayed in Wales, have become interwoven once again by family and cultural connections, and by the persistence of genealogy. Music and film remain a large part of my life and travelling between Wales and Patagonia is part of my inheritance.

I have heard so many people say that it was wrong for the Welsh people to emigrate to Patagonia, that they should have gone to the United States or Australia instead. Well, they could have gone, I suppose, but English was spoken in those countries and that was not attractive for the Welsh. As a result of all this my destiny was to be a Welshman who was born in Patagonia, brought up speaking Welsh, schooled in Spanish, and obliged to learn English when I came to

Wales. Even now, I dream in Spanish, I compose songs and poetry in Welsh, and I've written this book in English. I'm forever attracted by the open road but one of the pleasures of travelling is that whatever my experiences are on that road, I can always return to the cradle of Wales and its people, who I call 'family'.

Back once again in the hilly country of my 'great', *great*, great grandfathers in Wales, a journalist interviewed me recently with all the usual questions: 'Hello René, nice to see you. When did you arrive from Patagonia?'

I said, 'Yesterday.'

He said, 'How lovely. When you going back, then?'

— THE END —

APPENDIX

MICHAEL DANIEL JONES

by Terry Breverton

MARCH 2 1822 – DECEMBER 2 1899

THE FOUNDER OF THE WELSH COLONY OF PATAGONIA, FATHER OF THE MODERN WELSH NATIONALIST MOVEMENT, 'THE GREATEST WELSHMAN OF THE 19TH CENTURY'

MICHAEL Daniel Jones was born in the Manse, Llanuwchllyn, Merioneth, the son of another Michael Jones, who was minister of 'Yr Hen Gapel' (the old chapel) there. There was a huge theological controversy which split the congregation, and the minister later became Principal of the Independent College at Bala. After being educated by his father, Jones spent a few months as a draper's apprentice in Wrexham. However, Michael D. Jones wished to follow his father into the ministry, and went to Carmarthen Presbyterian College (1839-43) and then Highbury College in London. In 1847, he went to America, in the midst of the great emigration caused by the poor harvests and agricultural depression of 1840-50. He stayed with relatives in Cincinnati and was asked to stay for some time as a minister. While there, Jones set up a society to give financial assistance to poor people from Wales who wished to emigrate, and several branches of 'The Brython Association' started across the United States. This was to be the genesis of Jones' life mission, to establish a

Welsh-speaking 'Welsh Colony' for emigrants who wished to escape from the oppression of Tory landlords across Wales. He wanted a Welsh state where: '... *a free farmer could tread on his own land and enjoy on his own hearth, the song and the harp and true Welsh fellowship ... There will be chapel, school, and parliament and the old language will be the medium of worship, of trade, of science, of education and of government. A strong and self-reliant nation will grow in a Welsh homeland.'*

Returning to Wales, Michael D. Jones became pastor of Independent churches in Carmarthenshire. His father died in 1853, and Michael was asked to succeed as a minister of Bala, Tyn-y-Bont, Soar, Bethel and Llandderfel, and as Principal of Bala College. However, a constitutional dispute meant that for a time a rival college operated in Bala, before moving to Bangor in 1886. This was known as '*the Battle of the Two Constitutions*' (1879–85). Jones wanted the subscribers to be able to control the government of the college, whereas his antagonists wanted the controllers to be representatives appointed by the churches of each county of Wales. (Bala was the major Welsh-speaking college at this time.) The problem was exacerbated by Jones' financial support for the Patagonian Colony. He was forced to sell off Bodiwan, which was his home and also the seat of the college to meet his debts, and the so-called '*Decapitation Committee*' held at Shrewsbury dismissed Jones from the Principalship. Jones resigned from Bala College in 1892 to allow it to also move to Bangor, the new Bala-Bangor College later became the University of Wales there.

In South America the existence of the Welsh-speaking colony, in Patagonia, stopped Chile claiming vast expanses of land from Argentina in 1865. One hundred and fifty three Welsh emigrants had boarded the sailing ship *Mimosa* and landed at Port Madryn there in the same year, trekking forty miles to found a settlement near the Chubut River. In 1885, some families crossed four hundred miles of desert to establish another settlement in Cwm Hyfryd at the foot of the Andes. *Y Wladfa* ('The Colony'), founded by the reformist preacher Michael D. Jones, was to be a radical colony where Non-conformism and the Welsh language were to dominate. Jones was deeply concerned about the Anglicisation of Wales – to preserve the heritage his people would have to move. He is regarded as the *founder of the modern Welsh nationalist movement.* The Argentine government was anxious to control this vast unpopulated territory, in which it was still in dispute with Chile, so had granted one-hundred square miles for the establishment of a Welsh state, protected by the military.

For ten years after 1865, this Welsh state was completely self-governing, with its own constitution written in Welsh. The immigrants owned their own land and farmed their own farms – there was to be no capitalist state with its hated landlord system. *Females were given the vote – the first democracy in the world to have egalitarianism, and this fifty years before British suffragettes started to try to change the British system. Boys and girls aged eighteen could vote, over a century before they could in Britain. Voting was by secret ballot and all were eligible – two more democratic innovations.* The language of Parliament and the law was Welsh, and only Welsh school books were used.

The colony grew to three thousand people by the time Welsh immigration halted in 1912, *and had been the first society in the world to give women the vote*. Interestingly, the Welsh code of law established by the settlers was the first legal structure in Argentina, and its *'influence in modern-day Argentinian law can still be seen'*. Three hundred and fifty people are currently learning Welsh in Patagonia, helping the language to survive there, and plans are underway with teacher exchanges to double this figure. However, only five thousand still speak the language regularly, most of them in their later years. The success of the colony attracted immigrants from Spain and Italy in the first decades of the twentieth century, and the Welsh influence is declining steadily.

The Eisteddfod Fawr is still held in Chubut, financially supported by the Argentinian government. It gives around a quarter of a million pounds a year to support eisteddfodau in Gaiman, Trevelin and Trelew in recognition of the service performed by the early settlers. Gaiman is the 'most' Welsh town in Patagonia, with signs on the road approaching *'Visit Tŷ Llwyd, the Welsh Tea House'*, *'Stop at Tŷ Gwyn'* and *'Come to Tŷ Te Caerdydd'*. In Tŷ Te Caerdydd, a costumed group from the local school sometimes dances, and the traditional Welsh tea is served by Welsh-speaking, Welsh-costumed staff.

Jones was almost broken financially by the strain of supporting the settlement in Patagonia – he had envisaged it as the pattern for an independent Wales, and laboured, travelled, wrote, addressed meetings, collected money and lost his son there. He also fought against the oppression of Tory landlords – he hated servility, and beat the candidate of Sir Watkin Williams Wynn as representative on the county council for Llanuwchllyn in 1889. This was a tremendous victory for Welsh radicalism. He is buried at Yr Hen Gapel. His vision, hope and enthusiasm helped develop Welsh patriotic feeling into a vigorous, practical nationalism. The great poet Gwenallt, in 'The Historical Base of Welsh Nationalism', described Michael D. Jones as *'a saint, a great and large-hearted Congregationalist; the greatest Welshman of the 19th century; and the greatest nationalist after Owain Glyndŵr.'*